# CLARENDON LAW SERIES

*Edited by*

R BIRKS

# CLARENDON LAW SERIES

# DISCRIMINATION LAW

### SANDRA FREDMAN

**OXFORD**
UNIVERSITY PRESS

# OXFORD

### UNIVERSITY PRESS

Great Clarendon Street, Oxford OX2 6DP

Oxford University Press is a department of the University of Oxford.
It furthers the University's objective of excellence in research, scholarship,
and education by publishing worldwide in

Oxford New York

Auckland Bangkok Buenos Aires Cape Town Chennai
Dar es Salaam Delhi Hong Kong Istanbul Karachi Kolkata
Kuala Lumpur Madrid Melbourne Mexico City Mumbai Nairobi
São Paulo Shanghai Taipei Tokyo Toronto

Oxford is a registered trade mark of Oxford University Press
in the UK and in certain other countries

Published in the United States
by Oxford University Press Inc., New York

British Library Cataloguing in Publication Data
Data available

Library of Congress Cataloging in Publication Data
Data available

ISBN 0–19–876566–5

5 7 9 10 8 6

Typeset in Ehrhardt
by RefineCatch Limited, Bungay, Suffolk
Printed in Great Britain
on acid-free paper by
Biddles Ltd
King's Lynn, Norfolk

This book is dedicated to
Jem, Kim, and Dan,
to Alan
and to my parents,
Naomi and Mike

# Preface

Despite the widespread belief in equality, we live in a world which is marred by deep inequalities. As a white South African Jewish woman, an immigrant and member of an ethnic minority, I personally have experienced discrimination in many guises. I have been both a victim and, involuntarily, one of the perpetrator class. Growing up in a society twisted by the systematic racism of apartheid, with the scars of the Holocaust still fresh, and in a deeply sexist world, I discovered both the central value, and the elusiveness of equality. This book aims to contribute to the search for equality, not by providing answers, but by articulating the questions. It introduces the reader to the controversies we confront as soon as we try to translate our ideal of equality into legal form, and, more difficult still, into social and political reality. The book does not attempt to provide a single solution, but points to a range of possible responses, drawing on the experience of different jurisdictions, and locating the issues firmly within their appropriate historical and political frame. It is to be hoped that the reader will come away both with renewed faith in the ideal of equality, and with a heightened sensitivity to the problems to be faced.

There are a great many people to whom I owe very special thanks for their help and support in writing this book. My thanks are especially due to Peter Birks, as editor and colleague, who has been unstinting in his support for the project and the outcome. My special thanks too to Bob Hepple, not only for his detailed comments on this book, but also for the friendship and inspiration he has provided over many years. I could not have written this book without the formative input of Chris McCrudden, Mark Freedland, and Paul Davies, who have always been immensely generous in sharing their thoughts and ideas. I have also benefited enormously from ongoing discussions with many students and colleagues from all over the world. My two research assistants, Christopher Stothers and Suzanne Lambert, gave invaluable assistance in putting the final touches to the manuscript. I owe too a particular debt to the Arts and Humanities Research Board for their assistance in funding this project.

I dedicate this work to my husband Alan, to my children, Jem, Kim, and Dan, and to the hope that the world of their adulthood will be one with fewer inequalities than that of their childhood. I dedicate this book too to my mother, Naomi Fredman, and to my late father, Mike Fredman, whose courage in facing illness and death have added a deep poignancy to the process of writing it.

Sandra Fredman
September 2001

# Contents

# Table of Cases

# Table of Legislation and Statutory Materials

# I

# Equality: Concepts and Controversies

... to labour in the face of the majestic equality of the law, which forbids the rich
as well as the poor to sleep under bridges, to beg in the streets, and to steal bread.

Anatole France (1897)[1]

We hold these truths to be sacred and undeniable, that all men are created equal
and independent, that from that equal creation they derive rights inherent and
inalienable, among which are the preservation of life, and liberty, and the pursuit
of happiness.

Thomas Jefferson (c.1775)[2]

Equality as an ideal shines brightly in the galaxy of liberal aspirations.
Nor is it just an ideal. Attempts to capture it in legal form are numerous
and often grand: all human rights documents, both international and
domestic, include an equality guarantee, and this is bolstered in many
jurisdictions with statutory provisions. This suggests that we all have an
intuitive grasp of the meaning of equality and what it entails. Yet the
more closely we examine it, the more its meaning shifts. Is equality captured by the familiar aphorism that likes should be treated alike? This
appears both logical and straightforward. But the initial logic fades as
soon as we begin to ask further questions. When can we say that one
person is so 'like' another that they should be treated alike? For centuries
it was openly asserted that women were not 'like' men and therefore
deserved fewer rights. The same apparent logic was used to deny rights to
black people, slaves, and Jews; and it is still current in respect to some
groups, such as gay men and lesbian women, non-citizens, and older or
disabled people. And even if we can agree on whether two individuals are
relevantly alike, we may still have doubts as to whether they should always
be treated alike. Experience has shown that equal treatment can in practice perpetuate inequalities. As Anatole France graphically depicts in the
above quotation, a law which appears equal on its face bears far more

[1] A. France, *Le Lys rouge* (Calmann-Lévy, 1927), p. 106.
[2] 'Rough Draft' of the American Declaration of Independence in J. P. Boyd (ed.), *Papers
of Thomas Jefferson* vol. 1 (Princeton University Press, 1950), p. 423.

heavily on the poor than the rich. A rule which requires a high level of formal education as a precondition for employment, will, although applied equally to all, have the effect of excluding many who have suffered educational disadvantage, often a residue of racial discrimination or slavery. A rule which requires full time working as a prerequisite for training, pension, or promotion opportunities will operate to exclude many of those with primary responsibility for children, the vast majority of whom are still women. A rule which requires all employees or pupils to dress according to Christian traditions and take religious holidays according to the Christian calendar will perpetuate the exclusion of religious minorities.

How do we explain then how equal treatment can in effect lead to inequality, while unequal treatment might be necessary in order to achieve equality? The apparent paradox can be understood if we accept that equality can be formulated in different ways, depending on which underlying conception is chosen. Equality of treatment is predicated on the principle that justice inheres in consistency; hence likes should be treated alike. But this in turn is based on a purely abstract view of justice, which does not take into account existing distributions of wealth and power. Consistency in treatment of two individuals who appear alike but in fact differ in terms of access to power, opportunities or material benefits, results in unequal outcomes. An alternative conception of equality, therefore, is based on a more substantive view of justice, which concentrates on correcting maldistribution. Such a principle would lead to a focus on equality of results, requiring unequal treatment if necessary to achieve an equal impact. Alternatively, the focus could lie on facilitating personal self-fulfilment, by equalizing opportunities. This differs from both the above conceptions, in that a notion of equality which stresses equal opportunities is consistent with inequality of treatment *and* inequality of results. Unequal treatment might be necessary to equalize the opportunities of all individuals, but once opportunities are equal, different choices and capacities might lead to inequality of results.

The choice between different conceptions of equality is not one of logic but of values or policy. Equality could aim to achieve the redistributive goal of alleviating disadvantage, the liberal goal of treating all with equal concern and respect, the neo-liberal goal of market or contractual equality and the political goal of access to decision-making processes. It is striking that, despite the widespread adherence to the ideal of equality, there is so little agreement on its meaning and aims.

Also complex is the relationship between equality and difference. It is an easy step to assume that 'difference' means inequality and inequality is synonymous with inferiority. This assumes a conceptual framework based on a set of dichotomies: reason and emotion, soul and body, good and bad, equal and different. In this schema, deriving from Aristotle, the second part of the pair is inferior to the first. Difference is characterized as the negative partner, legitimating detrimental treatment of those who are different. Yet in a plural society such as that in modern Britain, difference and diversity should be regarded as positive attributes. Equality, far from suppressing difference, should accommodate and even celebrate it. Nor is difference necessarily an all-or-nothing concept. As Young argues:

> To say that there are differences among groups does not imply that there are not overlapping experiences, or that two groups have nothing in common. The assumption that real differences in affinity, culture, or privilege imply opposi-tional categorization must be challenged. Different groups are always similar in some respects, and always potentially share some attributes, experiences and goals.[3]

The above discussion has assumed that equality is the prime value in society. But equality may well conflict with other basic social values, such as liberty from State interference, including freedom of speech and thought. How then do we decide which takes priority? Should individuals be able to assert their freedom of speech rights in order to protect their rights to make racist comments? Or to produce pornographic material which degrades and stigmatizes women? Should an unborn foetus be entitled to claim a right to life to defeat the claims of the mother to reproductive freedom? On a different scale are the conflicts between equality and utilitarian or economic goals. Should equality be defeasible on the grounds that its achievement is too costly, either for the State or for private individuals?

For law-makers, facing the task of translating abstract notions into law, these questions are particularly complex. Legal formulations of equality must be coherent and comprehensible; and, equally importantly, they must contain mechanisms for making equality effective. But traditional enforcement and compliance mechanisms are often inappropriate in the equality context. Civil rights are normally enforceable in adversarial pro-ceedings initiated by one party to the dispute and carrying a financial remedy. Yet a right to equality might be an empty promise if it requires each individual victim of discrimination to conduct proceedings against a

---

[3] I.M. Young, *Justice and the Politics of Difference* (Princeton University Press, 1990), p. 171.

particular defendant, particularly if the defendant is her employer, the factual and legal issues complex, and the remedy limited to compensation. A wholehearted commitment to equality might well require far more imaginative legal structures, including not just prohibitions of discriminatory behaviour or practices, but positive duties to promote equality. Indeed, closer attention to the causes of inequalities in society point to the need to institute broader social programmes, such as the provision of targeted training and child-care, the modification of working hours, and the alteration of premises to accommodate disability. Even so, at the end of the day, we may also have to acknowledge the limits of the role traditional legal provisions and processes can play in bringing about social change.

The aim of this chapter is to examine in more detail some of these basic controversies. Chapter Two, recognizing that equality is ultimately highly sensitive to the society which it affects, examines the historical and current social context in respect of each of the main groups to which anti-discrimination law applies in Britain. Chapter Three examines the scope of discrimination law. Chapter Four uses the discussion thus far to assess the actual legal tools used in discrimination law. Chapter Five focuses on one of the most contested aspects of discrimination law, namely reverse discrimination, and Chapter Six considers the role of legal processes and remedies.

## I THE PRINCIPLE OF EQUALITY

### (i) BACKGROUND AND DEVELOPMENT

Equality as an ideal is a relatively modern construct. Classical and mediaeval societies were not founded on a principle of equality. Instead, society was ordered in hierarchical form, with entitlements and duties determined by birth or status rather than by virtue of an individual's inherent worth as a human being. Indeed, thinkers from Aristotle to Aquinas found no difficulty in justifying the subordination of women and slaves on grounds of their inherent inferiority, their lack of rationality, and their need for supervision and guidance from free male householders.

It was only with the advent of mercantile capitalism and the loosening bonds of feudalism that equality began to emerge as an organizing social principle. Greater economic freedom of individuals to pursue trade within a free market was accompanied by greater political freedom as Parliament gained power from the monarchy. It was in this hot-house climate of change and expectation that liberal ideology blossomed. John Locke, writing in 1690, captured the spirit of the age in his well-known aphorism: 'Men [are] by Nature all free, equal and independent'.[4] Politically, this meant increasing challenges to the authority of the monarch. Its economic manifestation was in the principle of freedom of contract. Freedom of contract was premised on the notion of equal parties, an abstract contractual equality which was oblivious to market reality.

Yet even then the promise of equality was ambiguous and exclusive. Indeed, a glance at the legal framework in the centuries following Locke reveals a landscape pock-marked with inequalities. Numerous groups, including women, slaves, religious minorities, black people, gypsies, and the unpropertied classes were excluded from the promise of liberal equality. Exclusion was achieved by the apparently logical argument that the basic rights to liberty and equality only inhered in individuals by virtue of their rationality. The concept of rationality could then be easily manipulated in an exclusive way. Women, slaves, and others were characterized as irrational and emotional and therefore not entitled to the equal rights due to rational beings.[5] Thus the newly ascendant equality principle co-existed with continued and unchallenged relations of domination. Slavery was not outlawed; colonialism flourished and women were denied basic rights such as the franchise, property ownership, and rights over their own children.[6] Locke himself saw no inconsistency between his lofty proclamation of equality and his description of the family as 'a Master . . . with all these subordinate Relations of Wife, Children, Servants and Slaves'.[7]

Nevertheless, the ideology of equality and freedom gave feminists and other disadvantaged groups the necessary vocabulary to argue for the emancipation of all. 'If all men are born free, why are women born slaves?' asked Mary Astell in 1700.[8] It was as a focus for political activism, rather than as a legal concept, that equality began to emerge as a real force for combatting sex discrimination and racism. But since the groups claiming equality inevitably lacked political power, progress was painfully slow. Three main phases in the development of a legal principle of

---

[4] John Locke, *Two Treatises of Government* P. Laslett (ed.) (Cambridge University Press, 1988) 'The Second Treatise', para. 95.

[5] S. Fredman, *Women and the Law* (Clarendon Press, 1997), ch. 1.

[6] See Fredman, above n. 5, chs. 1 and 2.

[7] Locke, above n. 4, 'Second Treatise', para. 86.

[8] M. Astell, 'Reflections upon Marriage', in M. Astell and B. Hill, *The First English Feminist* (Gower, 1986).

equality can be discerned. The first required the dismantling of formal legal impediments, such as slavery and the exclusion of married women from property rights, rights over their own children, and the suffrage. It was well into the twentieth century before the major impediments were removed.[9] Women in Britain only achieved equal suffrage as recently as 1928. Although equality before the law was a major achievement, it soon became clear that it was far from sufficient to achieve genuine equality. Women and members of racial or ethnic minorities were actively discriminated against, in the labour market, in housing, in social security and on the streets. Women were routinely paid on separate and lower scales than men doing the same work; black people were subjected to prejudice and exclusion. A new impetus was needed, in the form of legal prohibitions on discrimination or unequal treatment whether by public or private actors. This heralded the second stage, that of anti-discrimination legislation. Beginning in 1968, with the first weak and ineffectual race discrimination statute, this phase saw the introduction of statutory restrictions on discrimination in employment, education, and services. The domestic legislation, the Equal Pay Act 1970, the Sex Discrimination Act 1975, and the Race Relations Act 1976, were complemented and strengthened by sex discrimination legislation from the European Community. In 1995, a similar statutory framework was created to deal with discrimination on grounds of disability.

These laws have played an important role. But their limits, in turn, have become apparent. Three decades of anti-discrimination legislation have not been able to address deep-seated discriminatory structures. There remains a yawning gap between the pay of women and men; and ethnic minorities still experience unacceptably high levels of unemployment. Particularly disturbing is the finding of institutional racism in the Metropolitan police service, a body which should be combatting racism.[10] Equally problematic is the exclusion from current legislation both of significant groups and important areas of activity. It is these limitations which have prompted a reconsideration of equality laws; indeed, sustained campaigning has meant that we are now standing at the threshold of a new or third phase of equality laws. This requires both a widening of the scope of unlawful discrimination, and a sharpening of the tools to achieve, not just a negative prohibition on discrimination, but also a positive duty to promote equality. There are several new initiatives to

---

[9] On women, see Fredman, above n. 5, ch. 2.
[10] Home Office 'Report of the MacPherson Inquiry' Cm. 4262 February 24, 1999.

widen the grounds of unlawful discrimination. A range of new grounds of discrimination have been introduced with the incorporation of the European Convention on Human Rights. In addition, prompted by new EU directives, legislation will shortly be introduced to prohibit discrimination on grounds of religion, sexual orientation, and age. Equally significant is the introduction of new kinds of positive duties to promote equality. The damning indictment of racism in the police forces has produced legislation not just prohibiting discrimination across the range of activities by public authorities, but also requiring the active promotion of equality laws. Equality laws imposing positive duties on a range of actors are also being actively developed in other jurisdictions, most particularly the pioneering legislation in Northern Ireland and the introduction of 'mainstreaming' of sex equality in the European Union. The achievements of this third phase remain to be evaluated. Coverage is still patchy, and their impact and effectiveness remain largely untested.

It is against this background that we can begin to dissect the meaning of the concept of equality. In the following section, I consider more closely different notions of equality, considering first formal equality or equality as consistency, and then turning to different types of substantive equality, including equality of opportunity and equality of results. The second section is concerned with more substantive bases for equality, the most important being dignity, restitution, redistribution, and participative democracy. In the final section, I consider two important competitors with equality, namely liberty and market concerns.

## (II) FORMAL EQUALITY OR EQUALITY AS CONSISTENCY

The most basic concept of equality is the Aristotelian notion that likes should be treated alike. The power of this formulation derives from the even more elementary notion, that fairness requires consistent treatment. This principle appears to be both morally irrefutable and straightforward. Indeed, as we have seen, it has some important strengths. Crucially, it has meant that formal exclusionary laws must be dismantled; and overtly prejudicial behaviour, such as paying differential rates for like work, are prohibited.

However, equality in its formal sense of consistent treatment raises at least four sets of problems. The first concerns the threshold question of when two individuals are relevantly alike. Not every distinction is discriminatory. Governments and individuals classify people into groups for a wide variety of reasons and many of them are legitimate. For taxation reasons, it is quite legitimate to distinguish between high income and low-income groups. In the allocation of council housing, it is quite legitimate to distinguish between people with families and people without. Yet, as we have seen, for many years it was thought to be legitimate to distinguish women from men, blacks from whites. What sort of distinctions, therefore, should be outlawed by the law as illegitimate and unacceptable? One of the biggest leaps in twentieth century struggles for equality has been the recognition that characteristics based on race, sex, colour, or ethnic origin should not in themselves constitute relevant differences justifying inferior treatment. In other areas, such as sexual orientation, this recognition has still not been fully achieved. This question is explored further in Chapter Three.

The second difficulty is that equality as consistency is merely a relative principle. It requires only that two similarly situated individuals be treated alike. This means that there is no difference in principle between treating two such people equally badly, and treating them equally well. There is no substantive underpinning. For example, it has been held that if an employer harasses both men and women, then there is no discrimination on grounds of sex because they are both treated equally badly. Similarly, equal pay laws are of no benefit to a low paid woman if the only similarly situated male comparator is equally badly paid. In such a situation, the substantive right to a minimum wage would be more useful. Even more problematically, the absence of substantive underpinning means that a claim of equal treatment can just as easily be met by removing a benefit from the relatively privileged group, and equalizing the two parties at the lower point (levelling down), as by extending the benefit to the relatively underprivileged individual, and equalizing the parties at a high point (levelling up). In a famous US case, a city which was required to open its 'whites only' swimming pools to blacks chose instead to close down all its swimming pools.[11] It was held that identical treatment had been applied to both whites and blacks and that therefore there was no breach of the equality guarantee. In Britain, for many years, women were given 'special' health and safety protection. When this was held to infringe the equality people, the UK government removed the protections from women rather than extending them to men. Both these responses fulfilled the equality as consistency principle without benefiting anyone.

The third drawback of equality as consistency is the need to find a comparator. Inconsistent treatment can only be demonstrated by finding

---

[11] *Palmer v. Thompson* (1971) 403 US 217, 91 S Ct 1940.

a similarly situated person of the opposite race or sex who has been treated more favourably than the complainant. In making the judgement that two individuals are relevantly alike, the law requires us to disregard the race or sex of the parties. This in turn assumes that individuals can be considered in the abstract, apart from their colour, religion, ethnic origins, and gender. Yet an individual's social, economic, and political situation is still heavily determined by these very characteristics. The comparator, far from being an abstract individual, is in fact white, male, Christian, able-bodied, and heterosexual. Unless the claimant conforms to this norm, she cannot surmount the threshold requirement of demonstrating that she is similarly situated to the comparator. The result of the assumption of a 'universal individual' is therefore to create powerful conformist pressures. In feminist literature this has been dubbed the 'male norm'. Equality as consistency requires an answer to the question: 'Equal to whom?' The answer is, inevitably, 'equal to a man'. In the powerful words of Catherine MacKinnon: 'Concealed is the substantive way in which man has become the measure of all things. Under the sameness standard, women are measured according to our correspondence with man . . . Gender neutrality is thus simply the male standard'.[12] This problem was graphically illustrated in a recent Canadian case, in which a woman forest firefighter was dismissed for narrowly failing to pass a fitness test based on an aerobic standard demonstrably based on male physiology. Far from accepting a female norm of measurement, the Canadian Court of Appeals held that to apply a different standard for women would be creating reverse discrimination, unfairly discriminating against men. Fortunately, the Canadian Supreme Court reversed.[13] The problem has been even more acute in respect of pregnancy rights. On a strict view of equality as consistency, there is simply no appropriate male comparator and therefore no equality right arises. This difficulty was initially overcome by the unsatisfactory mechanism of comparing the treatment received by a pregnant woman with that of an ill man. It was only when the court could move beyond the idea of equality as consistency and therefore beyond the need for a male comparator that real progress could be made.[14] But this problem continues to dog discrimination legislation. In the area of equal pay, job segregation means that a

---

[12] C. MacKinnon, *Feminism Unmodified* Harvard University Press (1987) p. 34.

[13] *British Columbia Public Service Employee Relations Commission v. B.C.G.E.U.* [1997] CCL 8468, Canadian Supreme Court.

[14] See further S. Fredman, 'A Difference with Distinction: Pregnancy and Parenthood Reassessed' (1994) 110 LQR 106.

low paid woman will frequently be unable to find a male comparator doing equivalent work in her establishment. A nursery nurse or a cleaner or a secretary is likely to find herself in an all-female workforce; or in an establishment where the only men are in managerial positions and therefore not useful comparators.[15] Similarly a Muslim employee wishing to take time off work to attend Mosque may not find a relevant comparator, since potential comparators would not need time off for this purpose. Parekh puts it starkly: 'The choice before the minorities is simple. If they wish to become part of and be treated like the rest of the community, they should think and live like the latter; if instead they insist on retaining their separate cultures, they should not complain if they are treated differently'.[16]

The fourth problematic aspect of equality as consistency is its treatment of difference. Only 'likes' qualify for equal treatment; there is no requirement that people be treated appropriately according to their difference. Thus if a woman is doing work of less value than a comparable man, it may be appropriate to pay her less. But the equality as consistency principle does not require that she be paid proportionately to the difference in the value of her work. Similarly, cultural and religious difference might require positive measures which value difference in order to achieve genuine equality. Conversely, as we have seen, 'like' treatment may in practice entrench difference.

Finally, equality as consistency is intensely individualist. Of course, the major contribution of equality has been its insistence that an individual be treated according to her own qualities or merits, and not on the basis of negative stereotypes attributed to her because of her race or sex. However, in rejecting the negative effects of taking group-based characteristics into account, the principle of equality has assumed that all aspects of group membership should be disregarded. Yet, as we have seen, cultural, religious, and ethnic group membership is an important aspect of an individual's identity. Indeed, to attempt to abstract the individual from that context is not to create a universal individual, but simply to clothe her with the attributes of the dominant culture, religion, or ethnicity. An equally problematic aspect of this individualism is the emphasis on individual fault as the only legitimate basis for imposing liability. The correlative of treating a person only on the basis of her 'merit', is the

---

[15] See further S. Fredman, above n. 5, pp. 185–193.

[16] B. Parekh, 'Integrating Minorities' in T. Blackstone, B. Parekh, and P. Sanders, *Race Relations in Britain* (Routledge, 1998), p. 2.

principle that an individual should only be liable for damage for which he or she is responsible. This in turn means that only a respondent who can be proved to have treated the complainant less favourably on grounds of her race can be held liable for compensation. Yet sexism, racism, and other forms of discrimination extend far beyond individual acts of prejudice. Such prejudices are frequently embedded in the structure of society, and cannot be attributed clearly to any one person.

While formal equality or equality of treatment has a role to play, particularly in eradicating personal prejudice, it is clear from the above that it needs to be allied to a more substantive approach. It is to these that we now turn.

### (III) EQUALITY OF RESULTS

On this view, the equality principle goes beyond a demand for consistent treatment of likes, and requires instead that the result be equal. The strength of this notion of equality lies in its recognition that apparently identical treatment can in practice reinforce inequality because of past or on-going discrimination. Thus if there has been race discrimination in the provision of education for black children, a requirement of literacy as a precondition for voting rights will, although applied equally to all, in effect exclude a significant proportion of black people. Similarly, given that many women have their children in their early twenties, an upper age limit of twenty-eight for entry into the civil service, although applied to both men and women, will in effect exclude more women than men. This description shows too that the aim of equality of results is different from that of equality as consistency. Equality of results is primarily concerned with achieving a fairer distribution of benefits; while formal equality is based on a notion of procedural fairness stemming from consistent treatment.

However, a closer look at the notion of equality of results demonstrates some worrying ambiguities. Results or impact can be used in at least three different ways. The first focuses on the impact on the individual. Has the apparently equal treatment had a detrimental impact on this individual because of her race or sex? On this version, the aim is not to achieve equality of results but to obtain a remedy for the individual. Take for example the case of the school which prohibited the wearing of head coverings. The result was to exclude an observant Sikh boy. The removal of the rule meant that the boy was no longer barred, and the discriminatory impact on him was remedied. The dismantling of this particular obstacle would not, however, lead to a proportionate representation of

Sikhs at the school. The focus on the individual could also have the opposite effect. Thus if an individual member of a group is considered to be capable of complying with a condition, it becomes irrelevant that the majority of the members of her group are excluded by the same condition. In a recent sex discrimination case, it was held that although the requirement of full-time working excluded more women than men, in this case, the woman 'could' comply with the condition because she earned enough to afford child-care.[17] Thus the employer's refusal to allow a relatively senior job to be reorganized as a job share was found to be non-discriminatory. As well as making problematic assumptions to the effect that there is no difference to a woman between paying for child-care and spending time herself with her children, the result of this approach is to leave the discriminatory structure intact.

The second way in which equality of results is used focuses not on the results to the individual, but to the group. However, its aim is diagnostic, demonstrating the existence of obstacles to entry rather than prescribing an outcome pattern. Underlying this approach is the presumption that in a non-discriminatory environment, a fair spread of members of different sexes, races, or religions would be found in any particular body, be it a workforce, an educational establishment, or a decision-making body. The absence of one group, or its concentration in less lucrative or important areas, is taken as a sign that discrimination is probably taking place. But this is only a presumption. If no exclusionary criterion or obstacle can be proved, then it is assumed that the maldistribution is due to other factors, such as personal preference. Alternatively, if there is such a criterion, but it can be justified by the needs of the job, the presumption of discrimination is displaced. For example, a glance at the statistics shows that there are almost no women airline pilots. This inequality of results raises a presumption of discrimination. If it can be shown that women are excluded because it is believed that they will not make good pilots, then the inequality of results has been diagnostic of discrimination. But if it is shown that they are excluded because there are not enough well trained women, then it could be argued, relying on this conception of equality, that despite the inequality of results, there is no discrimination.

The third and strongest meaning of 'equality of results' requires an equal outcome, that is that the spread of women or minorities in a

[17] *Clymo v. Wandsworth* [1989] IRLR 241, EAT.

category should reflect their proportions in the workforce or the population as a whole. Thus there is no need for proof of an intervening 'discriminatory' factor to trigger action. The mere fact of under-representation is discriminatory; and action should be aimed at achieving an equal outcome. Thus, as will be seen in later chapters, several jurisdictions have introduced legislation with the explicit aim of increasing the representation of minorities or women in employment or public office.[18] This notion of equality of results is at its most controversial when it goes beyond the removal of exclusionary criteria and requires the achievement of an equal outcome by preferential treatment of the under-represented group. The reconciliation of reverse discrimination with the principle of equality is considered in detail in Chapter Five. But equality of results need not be achieved through openly preferential treatment. It could be achieved through encouragement, training and other such measures. It is notable that even here, the notion of equality is not fully in focus: it is usually not equality but proportionality, fairness, or balance which is required.

There is a sense in which equality of results is a strategically straight-forward goal, since results are relatively easily quantifiable. However, the focus on results might itself be misleading. This is because monitoring of results does not necessitate any fundamental re-examination of the structures that perpetuate discrimination. A change in the colour or gender composition of a grade or sector, while to some extent positive, might reflect only an increasingly successful assimilationist policy. Thus women who achieve these positions might have done so by conforming to 'male' working patterns, contracting out their child-care obligations to other women, who remain as underpaid and undervalued as ever. Members of ethnic minorities who achieve these positions may be those who had assimilated, whether voluntarily or because of absence of available options, in terms of dress, religious observance, or language. Similarly, the increase in numbers of women or black people doing certain types of jobs might coincide with a decrease in the pay or status of the job in question. Such a pattern has been clearly demonstrated in catering. Here, in an apparently positive move towards equality of results, women have increased their share of management jobs dramatically. Yet on closer inspection, it is found that the newly feminized managerial positions are relatively low paid (sometimes even less than the national average pay).

[18] Fair Employment and Treatment (Northern Ireland) Order (FETO) 1998, art. 4(1); Fair Employment Act 1989; Canadian Employment Equity Act 1995, s. 2.

Thus quantifiable change might only partially reflect qualitative change. There is a danger too that a focus on equality of results pays too little attention to the equally important duty to accommodate diversity by adapting existing structures.

Nor is it always entirely clear which 'results' are relevant. The argument is usually concerned with jobs or places at schools or universities, but does it extend to all goods and social benefits, and to representation in Parliament and local authorities? As will be seen later, the justification for a redistribution of jobs in favour of an excluded minority is very different from that needed to explain a redistribution of representation, given that democratically elected representatives are not expected to mirror exactly the interests of the racial or gender group to which they belong— assuming of course that such interests are homogeneous or easily identifiable.

## (IV) EQUALITY OF OPPORTUNITY

An increasingly popular alternative to both equality as consistency and equality of results is the notion of equality of opportunity. This notion steers a middle ground between formal equality and equality of results. Proponents of this view recognize that equal treatment against a background of past and structural discrimination can perpetuate disadvantage. Using the graphic metaphor of competitors in a race, it is argued that true equality cannot be achieved if individuals begin the race from different starting points. However, according to this approach, to focus entirely on equality of results is to go too far in subordinating the right to individual treatment to a utilitarian emphasis on outcomes. Once individuals enjoy equality of opportunity, the problem of institutional discrimination has been overcome, and fairness demands that they be treated on the basis of their individual qualities, without regard to sex or race. This model therefore specifically rejects policies which aim to correct imbalances in the work force by quotas or targets whose aim is one of equality of outcome. Instead, an equal opportunities approach aims to equalize the starting point; allowing the competitors to be judged on individual merit once the race has begun.

However, the metaphor of equal starting points is deceptively simple. What measures are required to ensure that individuals are genuinely able to compete equally? Williams distinguishes between a procedural and a substantive sense of equal opportunities. On a procedural view, equality of opportunity requires the removal of obstacles to the advancement of women or minorities, but does not guarantee that this will lead to greater substantive fairness in the result.[19] For example, the abolition of word-of-mouth recruitment or non-job-related selection criteria removes procedural obstacles and so opens up more opportunities. But this does not guarantee that more women or minorities will in fact be in a position to take advantage of those opportunities. Those who lack the requisite qualifications as a result of past discrimination will still be unable to meet job-related criteria; women with child-care responsibilities will still not find it easier to take on paid work. In the famous words of US President Lyndon Johnson, it is 'not enough to open the gates of opportunity. All our citizens must have the ability to walk through those gates'.[20]

A substantive sense of equality of opportunity, by contrast, requires measures to be taken to ensure that persons from all sections of society have a genuinely equal chance of satisfying the criteria for access to a particular social good.[21] This requires positive measures such as education and training, and family friendly measures. It may go even further, and challenge the criteria for access themselves, since existing criteria of merit may themselves reflect and reinforce existing patterns of disadvantage. For example, criteria which stress a continuous work history would reflect a view that experience out of the paid labour force is of little value to a future job. Women who have left the paid work force to bring up children would thereby by subject to detriment. As Hepple argues, one is not supplying genuine equality of opportunity if one applies an unchallenged criterion of merit to people who have been deprived of the opportunity to acquire 'merit'.[22]

## II A VALUE DRIVEN APPROACH

Equality laws have traditionally been founded and legitimated on grounds that they further the liberal goals of State neutrality, individualism, and the promotion of autonomy. Neutrality is achieved by forbidding State preferences for any one group or one conception of 'the good life' and is expressed first and foremost through the notion of formal

---

[19] B. Williams, 'The idea of equality' in P. Laslett and W. G. Runciman (eds.), *Philosophy, Politics and Society Second Series* (Blackwell, 1965), p. 110 and see J. Waldron in S. Guest and A. Milne (eds.), *Equality and Discrimination* (F. Steiner Verlag Wiesbaden, 1985), p. 97.

[20] Lyndon B. Johnson, Address at Howard University (June 4, 1965) cited in A. Thernstrom, 'Voting Rights, Another Affirmative Action Mess' [1996] 43 UCLA Law Review 2031, n. 22.

[21] Williams, above n. 19, at pp. 125–6.

[22] B. Hepple, 'Discrimination and Equality of Opportunity—Northern Irish lessons' [1990] 10 *Oxford Journal of Legal Studies* 408 at 411.

equality before the law. Beyond that, neutrality is furthered through a focus on fairness as consistency, requiring likes to be treated alike. Individualism is a second fundamental tenet of liberal equality law. On this analysis, the chief mischief of discrimination is that a person is subjected to detriment because she is attributed with stereotypical qualities based on a denigratory notion of her group membership. Respect for the individual requires that she be treated on her individual merits and regardless of her group membership. Autonomy is thus furthered by freeing her to make her own choices as to her view of the good life.

These aims have an immediate appeal: it seems logical to respond to the identified problem of discrimination by requiring that each person be treated as an individual, according to her own merits. However, the values of neutrality, individualism, and autonomy are, on closer examination, highly problematic. Most fundamentally, the apparent commitment to neutrality and individualism masks an insistence on a particular set of values, based on those of the dominant culture. This is because the basic premise, namely that there exists a 'universal individual', is deeply deceptive. It is true that everyone has attributes which are independent of group identities. But at the same time, it must be recognized that each individual is constituted partly by group affinities,[23] in his or her sense of identity, history, affinity with others, mode of reasoning, and expression of feelings. In practice, then, the apparently abstract individual is clothed with the attributes of the dominant culture, religion, or ethnicity. It is not a coincidence that ethnicity is usually associated with minorities, as though the dominant group stands for a universality rather than its own ethnic specificity.

Legislatures and courts in several jurisdictions have attempted to articulate an alternate set of values or principles informing the equality principle. Thus a statement of values to be furthered by the equality guarantee may be included in a preamble to a bill of rights or constitution. Four intertwined themes can be discerned: the first stressing the primacy of individual dignity and worth; the second based on the restitutionary[24] notion of redressing past discrimination; the third articulating redistributive aims; and the fourth founded in democratic concerns. Each of these will be considered in turn.

---

[23] I.M. Young, above n. 3, at p. 45.

[24] L.W.H. Ackermann, 'Equality and the South African Constitution: The Role of Dignity', Bram Fischer Lecture delivered at Rhodes House, Oxford on May 26, 2000.

## (I) DIGNITY

The primacy of individual dignity and worth as a foundation for equality rights has been clearly articulated in a number of jurisdictions, both in constitutional or statutory documents and by courts. Thus the Canadian Supreme Court declared in a recent case that the fundamental values enshrined in the Canadian Charter's equality guarantee are the 'protection and enhancement of human dignity, the promotion of equal opportunity, and the development of human potential based upon individual ability'. The purpose of the equality guarantee is declared to be 'to prevent the violation of human dignity and freedom through the imposition of limitations, disadvantages or burdens, through the stereotypical application of presumed group characteristics, rather than on the basis of merit, capacity or circumstance'.[25] Dignity is also central to the articulated values of the new South African Constitution. Addressing directly the history of humiliation and degradation to which the previous apartheid regime was dedicated, section 1 of the Constitution states that, amongst other things, the new South African State is founded on the values of 'human dignity, the achievement of equality, and the advancement of human rights and freedoms'. The general limitation clause in the South African Constitution also states emphatically that a right entrenched by the Constitution can only be limited to the extent that the limitation is 'reasonable and justifiable in an open and democratic society based on human dignity, autonomy, and freedom'.[26] Most importantly, the South African Constitution requires every court, when interpreting human rights, to do so in a way which promotes the values of human dignity, equality, and freedom.[27] Similarly, the German Basic Law, also strongly influenced by recent history, provides in its first and absolutely entrenched article, that human dignity is unassailable and that it is the duty of all State authority to respect and protect it.[28] Notably too, the right to dignity is established in the first Article of the European Union Charter of Fundamental Human Rights proclaimed in Nice in December 2000.

Such a commitment to the underlying values of human dignity and freedom ensures that equality has a universal application. As the German Constitutional Court put it: 'Since all persons are entitled to human dignity and freedom and to that extent are equal, the principle of equal

---

[25] *Miron v. Trudel* [1995] 2 SCR 418 at 489.
[26] South African Constitution, s. 36(1).　　　[27] *ibid.*, ss. 39(1) and (2).
[28] Basic Law for the Federal Republic of Germany (Grundgesetz, GG), Art. 1(1).

treatment is an obvious postulate for free democracy'.[29] Most importantly, dignity replaces rationality as a trigger for the equality right. As we
have seen, the link of equality with rationality has been used to deny
access to the equality right; in particular to women, who were portrayed
as lacking the prerequisite rationality. The crucial advance represented by
substituting dignity for rationality is that dignity is seen to be inherent in
the humanity of all people.

There are several concrete ways in which the dignity value influences
the development of the equality principle. Firstly, dignity creates a substantive underpinning to the equality principle. This makes it impossible
to argue that the principle of equality is satisfied by 'equally bad' treatment or by removing a benefit from the advantaged group and thereby
'levelling down'. Equality based on dignity must enhance rather than
diminish the status of individuals. The second way in which the dignity
value influences equality relates to the coverage of equality laws. In many
human rights documents, the list of groups who are protected against
unlawful discrimination may be expanded by courts. The dignity concept
allows such expansion to take place in a principled manner. For example,
the Canadian Supreme Court has held that the decision as to whether the
equality guarantee in the Canadian Charter of Rights prevents discrimination on a ground not specifically enumerated should be decided by considering the primary mission of the equality guarantee. This mission,
according to L'Hureux-Dube J, is 'the promotion of a society in which all
are secure in the knowledge that they are recognized at law as human
beings equally deserving of concern, respect, and consideration'.[30] On
this view, a person or group has been discriminated against when a legislative distinction makes them feel that they are less worthy of recognition
or value as human beings, as members of society.[31] Similarly, the question
of whether differentiation on a ground not specified in the South African
Constitution amounts to discrimination is answered by considering
whether the differentiation is based on attributes or characteristics which
objectively have the potential to impair the fundamental dignity of
persons as human beings.[32]

The idealism behind the focus on dignity is apparent from these

---

[29] *Communist Party* 5 BverfGE 85 (1956). (I am indebted to Mr Justice L.W.H.
Ackermann for drawing my attention to this quote.)

[30] *Andrews v. Law Society of British Columbia* [1989] 1 SCR 143 at 171.

[31] *Egan v. Canada* [1995] 2 SCR 513 at 545 (para. 39); *Vriend v. Alberta* [1998] 1 SCR 493,
156 DLR (4th) 385, [1998] 4 BHRC 140 at 185 (para 182).

[32] Ackermann, above n. 24, p. 14.

quotations. But a closer look at the concept itself reveals that it could have a range of meanings. According to Ackermann, dignity in the South African Constitution connotes 'innate, priceless and indefeasible human worth'.[33] The value attached to individuals simply by virtue of their humanity logically connotes that all are entitled to equal concern and respect. The profound importance of this value is unquestionable. At the same time, this formulation is compatible with a range of different approaches to equality.[34] Dignity is often linked to autonomy or the freedom of the individual to choose according to his or her view of the 'good' life. But on one view, freedom means absence of State intervention. This would give rise to a minimal notion of equality as equal absence from interference, a notion of equality which is consistent with wide divergences in wealth and quality of life.[35] At the other end of the scale, dignity could entail policies which aim to achieve equal welfare of individuals, or, alternatively, equal share of the resources distributed by the economic structure.[36] Alternatively, dignity could entail, as the Canadian Supreme Court has stated, 'the development of human potential based upon individual ability'.[37] For individuals who can achieve well once the burdens of stereotyping and stigma are removed, this notion holds great promise. But for those whose capacities are either innately limited or have themselves been limited by the effects of cumulative disadvantage, an equality conditional on merit might well be a false promise.

## (II) REMEDIAL AND RESTITUTIONARY AIMS

The second value underlying equality laws focuses instead on remedial or restitutionary aims. In this more historically specific sense, equality is aimed at compensating individuals for the detriment caused by prejudice and the ongoing effects of past discrimination. This is arguably the primary aim of many anti-discrimination statutes, emanating as they do from a political recognition of injustice stemming from racism, sexism, and other sorts of discrimination, whether in the extreme forms found under apartheid, Nazi Germany, or slavery, or the more subtle but equally insidious forms found in most societies. A concept of equality infused with this aim would need to be responsive to the particular problems it is intended to deal with, and be continually shaped and reshaped in order to

---

[33] *ibid*, p. 8.

[34] See D. Feldman, 'Human Dignity as a Legal Value' *Public Law* Winter 1999, p. 682.

[35] R. Dworkin, *Sovereign Virtue: The Theory and Practice of Equality* (Harvard University Press, 2000), p. 131.

[36] *ibid*.     [37] *Miron v. Trudel* [1995] 2 SCR 418 at 489.

achieve this aim effectively. Thus it has become clear that formal equality or equality as consistency can make only limited inroads on ongoing disadvantage resulting from past or continuing injustice. It is for this reason that more attention has been paid to equality of results or of opportunity.

Again, however, this value is not in itself sufficient to generate a single formulation of equality. Further decisions need to be taken on the weight to be given to individual interests, particularly the acceptability of utilitarianism and the relationship between community responsibility and individual fault. A spectrum of responses to this question is available. Traditionally, remedial functions in the law have been premised on the view that only if individual fault has been proved can an individual be required to provide a remedy. This leads to a limited view of the remedial ability of equality laws, since the effects of past discrimination are usually diffuse and often embedded in social structures. Such a focus on fault or intention to discriminate is particularly restrictive when applied in the context of State action. In the US, for example, it has been held that an invidious discriminatory purpose must be proved before a law or other official act can be held to breach the constitutional equality guarantee.[38] This has substantially undermined the ability of the equality principle to reach beyond a requirement of equal treatment. Alternatively, instead of requiring fault or intention to discriminate, it is possible to stress broader questions of community justice. Here the notion of restitutionary justice is helpful, since it has the advantage of substituting the notion of 'unjust enrichment' for the need for fault. Thus an individual who has benefited by virtue of his or her race or sex may be required to participate in the removal of racism or sexism even if he or she cannot be proved to have been responsible for the fault.[39] An even more thoroughgoing notion of communal justice might go further and stress that past discrimination can only be properly remedied when there has been equality of results, even if this entails detriment to some individuals.

## (III) DISTRIBUTIVE JUSTICE

A third value underlying equality is more explicitly redistributive, aiming not just to redress previous disadvantage but to achieve an equal distribution of social goods. On this view, true equal concern and respect is

---

[38] *Washington v. Davis* (1976) 426 US 229, 96 S Ct 2040.
[39] I am indebted to Mr Justice L.W.H. Ackermann for this point.

incompatible with extreme disparities of wealth, with segregation of a particular group into low paying, low status jobs and with severe under-representation of some groups in positions of power or representative bodies. This aim, however, is only helpful if the social resources in question are clearly specified. It is a difficult but workable aim if it is focused on the achievement of better representation of particular groups in specific occupations or higher status jobs. Thus in Northern Ireland, legislation has been enacted with the explicit aim of fair participation of Catholics and Protestants in employment, where fair participation has been interpreted as proportional representation. In this sense, the complexity arises in relation to the means to achieve this end, and in particular whether preferential treatment is permitted. Far more difficult are other social goods. Better distribution of representation in Parliament or other elected bodies does not have the same meaning as redistribution of jobs. We have long moved beyond the idea that the status or group membership of a representative matters more than what he or she believes or stands for.[40] The argument in favour of greater representation of under-represented groups must be couched in different terms from an argument in favour of redistribution of material benefits. Equally complex is the question of distribution of money or resources. Dworkin has recently devoted a long and complex work to the elaboration of a theory of material equality which he calls equality of resources.[41] This is of course only one of a rich tradition of theories of egalitarianism in distribution, including seminal works of theorists such as Marx, Rawls, Beveridge, and Marshall.

The difficulty in specifying both the benefits to be redistributed and the meaning of distributive equality is not the only source of criticism of distributive justice as an underlying value to be achieved by equality. Young argues forcefully that the distributive paradigm, which defines social justice as the morally proper distribution of social benefits and burdens among society's members,[42] has been given a distorted significance in theories of justice. Because it focuses on the allocation of material goods, the distributive paradigm ignores social structures such as decision-making power, the division of labour and culture, or the symbolic meanings attached to people, actions, and things.[43] Power itself, in her view, is not appropriately defined as a distributive benefit, because this makes power appear to be a possession rather than a relationship.

---

[40] See generally A. Phillips, *The Politics of Presence* (Clarendon Press, 1995).
[41] Dworkin, above n. 35.     [42] Young, above n. 3, p. 16.     [43] *ibid.*

Instead, she argues, the focus should be on domination, or structures which exclude people from participating in determining their actions. Crucially, domination need not be attributable to the actions of any particular individual, but produces constraints which are the intended or unintended product of actions of many people.[44]

## (IV) PARTICIPATIVE DEMOCRACY

These insights introduce the fourth possible underlying value of equality, namely that of participative democracy. Thus Young argues that social equality, while referring in part to the distribution of social goods, primarily refers to the full participation and inclusion of everyone in major social institutions.[45] A rich idea of equality sees equality as participation and inclusion of all groups, which in turn requires valuing difference and at times treating groups relevantly differently.[46] On this view, equality laws aim to remedy a flaw in majoritarian democracy. Originating in a famous footnote to a US Supreme Court decision, this view focuses on the way in which 'prejudice against discrete and insular minorities . . . tends seriously to curtail the operation of those political processes ordinarily to be relied upon to protect minorities'.[47] This notion was taken up by John Hart Ely, who argued that courts had a legitimate role to play in reviewing legislation where '(1) the ins are choking off the channels of political change to ensure that they will stay in and the outs will stay out; or (2) though no one is actually denied a voice or a vote, representatives beholden to an effective majority are systematically disadvantaging some minority'.[48] Although he was dealing with judicial review in general, his views illuminate the central value to equality of democratic participation. Given that past discrimination or other social mechanisms have blocked the avenues for political participation by particular minorities, legal rights, particularly equality laws, are needed both to compensate for this absence of political voice and to open up the channels for greater participation in the future. This approach has been explicitly used to require that the equality guarantee be extended to specific groups. Thus in a recent Canadian case, Ely's work was cited in order to show that the equality guarantee should extend to non-citizens, for the very reason that

---

[44] Young, above n. 3, pp. 31–2.          [45] *ibid*, p. 173.          [46] *ibid*, p. 158.
[47] *United States v. Carolene Products Company* (1938) 304 US 144, at 152, n. 4 (*per* Stone J).
[48] J. H. Ely, *Democracy and Distrust: A Theory of Judicial Review* (Harvard University Press, 1980), p. 103.

they lack in political power and are vulnerable to have their interests overlooked and their rights to equal concern and respect violated.[49]

## III COMPETING VALUES: LIBERTY OR EQUALITY

Even when agreement is reached on a specific conception or set of conceptions of equality as a basis for a legislative formulation of equality, it is still necessary to consider whether and in what circumstances, other, non equality based values should trump equality concerns. Two related rivals with equality will be considered here: liberty and economic or market concerns.

### (I) LIBERTY

Possibly the most serious rival for priority with equality is freedom or liberty. Indeed, Isaiah Berlin in his famous work characterized liberty and equality as the two major but frequently conflicting values: 'Both liberty and equality are among the primary goals pursued by human beings through many centuries; but total liberty for wolves is death to the lambs, total liberty of the powerful, the gifted is not compatible with the rights to a decent existence of the weak and the less gifted'.[50]

Closer examination shows, however, that, just as equality can be interpreted in many differing ways, so can liberty. Liberty could, at one extreme, mean simply licence; but this is hardly a plausible interpretation, since that would prohibit even laws against murder and theft. Instead, liberty is normally allied with a substantive value, such as speech.[51] Moreover, the extent of conflict between equality and liberty depends in part on which conception of equality is chosen. Thus a laissez faire egalitarian might find no conflict between liberty and equality: individuals should be equally free from State interference in order to pursue their own goals, and their fate depends on their own abilities, initiative, and luck.[52] Dworkin, by contrast, argues for a much stronger conception of equality, but nevertheless formulates a principle of liberty which, far from conflicting with equality, is a crucial ingredient. Equality of resources, on his argument, can only be achieved if each individual is not only free to make choices but must also take responsibility for those choices based on the cost of their decisions to other people.[53]

---

[49] *Andrews v. Law Society (British Columbia)* [1989] 1 SCR 143.
[50] I. Berlin, *Four Essays on Liberty* (Oxford University Press, 1969).
[51] Dworkin, above n. 35, p. 127.
[52] *ibid.*, p. 131.  [53] *ibid.*, p. 122.

Nevertheless, the practical experience of equality laws demonstrates clear potential for conflict between liberty and equality. Thus courts have had to decide whether prohibitions on racist speech should be struck down as infringing freedom of speech, or upheld as promoting racial equality. While courts in the US have upheld the freedom of speech value, Canadian courts have upheld the equality value.[54] Similarly, a statute restricting expenditure on political campaigns could be construed as unduly restricting liberty. Alternatively, it could be seen as legitimately promoting the egalitarian aim of ensuring that the political voice of richer individuals did not drown out that of poorer people.[55] Particularly complex is the relationship of liberty to substantive equality based on socio-economic rights. Thus minimum wages and maximum hours laws could be struck down because they undermine individual freedom of contract or upheld because they promote substantive equality.[56]

## (II) BUSINESS OR MARKET ORIENTED CONCERNS

Apart from the conflict with fundamental liberties, the major modern rival for priority with equality is that of business or market oriented concerns. In most jurisdictions, statutes and case-law have specifically permitted individuals or States to defend incursions on equality on the grounds that this is justified as a pursuit of business needs or State macro-economic policies. The question then concerns the weight to be given to each of these concerns. Can a policy or business interest displace equality simply because it is convenient or strategic, or must it be demonstrably necessary to achieve the business needs in question? The formulation and application of the so-called justification test has been a central concern in numerous cases.

A particularly important symbiotic relationship between equality and economic concerns has developed at EU level. The European Economic Community was initially established with the primary purpose of creating a common market in goods, services, and labour. At most it was envisaged that social policy at Community level was to have the sole purpose of

---

[54] *RAV v. City of St Paul, Minn* (1992) 505 US 377, 112 S Ct 2538; *R v. Keegstra* (1996) 61 CCC 3d 1, Supreme Court of Canada.
[55] *Buckley v. Valeo* (1976) 424 US 1, 96 S Ct 612; *Bowman v United Kingdom* (1998) 26 EHRR 1.
[56] *Lochner v. New York* (1905) 198 US 45, 25 S Ct 539.

creating a European-wide labour market.[57] Yet such market based aims were seen as necessitating, at the very least, a principle of equal pay for equal work for men and women. If some Member States were permitted to pay women less for the same work as men, it was thought, those Member States would achieve an unfair competitive advantage over others. This was particularly important for France, which already had equal pay laws in place. Equality could not, however, remain indefinitely subservient to market based aims. Within two decades, it was acknowledged, particularly by the European Court of Justice, that the sex equality provisions also had their basis in the fundamental human right to equality.[58] The most recent anti-discrimination provisions at EU level now place economic and social concerns side by side.

It is notable that little attention has been paid as to why business needs should trump equality. One plausible justification is that of liberty itself: the liberty of employers or other powerful actors to pursue their own interests should not, on this view, be infringed. During the 1980s and the early 1990s, this view was in the ascendant, owing to the political dominance of a neo-liberal laissez-faire ideology. This blatant preference for liberty over equality is often softened by the assertion that the good of the individual business will further the good of all, even if it subordinates particular equality rights (such as the right of a woman to equal pay with a man doing work of equal value). In an attempt to counteract the power of this ideology, the more mellow final years of the twentieth century saw an attempt to a create convergence between the two notions. Thus it has been argued that, far from detracting from market concerns, equality laws are demonstrably capable of serving economic and particularly efficiency-based ends.[59] Indeed, in the European Union, possibly the most striking characteristic of the past five years has been the convergence, at least at the level of rhetoric, between fundamental rights justifications and labour market justifications for equal opportunities. This convergence is crucially related to the shift in the labour market objectives of the EU from market creation to job creation.[60] Crucially, the high rates of unemployment among women were identified as one of the areas of concern. The

---

[57] See, e.g. W. Streeck, 'From Market Making to State Building' in S. Leibfried and P. Pierson (eds.), *European Social Policy: Between Fragmentation and Integration* (Brookings Institution, 1995), p. 397.

[58] Case 149/77 *Defrenne v. Sabena (Defrenne No. 2)* [1978] ECR 1365.

[59] See S. Deakin 'Labour Law as Market Regulation' in P. Davies *et al.* (eds.), *European Community Labour Law: Principles and Perspectives* (Clarendon Press, 1996); S. Deakin and F. Wilkinson, 'Rights vs Efficiency?' [1994] 23 ILJ 289.

[60] See M. R. Freedland, 'Employment Policy' in Davies *et al.* (eds.), above n. 59.

result is that the impetus for gender equality has been seen through an 'economic prism', which characterizes the disadvantaged position of women in the labour market as a source of economic inefficiency, and therefore includes sex equality within its strategy to achieve economic competitiveness.[61]

Of course, there is always the danger that instead of a genuine and mutually reinforcing coincidence of aims, the rhetoric of convergence has merely obscured the extent to which market concerns have stunted the growth of a truly rights-based equality principle. When the court holds the balance between the equality value and that of market or business concerns, the weight given to the various values becomes crucial. A bias towards business needs would yield a test which allowed mere convenience to justify an infringement on equality, whereas a greater (although not absolute) commitment to equality would require that it only be limited to the extent strictly necessary to achieve the stated aim. For example, if an employer wishes to justify paying female part-time workers less than male full-timers doing the same job, a lenient standard would allow him or her simply to assert that part-timers are less valuable, or that it is more profitable to pay them less. A strict standard would require that the employer prove that there is no less discriminatory alternative to achieving the stated aim of increased profits or creating a more productive workforce.

## IV CONCLUSION

This chapter has examined some of the major conceptual issues surrounding the equality principle. It has considered differing conceptions of the equality principle and sketched out possible limitations and complexities. The next chapter, recognizing that equality cannot be considered in the abstract, but must be understood in its historical and political context, turns to a consideration of the causes and patterns of inequality.

---

[61] See S. Duncan, 'Obstacles to a Successful Equal Opportunities Policy in the EU' (1996) 3:4 *European Journal of Women's Studies* 399–422.

# Sources of Discrimination: Racism, Sexism, and Prejudice

Anti-discrimination law is necessarily a response to particular manifestations of inequality, which are themselves deeply embedded in the historical and political context of a given society. Discrimination laws are only
effective if they are moulded to deal with the types of inequalities which
have developed in the society to which they refer. It is therefore particularly important to trace the history of prejudice and discrimination in
Britain, and, where relevant Europe, in order to understand the strengths
and weaknesses of the framework of discrimination legislation, and to be
in a position to propose sensible reforms. This chapter briefly sketches
the history and context of some of the main sources of discrimination in
modern Britain. A comprehensive survey is impossible within the bounds
of a brief work such as this, particularly because, as was noted in Chapter
One, 'discrete and insular' minorities are in the process of evolving. The
chapter therefore focuses on women, ethnic and religious minorities, gay
men and lesbian women, and disabled people.

## I  WOMEN

The development of equality for women in any real sense is disturbingly
recent.[1] Until well into the twentieth century, women were legally subordinate to men in a host of different ways. This was especially true of
marriage. Under the common law, known as 'coverture', marriage constituted of a legal obliteration of women's identity. 'The very being or legal
existence of the wife is suspended during the marriage or at least
incorporated and consolidated into that of the husband under whose
wing, protection and cover she performs everything',[2] wrote Blackstone

---

[1] This section is drawn substantially from S. Fredman, *Women and the Law* (Clarendon
Press, 1997), ch. 2.
[2] W. Blackstone, *Commentaries on the Law of England* (15th ed., T. Cadell & W. Davies,
1809), book I ch. XV p. 430.

in 1809. A married woman was a perpetual legal minor: her husband had near-absolute control over her property as well as her person. She had no right to custody of their children and no right to testamentary freedom. Her husband even had the power of 'domestic chastisement'. Even when this power had come to be doubted, substantial levels of violence perpetrated against wives were tacitly condoned. Nor was a married woman entitled to refuse consent to sexual intercourse with her husband. Indeed, it was not until the last decades of the twentieth century that rape in marriage was recognized as a crime. Not surprisingly, John Stuart Mill described the law of marriage as 'the only legal bondage known to our law'.[3]

Why then was marriage the focus of women's legal subordination? O'Brien has powerfully demonstrated the important influence of the difference in women and men's reproductive capacities.[4] Not only has women's ability to give birth meant that she has consistently had prime responsibility for child-care. In addition, men's inability to be absolutely certain of their paternity, has generated deep anxiety, leading to elaborate legal mechanisms designed to ensure to the husband absolute rights to the wife's sexual fidelity and the children of the marriage. This was the basis of the double standard of adultery, which condoned a husband's adultery, but imposed harsh penalties on the wife. As Lord Chancellor Cranworth explained to the House of Lords, 'The adultery of the wife might be the means of palming spurious offspring upon the husband, while the adultery of the husband could have no such effect with regard to the wife'.[5]

Nor was marriage the only source of women's inequality. Until well into the twentieth century, women were barred from political participation. The contradictions between the liberal ideal of equality and the subordination of women were addressed by characterizing women as irrational, temperamentally unsuited to political life, and by nature consigned to the home. Rejecting a proposal to extend the suffrage to women in 1892, Asquith justified his position to Parliament by arguing that '[Women's] natural sphere is not the turmoil and dust of politics but the circle of social and domestic life'.[6] The refusal of nineteenth century legislatures to accept women as equal citizens was supported by an

---

[3] J. S. Mill, *The Subjection of Women* (Wordsworth Classics, 1996), p. 135.
[4] M. O'Brien, *The Politics of Reproduction* (Routledge & Kegan Paul, 1981), p. 53.
[5] Quoted in M. Finer and O. R. McGregor, 'The History of the Obligation to Maintain' in *Report of the Committee on One-Parent Families* Cmnd. 5629–1 (1974), appendix 5.
[6] Parliamentary Debates (series 4) vol. 3, col. 1513 (April 27, 1892).

intransigent judiciary.[7] Legislation granting women the municipal franchise in 1869[8] was immediately interpreted by the judges to exclude married women. On marriage, it was held, a woman's 'existence was merged with that of her husband', and therefore she could not vote.[9] Even when the right to vote at local level was established, judges moved quickly to hold that this did not include the right to stand for election. 'By the common law of England, women are not in general deemed capable of exercising public functions' and therefore only express words of a statute could change this.[10]

Within the workforce, women were similarly disadvantaged. Women have always participated in the workforce, a phenomenon often concealed by statistics which chart only formal work. But the most striking feature of women's work until well into the twentieth century was the pervasive principle that women's work attracted a lower rate than that of men, even when they were engaged on identical work with men.[11] Again, this was justified by the well-worn myths that a woman's natural role was in the home; that she should depend on her husband for subsistence; that she did not have to support a family; or that she was less productive than a man. Again, the courts were active proponents of such discrimination. When the Poplar Borough Council instituted equal pay for men and women on the lowest grade, the House of Lords took the view that the Council had allowed itself to be guided by 'some eccentric principles of socialistic philanthropy, or by a feminist ambition to secure the equality of the sexes in the matter of wages in the world of labour'.[12] The policy was struck down as irrational. An attempt by women teachers to enlist the aid of the courts to strike down the widespread policy of dismissing women teachers on marriage was met by a similar rebuff. 'It would in my view be pressing public policy to intolerable lengths to hold that it was outraged by this Authority expressing a preference for unmarried women over married women as teachers, in view of the fact that the services of the latter are frequently . . . liable to be interrupted by absences extending over several months'.[13] This view was later endorsed by the Court of Appeal, which accepted the argument by the education authority that the

---

[7] *Chorlton v. Lings* [1864] LR 4 CP 374.
[8] Municipal Franchise Act 1869.
[9] *R v. Harrald* [1872] LR VII QB 361.
[10] *De Souza v. Cobden* [1891] 1 QB 687 CA at 691.
[11] See Fredman, above n. 1, pp. 107ff.
[12] *Roberts v. Hopwood* [1925] AC 578 (HL) at 591 (*per* Lord Atkinson).
[13] *Price v. Rhondda UDC* [1923] 1 Ch 372 at 379.

duty of the married woman was primarily to look after her domestic concerns.[14]

As well as low pay for like work, job segregation was endemic. Women were formally excluded from important spheres of work, including medicine and law, until the late nineteenth century. In addition women workers were often physically segregated from men, in separate rooms or floors; and possibilities for training or promotion were minimal. These patterns were often reinforced by trade unions, whose male membership perceived that equal pay for women would constitute a threat to the legitimacy of their demand for a 'family wage'; and that permitting women to compete for 'male' jobs might undercut their own position. It was only when trade unions came to the view that equal pay for women would in fact prevent cheap substitution of female labour that it was decided to support the campaign for equal pay.

The battle for juridical equality was a long and painful one. It was only in the late nineteenth century, and then at an excruciatingly slow pace, that these legal disabilities were gradually dismantled. Thus genuine progress towards formal equality in property rights between husband and wife was only clearly evident after 1882, a process which was not complete until 1935. Similarly, the father retained absolute rights to custody of the children, a right which was only slightly modified in 1839, but real equality in this context was not achieved until 1925. Most glaring in its contradiction of liberalism's promise of equality was the refusal to extend political rights to women. Women were not permitted to vote in national elections until 1918, and even then, a minimum voting age of thirty was imposed. True equality was not fully conceded until 1928, when the minimum voting age for men and women was equalized at twenty-one. Even then, women were still barred from the House of Lords, in which formal equality was not achieved until as recently as 1963.

Juridical equality was not, however, the end of the struggle. It was with deep disappointment that feminists and women's rights campaigners realized that lifting legal impediments was not sufficient to dislodge deeply ingrained patterns of prejudice and disadvantage suffered by women. The radical shake-up of the First World War, when women were of necessity precipitated into male jobs, was not sufficient to dislodge these deep-seated patterns. After the War, pay differentials between men and women were institutionalized across the public and private sectors. In the civil service, women's pay was pegged at a maximum of 80 per cent of

---

[14] *Short v. Poole Corp* [1926] Ch 26 (CA).

that of men; and statutory instruments prescribing pay in the police forces and teaching profession prescribed similar discrepancies for men and women doing the same work. Returning veterans were given priority over jobs, and women were forced back into domestic work and other menial work by fierce polemical campaigns directed against women accused of taking men's jobs. It was not until 1955 that equal pay was introduced in the civil service, and an attempt to provide for equal pay in the teaching profession was vetoed by Churchill in 1944.

During the post-war period, women became a far more visible part of the workforce; helped by increasing availability of contraception, falling family sizes, and rapidly advancing technology creating electrical appliances to assist with domestic work. But job segregation and pay disparities persisted. Women were still dismissed on marriage in many occupations until well into the post-war period; and the practice of paying women less than men for performing the same work was widespread and officially endorsed. Indeed, the principle of sex differentiation was openly declared to be a matter of government policy after the Second World War, and women in the civil service were paid on separate and lower pay scales than men doing the same work until 1962.[15] Jobs were highly segregated with women clustered in low paid low status 'women's work'.

It was clear that such entrenched discrimination would persist unless it was prohibited by law. However, attempts to give statutory force to a more far-reaching notion of equality met with determined resistance. Thus instead of the wide-ranging Women's Emancipation Bill of 1919 the legislature enacted only the Sex Disqualification (Removal) Act 1919. This Act, in principle, opened more doors for women, making it unlawful to disqualify anyone on the grounds of sex or marriage from the holding of a civil or judicial office, the exercise of a public function, or the entry into a civil profession or location. However, broad exceptions undermined its impact. Most importantly, it permitted the retention of specific policies requiring women to resign from paid employment on marriage, policies which the courts enthusiastically endorsed.[16]

Pay discrimination was the first to be tackled. At European level, the first moves to provide for equal pay were found in the Treaty of Rome itself. Although the EEC was fundamentally conceived as an economic rather than a political entity, France, which itself already had an equal pay law, successfully argued that it would be placed at an unfair competitive

---

[15] See Fredman, above n. 1, p. 134.     [16] *ibid.*, pp. 80–82.

disadvantage if other Member States were permitted to pay women less for the same work. Article 141 (ex 119) lay dormant for two decades; but in the mid 1970s it was resurrected by a landmark decision of the ECJ that the right to equal pay was directly effective.[17] This meant that individual women in Member States could bring claims in their own domestic courts for breach of Article 119 even if there was no domestic legislation to this effect. This was reinforced by new legislation, the Equal Pay Directive, which provided that equal pay for equal work should include work of equal value. In the meantime, in the UK, the Equal Pay Act was enacted in 1970, and the entry of the UK into the European Economic Community in 1972 brought with it the directly effective Article 119. The Equal Pay Act was more limited than EC law, in that it did not provide for the right to equal pay for work of equal value, as required by the Equal Pay Directive.[18] As a result of infringement proceedings brought by the European Commission, the legislation was amended in 1983 to include the right to equal pay for work of equal value. Moreover, throughout the 1980s and early 1990s, the ECJ consistently expanded the reach of Article 119 by interpreting the concept of 'pay' widely to include pensions, redundancy compensation, and other equivalent benefits. In an even more recent development, the EU equal pay provisions have been streamlined and amended. Now known as Article 141, the new provisions incorporate the Equal Pay Directive and give express powers to the Community to legislate on matters of equal treatment and pay.

The second major piece of anti-discrimination legislation was the Sex Discrimination Act 1975, which made it unlawful to discriminate directly or indirectly on grounds of sex or marriage in employment, education, or the provision of services. This complemented the Equal Pay Act by prohibiting discrimination outside of pay issues, including recruitment, promotion, and training. It too is buttressed by EU legislation, in the form of the Equal Treatment Directive, passed in 1976. Unlike Article 141, the Equal Treatment Directive is only directly effective against State bodies. Although the ECJ has interpreted the concept of 'State' widely, this has inevitably limited its impact.

The effect of the legislation was initially dramatic. The practice of paying women on a lower scale than men for the same work was eliminated and the pay gap between men and women narrowed significantly. Whereas the average hourly pay of women in 1970 was only 61.8 per cent

---

[17] Case 43/75 *Defrenne v. Sabena* [1976] ECR 455.
[18] Except where the employer had initiated a job evaluation study.

of that of men, it had shot up to 74.2 per cent in 1977. However, momentum was quickly exhausted. By 1980, the gap had widened again; and there was little further progress until the mid 1990s, when women's pay began to inch up again. Indeed, the extension to equal value has seemed to have little immediate impact.

At the end of the twentieth century, then, and despite twenty-five years of anti discrimination legislation, women's disadvantage is still embedded in the institutions and structures of our society. In 1999, the average hourly pay of full time women workers had barely reached 80 per cent of that of full time men. The figures for weekly earnings are even more disappointing: full time women workers take home only 72 per cent of the pay of average full time men.[19] The gulf between men and women is at its deepest when we examine the pay of part-time workers, the vast majority of whom are women. Part-time workers earn on average per hour as little as 59 per cent of the average hourly pay of male full time workers. Low pay for women is not just a relative issue: women constitute an astonishing four-fifths of the two million workers who have weekly earnings below the National Insurance lower earnings limit. Particularly problematic is the effect of low pay on women's ability to support themselves in old age. Those who earn below the level at which National Insurance contributions are payable are not eligible for a State pension at all. Those who do qualify are likely to find that the level of their pension payments is severely depressed if they have worked in low paid jobs, or have taken periods out of paid work for child-rearing. These limitations are not compensated for outside of the State pension scheme: fewer women than men work for employers with an occupational pension scheme, and low income and breaks in employment are not compatible with personal pension arrangements. Finally, the fact that women tend to live longer than men is often used as a pretext for making it more expensive for a woman to buy the same pension as a man of the same age. It is not surprising, given all these facts, that elderly women are amongst the poorest in society.

A closer look at the reasons behind this continuing pattern of disadvantage reveals that low pay is closely associated with the structure of the employment market itself. Jobs remain highly segregated, with women concentrated in low paying, low status jobs. Thus 93 per cent of engineers and technologists are male; and men constitute 96 per cent of all drivers of road goods vehicles and 91 per cent of all those employed in

---

[19] Thus reflecting the shorter hours worked by women.

craft and related occupations. By contrast, women cluster in caring jobs: women comprise 90 per cent of all nurses; 92 per cent of care assistants and attendants, and 85 per cent of primary and nursery school teachers.[20] It is a sad reflection on our society that these jobs are poorly paid relative to their demands in terms of skill, effort, responsibility, and contribution to society. Even when men and women are in the same profession or industry, women tend to cluster on the lowest rungs of the ladder. Men comprise 80 per cent of computer analysts or programmers, while women constitute 72 per cent of computer and office machine operators. Again, as we have seen, women form the vast majority of primary and nursery teachers, but this proportion dips steeply to only 50 per cent of head teachers. As well as being segregated into lower paying jobs, women are seriously under-represented in most of the areas of influence in society. Thus in 1999, they formed only 18 per cent of MPs at Westminster, a figure which despite having doubled in the 1997 election, still puts the UK nineteenth in the world league table. Compared to this, the figures for the Scottish Parliament (37 per cent) and the Welsh Assembly (40 per cent) look rosy indeed. Similarly, there are very few women in the police force, and only a tiny handful in the top ranks. Only 7 per cent of High Court judges in England and Wales in 1998 were women; there was only one female Lord Justice; and no female Law Lords. A similar pattern is evident in management, where the boardroom remains essentially a male preserve. In 1998, women comprised a mere 3.6 per cent of directors. Even when they reach senior levels of management, women tend to be paid significantly less than men. Thus in 1996, the average earnings of female directors trailed about £18,000 behind those of male directors.

But it is in the interaction between family and paid work that the key to the understanding of women's continued disadvantage lies. Economic pressures have made it essential for many women to undertake paid work; yet there has been little diminution in their responsibility for unpaid family work. Nor has the labour market adjusted to accommodate the needs of parents with young families. The best opportunities for pay, training, promotion, job security, and employment related benefits are still found in full-time working. It is true there has been a marked shift in the labour market towards 'flexible' jobs, which are, in principle, compatible with family responsibilities. However, such jobs are, in practice, fashioned to accommodate the needs of the employer, rather than those of the

---

[20] Figures used here are taken from Equal Opportunities Commission *Facts about Women and Men in Great Britain 1998*.

employee with young children. Flexibility for an employer requires working practices which fluctuate according to the needs of the business, and which therefore save labour costs. The resulting jobs are often poorly paid, lacking in job security, and require employees to work at times which conflict with family responsibilities. Conversely, there is great pressure on many employees to work overtime, attracting significant extra earnings. Indeed, men in Britain work longer hours than employees in any other European country. The result is that women with young children tend to congregate in poorly paid, low status part-time work, a pattern which has a lasting effect on their lifetime earnings. At the same time, there are many women who cannot enter the workforce at all. For lone mothers, the dual role of home-worker and breadwinner is increasingly difficult to sustain. Lone mothers are less likely to be working in the paid labour force than other mothers; and lone mothers are particularly likely to be living in poverty. Paradoxically too, increases in male unemployment have not had the effect of reversing the gender roles. Instead, there has been a rising dichotomy between work-rich households (with two earners) and work poor households (with no earners). This is because a family on benefit is only better off if one or both partners can find jobs with reasonable pay and security. If the woman can only find a poorly paid part-time job, the family might well suffer a net loss in benefit.

Economic disadvantage is not the only manifestation of continuing sexism in society. Women also find themselves the victims of sexual violence and harassment, whether in the home, at work, or in the street. Sexual harassment at work is problematic in a unique and corrosive way. Its perpetrators feel entitled to invade a woman's privacy and to strip her of the public identity owed to her as an equal participant in the public sphere of the workplace. It is particularly destructive in that it threatens not just her personal dignity but also her ability to continue in employment. The choice between loss of a job and succumbing to sexual pressure is an invidious one. More serious still is violence in the home and on the streets. The attitude of police to complaints of rape is particularly problematic. In 1997, there were 6,281 recorded rapes, but only 9 per cent led to a conviction. Even this low conviction rate probably over-estimates the true figures; since a significant number of rape complaints are not even recorded as crimes in the first place. Indeed, a recent Home Office study showed that over half of all reported rapes were not proceeded with. Although the courts have belatedly recognized that rape can occur within marriage, the police seem still to dismiss out of hand any complaint of rape by a woman who knew the alleged perpetrator.[21]

## II  RACE, RELIGION, AND ETHNICITY

Race relations in Britain have been similarly marked by deep-seated and institutionalized inequalities. However, this history differs from that of gender discrimination. Indeed, the complex interaction of race, nationality, religion, and culture make for a tangle of forces which do not yield to a straightforward narrative. While religious discord had been a feature of British history for many years, Britain came into the twentieth century with a fixed self image as a homogeneous, white Christian society. This self image not only obscures but negates the existence of small internal minorities, many of whom suffered prejudice and legal disabilities. Most conspicuous was the slave trade. Slavery was an accepted reality in eighteenth century Britain with black men and women sold openly at auctions. The use of black slaves as domestic servants was fashionable and widespread; and in 1770, there were between 14,000 and 20,000 black slaves in London alone.[22] The legality of slavery was, however, ambiguous, and judges from 1670 delivered a series of conflicting opinions. As Hepple concludes, 'the majority of judges were slow and reluctant emancipators'.[23] Slavery was not formally abolished in both England and the colonies until 1833.

Other minorities were less openly oppressed, but still suffered significant discrimination. Possibly the largest minority were the Irish Catholics, who formed a significant presence throughout the nineteenth century. Yet 'there was a shared pool of insidious stereotypes about Irish Catholics ... For the Protestant and liberal imagination they were the significant "other" in contrast to whom identity was defined'.[24] Catholics were given the vote in 1820; but it was only when State funding was provided for Catholic schools in 1902 that Catholics began to feel that they were accepted members of society. By the mid twentieth century,

---

[21] K. Cook, 'When is rape a real crime?' *New Law Journal* December 10, 1999, p. 1856; and see J. Harris and S. Grace, *A Question of Evidence?: Investigating and Prosecuting Rape in the 1990s* Home Office Research Study 196 (Home Office, 1999).

[22] For a valuable discussion, see B. Hepple, *Race, Jobs and the Law in Britain* (2nd ed., Penguin Books, 1970), pp. 59–62.

[23] *ibid.*, p. 61.

[24] P. Lewis, 'Arenas of Ethnic Negotiation' in T. Modood and P. Werbner, *The Politics of Multiculturalism in the New Europe: Racism, Identity and Community* (Zed Books, 1997), p. 128.

Hepple could argue that, while 'social inequality remains, Irish workers in Britain are rarely thought of with hostility as an alien group'.[25]

Jews, expelled from Britain in 1290, were only readmitted by Cromwell in 1656 because of the financial and political services which they could render him. They were tolerated rather than welcomed, and although their community flourished, they continued to labour under severe legal disabilities. A particular obstacle was the requirement to take a Christian oath: until the mid nineteenth century, all Crown appointments and most professions were required to subscribe to a Christian oath before taking up their posts.[26] This is a good example of the way in which formal equality can operate to deny substantive equality. Many observant Jews were precluded by this condition from entering such occupations. Indeed, the first Jewish MP, Baron Lionel de Rothschild, refused to swear the Christian oath of allegiance, and could not take up his seat in Parliament until 1858, eleven years after he had been elected.[27] Indeed, it was a mark of progress to substantive equality when different treatment was permitted in such circumstances. Thus the declaration of a court in 1764 that a Muslim witness could swear an oath on the Qur'an was a rare example of judicial insight.

The settled Jewish community had achieved a measure of integration by the end of the century. But the influx, after 1881, of over 100,000 Jews fleeing pogroms and political and economic restriction in Russia and Eastern Europe alarmed the authorities sufficiently to pass the Aliens Act 1905, which gave immigration officers the power to refuse entry to 'undesirable' immigrants.[28] This of course failed to address the desperate poverty of those Jews who had already arrived. Instead, the fact that Jews worked extremely long hours in the worst-off section of sweated labour triggered a spate of anti-Semitism which in effect blamed the Jews for their own plight and accused them of undercutting local labour conditions. It was only the enactment of effective factory legislation from 1901, and the growth of Jewish trade unions, which led to the elimination of Jewish sweated labour.[29]

Nor were these the only minorities. Gypsies had lived in Britain since

[25] Hepple, above n. 22, p. 70.
[26] D. Cooper and D. Herman, 'Jews and Other Uncertainties: Race, Faith and English Law' [1999] 19 *Legal Studies* 339 at 345.
[27] Jewish Disabilities Removal Act 1845; Jewish Relief Act 1858.
[28] Repealed April 12, 1920 by Aliens Order 1920 under Aliens Restriction (Amendment) Act 1919.
[29] Hepple, above n. 22, pp. 68–9. Note that by 1939 a further 50,000 Jews sought refuge here from the Nazis.

the beginning of the sixteenth century. Although their presence was initially tolerated, within a short time they were subjected to a spate of repressive legislation aimed at expelling them from the country and outlawing their life style and methods of making a living. Gypsies or Roma people have nevertheless retained a clearly delineated ethnic and cultural identity, and in 1995, it was estimated that there were 33,000 gypsies living in caravans and a further 30,00 living in houses. There are between 12,000 and 13,000 gypsy caravans.[30] The main source of discrimination against gypsies in the modern legal system is found in planning laws, reflecting and reinforcing long-standing hostility by the resident population to gypsies. As in other parts of Europe, government policy towards gypsies was primarily assimilationist, and although it was often stated that government policy was to accept the gypsy's right to a nomadic existence, in fact the underlying assumption was always that gypsies would eventually be assimilated into the dominant culture.[31] In particular, and crucially, 'site provision was equated with settlement, and in turn equated with assimilation'.[32] Legislation passed in 1968 placed an obligation on local authorities to make provision for gypsy sites.[33] An authority which provided such sites could apply for 'designation' of their areas, giving the authority additional powers to remove any gypsies camping in unauthorized sites.[34] Not surprisingly, gypsies viewed this legislation as an attempt to impose assimilation and permanent settlement, by closing off traditional stopping places and insisting on regularization.[35] This was aggravated by the fact that local authorities routinely and blatantly ignored their duty to provide sites. The result was, according to an authoritative report, that the majority of gypsies were deprived of the opportunity of finding a legal abode. 'Only when they are travelling on the road can they remain within the law; when they stop for the night, they have no alternative but to break the law'.[36] Instead, however, of insisting on proper compliance, the government decided in 1994 to repeal the statutory duty on local authorities to provide sites, as well as to terminate the central government subsidy to local authorities who did

[30] S. Poulter, *Ethnicity, Law and Human Rights: The English Experience* (Oxford: Clarendon Press, 1998), p. 148.
[31] *ibid.*, p. 163.
[32] J. Okely, *The Traveller-Gypsies* (Cambridge University Press, 1983), p. 113.
[33] Caravan Sites Act 1968.                                    [34] *ibid.*, ss. 10–12.
[35] P. Panayi, *An Ethnic History of Europe since 1945: Nations, States and Minorities* (Longman, 2000), p. 53.
[36] J. Cripps, *Accommodation for Gypsies: A Report on the Working of the Caravan Sites Act 1968* (HMSO, 1977); and see Poulter, above n. 30, p. 162.

provide sites. The result is to leave the provision of sites entirely to the private sector. This was accompanied by the extension of criminal sanctions for unauthorized encampments.[37] The semblance of pluralism has been replaced with an explicitly assimilationist policy, using the criminal law to repress the nomadic tradition of gypsies.[38]

Gypsies have received little support from equality laws, either at international or domestic level. Attempts to argue that their rights to private and family life have been violated in a manner which is discriminatory under Articles 8 and 14 of the ECHR have been rebuffed.[39] Although the European Court of Human Rights has finally acknowledged that a gypsy's caravan counts as a 'home' which is entitled to respect under Article 8, it has been quick to equate 'public policy' with the interests of the settled population, and therefore to hold that gypsy's rights could not override the 'general interest' in conforming with planning policy.[40] More recently, the Council of Europe has taken more explicit responsibility for guiding policy at European level. The Framework Convention for the Protection of National Minorities, which entered into force in 1998, sets out more explicitly the principles to be respected and implemented by the Sates Parties to promote full and effective equality between national minorities and the majority. This should give more explicit protection to gypsies than the ECHR, although its main enforcement mechanism is not by complaint to the court, but by a report and monitoring requirement. In 2000, the Council of Europe issued a recommendation to Member States providing guidelines for the provision of education for Roma/ Gypsy people in Europe which catered specifically for their needs as an itinerant population. It is not yet clear what effect this will have on States policies in practice.

The existence of significant minorities notwithstanding, it was the decline of Britain's role as a colonizer which had the most lasting effect on the nature of modern day plural society.[41] Although the process of decolonization took place over a substantial period, the full political independence of Britain's colonies in Africa, Asia, and the Caribbean were all achieved in the period immediately after the Second World War. This coincided with the urgent need for reconstruction of the battered

---

[37] Criminal Justice and Public Order Act 1994, s. 77.

[38] Poulter, above n. 30, p. 184.

[39] *P v. United Kingdom* Application 14751/89, (1991) DR 264.

[40] *Buckley v. United Kingdom* (1993) 23 EHRR 101.

[41] For a useful brief synopsis, see H. Goulbourne, *Race Relations in Britain Since 1945* (MacMillan Press, 1998), ch. 2.

British economy, which had lost many of its own workers in the war. Systematic underdevelopment of the local economy in many of the former colonies had created a pool of desperate workers, who responded with alacrity to the policies of active recruitment instituted after the war. In particular, faced with grinding poverty at home, people from the Caribbean flocked to the 'economic magnet, which lured so many of us to the Mother Country in the late forties and fifties'.[42] They were joined by increasing numbers of people from Africa, including significant numbers of East African Indians who were squeezed out by the Africanization policies in Kenya and Tanzania, and later expelled from Uganda. Even greater numbers came from India after independence in 1947, and after the break up of colonial India. In addition, Ireland, starved of capital to develop its own domestic economy, remained a ready source of cheap labour for Britain. The Irish now form the largest ethnic minority in Britain: during the 1990s, there were more than two million Irish people in Britain, forming 4.6 per cent of the total population.

   While discrimination against women manifested itself in express legal prohibitions, issues of race and colour were dealt with in the post-war period by manipulating the basic condition for belonging in society, namely citizenship. The initial self confidence of post-colonial Britain in its own identity was expressed in the inclusive principle of citizenship introduced in 1949 to replace the colonial notion of the 'British subject'. The status of 'citizen of the United Kingdom and Colonies' enabled the post-war economic migrants to arrive unimpeded as citizens. It also furthered Britain's economic needs, facilitating the active recruitment of migrants from the Commonwealth to meet the demand for labour. However, once the need for labour abated, and policy-makers became more concerned with keeping jobs for indigenous people, there was a rapid retreat from an inclusive notion of citizenship. Beginning with the Commonwealth Immigration Act 1962, the resulting web of immigration controls, although ostensibly neutral, were widely perceived as primarily aimed at the restriction of entry of black and Asian people. Most obvious was the Commonwealth Immigration Act 1968, which severed nationality rights from the right to live in the UK. British nationality no longer carried with it the right to enter the UK, unless the holder was born in the UK, or one of his or her parents or grandparents had been born or acquired citizenship through residence there. This impacted most

---

[42] B. Bryan, S. Dadzie, and S. Scafe, *The Heart of the Race: Black Women's Lives in Britain* (Virago, 1985), p. 16.

forcefully on the East African Asians who, despite opting for British nationality at the time of independence, found themselves in the no-man's land of being a national without rights of residence. By contrast, a white settler in Kenya or elsewhere, whose parents or grandparents had left Britain to live in Kenya during the colonial period, had an automatic right of abode. The inherent racism of this provision was sufficiently striking to prompt the European Commission of Human Rights to find it to be 'inhuman or degrading treatment' in breach of Article 3 of the ECHR. According to the Commission, 'publicly to single out a group of persons for differential treatment on the basis of race might, in certain circumstances, constitute a special form of affront to human dignity'.[43] The UK government's response was to allow limited entry by issuing special vouchers. It was also forced to admit 25,000 Ugandan Asians expelled from Uganda by Idi Amin in 1972 because international law requires citizens to be permitted entry if they are expelled by their country of current residence.

Nevertheless, successive British governments pressed on with their programme of redefinition of British nationality to exclude new Commonwealth immigrants. As a result of the Immigration Act of 1971 and the Nationality Act of 1981, which, albeit much amended, still form the basis of immigration controls today, the gate has clanged shut on new migration from the Caribbean and Indian sub-continent. The only channel for further immigration is in order to re-unite families of men settled here on January 1, 1973 and this channel has proved to be narrow and twisted. Paradoxically, such controls have been justified in terms of achieving good race relations. Thus, according to the Home Office in 1981: 'The basis of the Government's policy is the belief that firm immigration control is essential to achieve good community relations'.[44] Such a view is difficult to reconcile with the most recent measure, which from January 27, 1997, made it an offence for an employer knowingly to employ a person who is not permitted to work under the immigration rules.[45] Employers must check a worker's documents to ensure that he or she has such permission; and proof of such a check is a defence against possible prosecution. This provision may well result in discrimination in recruitment against black and people who appear foreign, and it is particularly disappointing that the Labour government, elected in 1997, has

---

[43] *East African Asians v. United Kingdom* [1970] 13 Ybk 928 at 944.

[44] *Home Affairs Committee on Immigration from the Indian Sub-continent 5th Report* (HC Paper (1981–82) 90-I Vol. II), p. 1 para. 2.

[45] Asylum and Immigration Act 1996, s. 8.

dropped its election pledge to repeal this position in favour of enacting a statutory code of practice as a safeguard against unfair discrimination.

The most recent pressure has come from the many people fleeing from oppression and poverty in their home countries, seeking asylum in Britain. As many as 32,500 people applied for asylum in 1997, the vast majority being from Africa and Asia. This has created a great deal of fluster and alarm in official circles, a reaction which conceals but also permits the often inhuman treatment of many of the people who arrive uninvited but desperate. A whole new legislative and administrative structure has been created to deal with 'the problem'; but this has not expedited decision-making, so that some people have had to wait up to seven years for a first decision on their application. The assertion that strict immigration controls and tough measures against asylum seekers are compatible with good race relations internally has been used to justify such heavy-handed measures as the withdrawal of benefits from many asylum seekers.[46] These measures are likely to deter many who are anxious and confused about their status from applying for benefits to which they are entitled. Allied with the requirement on employers to check immigration status of recruits[47] and increased police powers to raid premises, these approaches are likely to lead to a new and different sort of race discrimination. Indeed, the danger of open hostility was so marked that in the run-up to the debates on new legislation in 1999, the leaders of all the political parties called on their supporters and the media to ensure that the debates did not become an excuse for displays of prejudice on grounds of race, religion, or nationality. This has not, however, deterred legislators from putting into place severely restrictive measures. Nor has judicial intervention had much effect. Regulations removing benefits from asylum seekers were quashed in 1997 on the grounds that they were 'so uncompromisingly draconian that they must indeed be held to be *ultra vires*. Parliament cannot have intended a significant number of genuine asylum seekers to be impaled on the horns of so intolerable a dilemma: the need either to abandon their claim to refugee status or alternatively to maintain them . . . in a state of utter destitution'.[48] Nevertheless, Parliament enacted the substance of the regulations in primary legislation with retrospective effect shortly thereafter.[49] This was only slightly softened by

---

[46] Asylum and Immigration Act 1996, s. 11 and sched. 1.                         [47] *ibid.*, s. 8.
[48] *R v. Secretary of State for Social Security, ex p Joint Council for the Welfare of Immigrants* [1997] 1 WLR 275 (CA).
[49] Asylum and Immigration Act 1996, s. 11. See W. Wade and C. F. Forsyth, *Administrative Law* (8th ed, Oxford University Press, 2000), p. 858.

1999 legislation which provides welfare support for destitute asylum seekers and their dependants predominantly by means of vouchers rather than cash.[50]

Meanwhile, Britain had become, in effect, a multicultural community. However, the process of integration has been a painful one, and equality is still illusory. The early decades were particularly difficult for the newly migrated communities.[51] Thus the First National Survey of Ethnic Minorities, conducted in 1966, found that migrants were overwhelmingly in manual work, confined to a limited number of industries and often trapped in jobs below their level of qualification. Racial prejudice was widespread: there was overt refusal by some employers to employ 'coloured' workers and employment opportunities were often available only in areas in which there were insufficient white workers to fill the posts. Such prejudice also made it very difficult to gain access to housing. Private landlords often overtly excluded black or Asians from private tenancies, mortgages were frequently only available on exorbitant terms and very few migrants were in council housing. This left migrant families with little choice but to live in the worst available private rented housing in slum areas, with inevitably detrimental consequences for schooling and health.

Yet prior to 1965, there was no legal protection against discrimination, racial or otherwise. The judges were on occasion willing to endorse ingenious legal arguments;[52] but judge-made common law never recognized racial discrimination as a distinct legal wrong.[53] Nor were judges prepared to allow complainants to rely on the well-known if ill-defined principle that contracts, wills, or other documents could be declared void as contrary to public policy. Racial or religious discrimination, although on several occasions declared to be 'deplorable', was simply not considered to be contrary to public policy.[54] This was justified in part on the grounds that it was for Parliament, not the courts, to develop public policy. Responsibility was therefore laid firmly in the lap of the legislature. Yet here too considerable reluctance was evident: the years from 1950 to 1965 saw the failure of at least ten attempts to persuade

---

[50] Asylum and Immigration Act 1999, ss. 90–91.

[51] The information in this section is taken from T. Modood *et al.*, *Ethnic Minorities in Britain: Diversity and Disadvantage* The Fourth National Survey of Ethnic Minorities in Britain (Policy Studies Institute, 1997), ch. 10.

[52] *Constantine v. Imperial Hotels Ltd* [1944] KB 693.

[53] Hepple, above n. 22, p. 144.

[54] *Re Lysaght, Hill v. Royal College of Surgeons* [1965] 3 WLR 391 at 402.

Parliament to legislate against race discrimination. When legislation finally emerged, in the form of the Race Relations Act 1965, it was severely limited. Instead of covering the most important areas of discrimination, namely employment and housing, it applied only to discrimination in an oddly assorted list of places of public resort. Discrimination in hotels, restaurants, public houses, theatres, sports grounds, swimming pools, and public transport services was unlawful; but discrimination in shops and boarding houses was not. The Act did not bind the Crown; and it relied wholly on administrative, as against legally enforceable, remedies. The ineffectiveness of the 1965 Act was clearly highlighted by research findings of widespread and overt prejudice, particularly in housing and employment. These gave renewed impetus to a remarkable political campaign, spearheaded by organizations of ethnic minorities as well as the Labour Party and other left wing political organizations. The campaign led to the enactment of the Race Relations Act 1968, which moved into the centre arena of discrimination by covering employment. However, the effectiveness of the Act was seriously undermined by the use of voluntary industrial disputes procedures as the primary means of enforcement in industries covering one third of the workforce; and by the absence of any right by individuals to enforce the law. By 1975, the Race Relations Board was forced to conclude that the experiment of using voluntary panels had failed.

Further evidence of the failure of the legislation to make any impact on discrimination and disadvantage emerged with the publication of the results of the second national survey, in 1974, which found that minority groups were still disproportionately concentrated in semi-skilled and unskilled work, and very few had succeeded in obtaining professional or managerial jobs. Equally serious was the persistence of overt discrimination on grounds of race: experimental work carried out by researchers who applied for the same job under different names showed that in one in three cases in which a white man and an ethnic minority man applied for a job, only the white man was offered an interview or job. Ethnic minorities continued to live in cheaper properties in inner-city areas, which were more crowded and had poorer amenities than white people. Although the level of home ownership had climbed steeply between 1968 and 1974, particularly among Asians, this was at least in part a result of exclusion from desirable rented accommodation and the quality of homes was often poor. Many members of the Asian communities could speak English only slightly or at all: this was true of the majority of women and as many as a third of men. Similarly, the considerable efforts by some members of minority groups to improve their qualifications had not yet paid off: as many as a fifth of all ethnic minority men with degrees of British standard were still in manual jobs.

Renewed impetus for change led to the enactment of the Race Relations Act 1976, which remains the central legislative source of protection against discrimination on grounds of race, colour, nationality, and ethnic or national origins. This signified an important step forward, both in the introduction of a right of individual enforcement and in the use of the relatively sophisticated conceptual framework encompassing both direct and indirect discrimination. Nevertheless, its immediate impact on patterns of disadvantage were scarcely discernible. Indeed, the deep and protracted recession of the early 1980s represented a severe setback for many members of ethnic minorities. Although all workers in the stricken manufacturing sector suffered, unemployment was disproportionately high among ethnic minority workers. Indian and African Asian men were somewhat protected because many had turned to self employment as a response to the continuing obstacles to access to higher paid work. But the rate of unemployment among other minorities was twice as high as that of whites. Moreover, because Asian households tended to be bigger than those of whites, the gulf between household income of whites and those of Asians was particularly large. There were, however, clear signs that change might be on the horizon, at least for the better qualified. Education emerged as a major commitment among all ethnic minority groups, who (with the exception of Caribbean men) had higher rates of post-16 education than whites. As Modood noted: 'Qualifications, and the changing climate of opinion as reflected in legislation, were capable of loosening the barriers of discrimination and altering the initial allocation of migrants to the bottom of the pile . . . '.[55] At the same time, there was increasing polarization: for those who did not succeed in obtaining qualifications, the mere symbolic and educational aspect of the Race Relations Act was clearly insufficient. After nearly two decades of political concern, they continued to be in low-status and low-paid work and to be disproportionately represented among the unemployed.

Developments in the 1990s have to some extent borne out these predictions. There has been a clear upward movement in job levels of ethnic minorities and a narrowing of differentials between ethnic minorities and the ethnic majority. Particularly important is the finding that different groups with the same qualifications doing the same types of jobs in the

---

[55] Modood *et al.*, above n. 51, p. 342.

same areas are generally paid similar amounts. Thus whereas it was argued in the 1970s that qualifications did little to improve the earning prospects of minority groups, this no longer seems to be true in the 1990s. This suggests that the strategy of encouraging young people to maximize their qualifications is crucial in changing the pattern of earnings among minority groups.[56]

But the most striking finding of the 1990s is that the differences between the minorities are often as great as those between the majority and the minority. By far the most disadvantaged group consists of families of Bangladeshi and Pakistani origin and their British born children.[57] 'Name any group whose poverty causes national concern—pensioners, disabled people, one-parent families, the unemployed—Pakistanis and Bangladeshis were poorer'.[58] In 1994, more than four out of five households of Pakistani or Bangladeshi origin had an equivalent income below half the national average, four times as many as white non-pensioner households. Unemployment rates among men of Pakistani or Bangladeshi origin are high and for those in work, pay tends to be low. In addition, women are discouraged from undertaking paid work especially when their children are young. Families tend to be far larger than those of other groups, and households are often multi-generational, including grandparents as well as children. Finally, families of Pakistani or Bangladeshi origin continue to be the worst housed. They are still disproportionately located in inner city areas, and are the most residentially segregated of all groups.

By contrast, East African Asians and Chinese have reached parity with whites, and Indians are fast closing any remaining gaps. In effect, the downgrading effect of migration has finally been overcome, and these groups have reached pre-migration levels. Thus in 1994, men of African Asian origin were as likely as whites to be professional, managers, and employers, and in terms of income, those of African Asian origin had in fact overtaken whites. However, it is still the case that more households of African Asian origin are in poverty than whites. In many respects too, people of Indian origin have reached parity with whites. The average household of Indian origin has a slightly higher total income than a white household (including pensioners), their unemployment rate is only

---

[56] Modood *et al.*, above n. 51, p. 120.

[57] Statistical literature refers to ethnic minority members by their country of origin. For example, people of Pakistani origin and their British born families are referred to as Pakistani. This should not be read as implying that such people are not full British citizens.

[58] Modood *et al.*, above n. 51, p. 180.

slightly higher than whites, and a 1999 study found that young men of Indian origin had almost the same earning power as their white counterparts; compared to young men of Pakistani and Bangladeshi origin, who had not much more than half of whites' earning power.

A more complex pattern is found among people of Caribbean or African origin, where there is a very strong variation between individual members of the groups. Thus a study published in 1999 showed that young men were more than twice as likely to be unemployed as young white men, and had lower earnings. People of Caribbean origin are rather more likely to stay on at school after 16 than their white counterparts, although both whites and Caribbeans lag well behind those of African or Indian origin. Overall, the rate of poverty among people of Caribbean origin is only slightly higher than that among white households. So far as those of African origin are concerned, the earning power of young men of African origin tends to be considerably less than whites'. In addition, they have a higher than average risk of unemployment. For those in work, many individuals receive a substantially lower return for the same level of qualification than their white counterparts.

It is essential in the analysis of race to consider gender, which intersects with class, ethnic origin, and religion to produce an increasingly complex pattern. We have already seen that women of all ethnicities earn substantially less than men, but there are important ethnic variations. Indeed, the weekly earnings of full-time ethnic minority women were found in the 1994 survey to be higher than those of white women; and while there was a gender gap in all minority groups, the biggest gap was between white men and white women. The highest average earnings were those of women of Caribbean origin, despite having a greater incidence of lone parenthood. They also hold an above average share of supervisory posts and are much less likely to work part-time than their white counterparts. However, they have not surmounted the basic obstacles facing all women. Like all women, women of Caribbean origin are grossly underrepresented in the top jobs category, and have a high rate of unemployment.[59] Women of Bangladeshi or Pakistani origin, by contrast, are strongly discouraged by their families and communities from undertaking paid work at all, and the minority who do work are often poorly paid and highly exploited, particularly if they are home workers in the textile industry. It is also crucial to recognize the extent to which the statistics obscure class divisions internal to groups. Thus some individuals in all

[59] *ibid.*, p. 144.

these groups have succeeded, while others remain disadvantaged. This in turn raises the question as to what is the aim of equality. Is it ultimately to reproduce within ethnic groups the pattern of advantage and disadvantage found in white groups, the assumption being that any divergence is a result of discrimination? Or is it to reduce the total sum of disadvantage, amongst whites as much as amongst others?

Socio-economic factors are not, however, the only measure of discrimination. In addition, there is a disturbing persistence of violence, harassment, and prejudice on the grounds of race, religion, and ethnicity. Over 23,000 complaints of alleged racist attacks were received by police in the twelve months up to March 1999. A recent Home Office study found that perpetrators of racial harassment are of all ages and sexes, including young children and pensioners, with a disturbingly high proportion of racial incidents attributed to young people. Particularly seriously, the research found that the views of the perpetrators were often shared by the wider communities to which they belong, with a high level of racism found in children of primary and even pre-school age. The failure to condemn perpetrators, and active reinforcement of their behaviour, makes perpetrators feel that their behaviour is legitimate. Thus the attempt to combat racial harassment requires not just effective action against perpetrators, but also the development of strategies to address the attitudes of the 'perpetrator community' towards ethnic minorities.[60] Of especial importance is the need to address racism in the education system itself, so that children are taught to value cultural diversity and to respect each other for what they are.

Perhaps the most serious is the lack of confidence in the police. A significant number of people have experienced racial harassment at the hands of the police themselves, and even more believe that the police have not responded appropriately to complaints of racial violence or harassment. This perception is borne out by Home Office statistics for 1998–9, which found that black people were six times more likely than whites to be stopped and searched under police powers to detect and investigate crime. This lack of confidence extends to the criminal justice system as a whole. Black people were found to be more likely to be arrested than whites, and a higher proportion of cases against blacks were later discontinued on grounds of lack of evidence than against whites. Ethnic minorities were over-represented among the prison population.

[60] R. Sibbit, *The Perpetrators of Racial Harassment and Racial Violence* Home Office Research Study 176 (Home Office, 1997).

These issues were forced to the surface by the case of Stephen Lawrence, the victim of a racist assault and murder. Allegations of racism about the police failure to investigate the murder properly and to prosecute the perpetrators led to the establishment of what has been labelled a 'watershed' inquiry, led by MacPherson. The Report of the Inquiry[61] took a crucial step forward in recognizing that racism can extend beyond individual acts of prejudice to the institutional culture and organization of the police itself. Such 'institutional racism' was found to be a pervasive influence in police decisions as to how to conduct the murder investigation; indeed the deficiencies in policing identified in the Report were attributed in part at least to the failure to recognize and accept racism as a central feature of the murder.[62] But the Report went further and tackled the broader culture and structure of both the police and other agencies. Institutional racism was defined as the 'collective failure of an organization to provide an appropriate and professional service to people because of their colour, culture, or ethnic origin. It can be seen or detected in process, attitudes, and behaviour which amount to discrimination through unwitting prejudice, ignorance, thoughtlessness, and racist stereotyping which disadvantage minority ethnic people'.[63] It persists because of organizational failure to recognize and address its existence. Such institutional discrimination was found to be endemic in the Metropolitan Police Service as well as other police services.[64] Thus racist stereotyping was an important contributory influence in the disparity in the statistics on the use of stop and search powers mentioned above. Failure to recognize and correct such racism was clearly evidenced in the fact that none of the officers involved in the Lawrence investigation had had any training in race relations throughout the course of their whole career. The resulting lack of confidence in the police was manifested in the widespread under-reporting of racist incidents. To address these issues, it was crucial that the police service be made open and accountable.

Despite the strength of criticism by the MacPherson Commission, racism in the public services continues. Particularly disturbing is a finding of institutional racism within the very institution charged with prosecuting crime, the Crown Prosecution Service. In a report published in 2001, the Commission for Racial Equality found that staff at one of the Service's offices were almost wholly segregated on racial lines, largely as a result of preferences among the white group not to be under the

---

[61] Home Office 'Report of the MacPherson Inquiry' Cmd. 4262 February 24, 1999.
[62] *ibid.*, para. 6.21.          [63] *ibid.*, para. 6.34.          [64] *ibid.*

management of a black person. In addition, several members of the white
staff held stereotypical negative images of the black staff. Despite know-
ing about the problem, the senior management of the service failed to
take any action. In the view of the CRE, so serious a degree of managerial
failure amounted to 'institutional' discrimination.

Two proposals have been made to address the problem of racism both
within the public services and in the broader community. First, amendments to the Race Relations Act 1976 will make the police liable for
discrimination in a wide range of circumstances. These are described in
Chapter Three below. Secondly, the Crime and Disorder Act 1998 introduced a set of new offences to deal with racially aggravated violence.
Assault, battery, malicious wounding, and assault occasioning actual bod-
ily harm are racially aggravated if 'the offender demonstrates towards the
victim hostility based on the victim's membership of a racial group', or
'the offence is motivated (wholly or partly) by hostility towards members
of a racial group based on their membership of that group'.[65] Because
'racial group' is defined in the same way as under the Race Relations Act
(see Chapter Two below), this protection does not extend to victims of
purely religious abuse. Sentences for these offences are higher than for
those of the non-racially aggravated equivalent offences. In addition,
there is a new offence of racially aggravated harassment and courts must
take account of racial motivation as an aggravating factor when passing
sentence.[66] The use of the criminal law in this way is outside the scope of
this book, except to note that, as a legal tool, it is beset with problems. [67]

Cultural diversity is not, however, entirely characterized by negative
features. Britain's society is instead enriched by its newly attained multicultural qualities. Differences in family structure, religion, language, and
dress all contribute to a rich and diverse society. Dress is perhaps the
most visible feature of cultural diversity, and is often intimately bound up
with religion. The majority of women of South Asian origin, particularly
women of Pakistani origin, wear Asian clothes (although few men of
Asian origin do); and most women of Pakistani and Bangladeshi origin
wear their heads covered, even among the younger generations. At the
same time, there are clear assimilationist trends. A distinctive way of
dressing is becoming less common among younger members of minority
groups, particularly among Hindus. Notably, too, fewer young Sikh men

---

[65] Crime and Disorder Act 1998, s. 28(1)(a) and (b).                    [66] *ibid.*, s. 96.
[67] See, e.g. R. Leng, R. Taylor, and M. Wasik, *Blackstone's Guide to the Crime and Disorder
Act 1998* (Blackstone, 1998); J. Holroyd, 'Racially Aggravated Offences' *New Law Journal*
May 14, 1999, p. 722.

wear turbans than older men. By contrast, Caribbean cultural dress is a growing, dynamic force with a charisma which has influenced the dominant cultural dress. It is the younger generation of Caribbeans who are infusing Caribbean culture with new energy and vitality, a vitality often attractive to members of other ethnic groups, particularly young whites. Religion is also a distinguishing feature. Whereas only a tiny minority of young whites see religion as very important to how they lead their lives, the large majority of those of Pakistani and Bangladeshi origin consider religion a central defining characteristic of their identity. Significant minorities of those of Indian and Caribbean origins are religious; but it is notable that, according to the Fourth National Survey, their black identity is much more prominent in the self description of people of Caribbean origin than is religion. By contrast only a minority of people of South Asian origin think of themselves as black. Language is a further measure of cultural identity. The Fourth National Survey found that, with the exception of those of Caribbean origin, nearly all ethnic minority persons speak a language other than English, with Punjabi being the most commonly used South Asian language.

Different ethnic groups also exhibit quite different social and cultural characteristics. Thus families of Pakistani and Bangladeshi origin tend to be larger than average, many families having four or more children, and a significant proportion having six or more. These families are usually multi-generational, often living with the father's parents. This family structure therefore plays a central role in the care of the elderly, with as many as two thirds of Asian elders living in Britain residing in the same household as one or more of their adult children.[68] Arranged marriages are still customary although there are fewer among British born Asians. These patterns are not of course static, and it is notable that households of Indian and Pakistani origin contain fewer children in 1999 than they did in the early 1980s. By contrast, there has been no change in the size of families of Bangladeshi origin. Religion plays a central communal role. Families of Afro-Caribbean origin are at the other end of the spectrum, with a large number of unattached single adults (particularly men) and an unusually high proportion of single parent families. A recent survey found that the most striking characteristic of families of Caribbean origin was the low emphasis on long-term partnerships, and especially on formal marriage. Nearly a third of families of Caribbean origin with children had a mother who had never been married.[69] White families differ again:

---

[68] Modood *et al.*, above n. 51, p. 58.    [69] *ibid.*, pp. 56ff.

the number of children in white families is falling, and there is a striking increase in marital breakdown, single parent families and cohabitation. In addition, there is a striking decrease in religion among white families.

The combination of cultures can produce new and exciting syntheses. Nowhere is this better manifested than in marriage or partnership between men and women of different ethnic backgrounds. The Fourth National Survey of Ethnic Minorities found that of those Caribbeans in the survey who had married or lived as married, a high proportion had chosen a white partner. Indeed, half of the men and a third of women had entered into relationships with white people. This is in one sense an important indicator of the relative openness of British society to a common sense of belonging. In other countries, such as South Africa and the USA, a core perpetuating feature of racism were the prohibitions, both legal and cultural, on any form of racial intermarriage. Nor has this meant that Caribbean culture has been simply subsumed within British culture. Instead, Caribbean people have contributed a vibrant new dimension to British culture, particularly in contemporary youth culture, where studies have shown that many young people admire their black contemporaries not in spite but because of their blackness.[70] Equally important are internal taboos on inter-marriage which keep some cultures insulated from their broader society. Thus Pakistani and Bangladeshis were much less likely to have white partners or spouses than Caribbean families, with just 1 per cent of those covered by the Fourth National Survey stating that they had a white partner. By contrast, a growing proportion of Indians and African Asians, particularly those born in this country, have white partners. As the authors of the survey point out, this will eventually have implications for the definition and concept of ethnic identity itself. [71]

This complex picture of ethnic diversity and differential disadvantage prompts an equally sophisticated explanation. In the first energetic drive against racism it was of fundamental importance to stress the unity of oppressed peoples rather than their diversity. Thus 'blackness' became a political epithet rather than a description of individual characteristics. Assertions of ethnicity were thought to represent a strategy of 'divide and rule'. However, the diversity of cultural and socio-economic experiences among Britain's minorities has made it essential to reconsider the strategic value of an analysis based wholly on a black-white dichotomy. Modood, in his important contribution to the debate, has demonstrated

---

[70] Modood *et al.*, above n. 51, p. 352.          [71] *ibid.*, p. 31.

how in practice such an analysis negated the specificity of different experiences of oppression, particularly those of British Asians. South Asian Muslims, he argues, are victims of a distinctive kind of racism, based on antithetical images of Islam. By contrast, Caribbeans suffer from a different set of stereotypes.

Thus contemporary racism cannot be understood simply as prejudice against individuals on the grounds of their colour. Attempts to supply a physiological or evolutionary content to the notion of 'race' are familiar. However, under the guise of 'scientific knowledge', such theories have almost invariably been used to justify exclusion, subordination or even extermination of some 'racial' groups by others. It is therefore increasingly recognized, that race is itself a social construct, reflecting ideological attempts to legitimate domination, and heavily based on social and historical context. As Stuart Hall argues, ' "Black" is essentially a politically and culturally constructed category, which cannot be grounded in a set of fixed transcultural or transcendental racial categories and which therefore has no guarantees in Nature. What this brings into play is the recognition of the immense diversity and differentiation of the historical and cultural experiences of black subjects'.[72] Racism is, therefore, not about objective characteristics, but about relationships of domination and subordination, about hatred of the 'Other' in defence of 'Self', perpetrated and apparently legitimated through images of the 'Other' as inferior, abhorrent, even sub-human.

Because racism is based on a polarization of opposites: 'we' and 'they'; 'White' and 'Black'; 'Self' and 'Other', it also has the effect of assuming that there is a uniform, undifferentiated 'Other'. This has several consequences. First, racism is insensitive to diversity between groups. Thus it is common to refer to 'ethnic minorities' as a homogeneous group, without noting the differences between those groups. For example, talk in Britain about ethnic minorities fails to capture the very real differences between people of Afro-Caribbean origin and those from India, which in turn differ from those of Pakistani origin. Second, the assumption of an undifferentiated 'Other' assumes that a group has a fixed essence, and that individuals can be wholly defined by their membership of their group. This in turn makes it easy to stereotype individuals, often linking their group identity to denigratory ascriptions. Third, such essentialism creates a rigid and static view of culture, described from the outside,

---

[72] Hall, 'New Ethnicities' in J. Donald and A. Rattansi (eds.), *Race, Culture and Difference* (Open University, 1992), p. 254.

ignoring the dynamic evolution of culture and religion. In addition, while membership of a cultural or religious group is an important aspect of people's lives, many people belong to several different overlapping and intersecting groupings. It is therefore, more appropriate to speak, not of racism, but of multiple racisms.[73] Indeed, as Modood argues, it is no longer adequate to think that racism is based entirely on colour. Besides 'colour-racism', it has become clear that there is a developing set of 'cultural racisms', which 'use cultural difference to vilify or demand cultural assimilation from groups who also suffer colour racism.'[74] Modood identifies, in particular, anti-Muslim prejudice, a white reaction to the revival of Islamic self-confidence.

The fragmentation of the political concept of 'blackness' is a crucial step towards framing a more sophisticated legal framework. However, there remains an overarching commonality of experience of racism. This is harshly demonstrated by the pervasiveness of racist attacks to which all ethnic groups are vulnerable. The overarching concept of racism therefore needs to be retained because it captures the underlying power relationship, a relationship where naked power is premised entirely on arbitrary assumptions of superiority. Also crucial is the recognition that disadvantage is not only explicable in terms of such discrimination. Structural forces in the economy play a crucial role in shaping the opportunities of both minorities and majorities. If these complex issues are to be dealt with effectively, a correspondingly sensitive and sophisticated legal framework is required.

## III SEXUAL ORIENTATION

Discrimination on grounds of sexual orientation is a particularly vicious denial of dignity and equality, since it strikes out against the sexual intimacy at the very core of an individual's identity and well-being. It involves not just the equality right, but also the right to privacy and family life; and even more fundamentally, the basic right to the free development of one's personality. Yet there has been less progress in the quest for equality on grounds of sexual orientation than there has been for race and sex discrimination. This manifests in three main ways: first, greater restrictions are placed on same sex activity than on heterosexual sex; second,

---

[73] R. Bhavnani, *Black Women in the Labour Market: A Research Review* (EOC Research Series, 1994); T. Modood, 'Ethnic Diversity and Disadvantage' in Modood *et al.*, above n. 51, p. 353.

[74] Modood *et al.*, above n. 51, p. 353.

there is less respect for the family life of same-sex partners than for heterosexuals; and third, the protection against discrimination and harassment on grounds of sexual orientation in the workplace is minimal.

Same-sex sexual activity between men remained a criminal offence until 1967. The Sexual Offences Act of 1967 made some progress towards equality by creating an exception for sexual activity between two consenting men in private. The age of consent, originally set at twenty-one was reduced to eighteen in 1994.[75] However, this fell short of equality in that the age of consent was still higher than that for heterosexuals, who are free to engage in consensual sexual activity over sixteen.[76] The impetus for change finally came in 1997 when the European Commission of Human Rights declared admissible a claim by a gay man that the higher age of consent violated his right to respect for his private life and was discriminatory.[77] Nevertheless, the deep-seated reluctance to give equal respect to homosexuality as to heterosexuality meant that attempts to amend the legislation found themselves obstructed on several occasions in the House of Lords. Thus on two occasions an amendment to equalize the age of consent was passed in the House of Commons on a free vote, but rejected by the House of Lords. It was not until 2000 that the Sexual Offences Amendment Act was finally passed equalizing the age of consent for sexual activity so that it is the same for male homosexuals as for heterosexuals and lesbians.[78] However, even this does not constitute full equality. Adult consensual sex between two gay men is still an offence punishable by up to two years' imprisonment unless it takes place in private. By contrast, heterosexual sex in equivalent circumstances is not an offence unless it outrages public decency, and on conviction the penalty is usually a small fine.[79]

Perhaps the most blatant pattern of persecution of gay men and lesbian women has been the policy of exclusion from the military. Not only has this meant that those who are open about their sexual orientation are excluded or dismissed, it has also made 'suspected' gay men or lesbian women the target of intrusive investigations and interrogations. An attempt to put an end to this policy in Parliament, in the EU and the

[75] Sexual Offences Act 1967, s. 1 as amended by Criminal Justice and Public Order Act 1994.
[76] Sexual Offences Act 1956, s. 12(1).
[77] *Sutherland v. United Kingdom* Application No. 25186/94 (Commission Report July 1, 1997).
[78] Sexual Offences (Amendment) Act 2000.
[79] See generally R. Wintemute, 'Sexual Orientation Discrimination' in C. McCrudden and G. Chambers (eds.), *Individual Rights and the Law in Britain* (Clarendon, 1994).

domestic courts all failed; but a set of robust decisions of the European Court of Human Rights as recently as 1999 found this to be a breach of the right to privacy and respect for one's private life.[80] The policy of exclusion has now finally been lifted.

However, progress towards equality has been far from consistent. The Conservative government in power from 1979 to 1997 carried its hostility to homosexuality so far as to enact the notorious section 28 of the Local Government Act 1988, which actively prohibited local authorities from intentionally promoting homosexuality or promoting the teaching of the 'acceptability of homosexuality as a pretended family relationship'. Attempts by the Labour government elected in 1997 to repeal the legislation have been met with vociferous opposition by the top levels of the Conservative Party leadership and repeatedly been blocked by the House of Lords. The result has been that instead of a full repeal, a caveat has simply been inserted into the relevant legislation stating that the prohibition on the promotion of homosexuality does not prevent head teachers, teachers, or governing bodies in maintained schools from taking steps to prevent any form of bullying.[81] Only in Scotland has this provision been removed.

The begrudging gestures towards recognition of the legitimacy of male same-sex sexual activity have yet to be accompanied by any acknowledgement of the depth and permanency of same sex relationships. Gay couples are denied the right to marry by the Matrimonial Causes Act 1973, which specifies that marriage partners must be of opposite sexes. Nor do gay partners have access to benefits accorded to co-habiting heterosexual couples. Thus a gay man or lesbian woman has no right to have his or her partner recognized for such crucial purposes as immigration, succession on intestacy, National Insurance pensions for spouses, or employment related benefits. Similarly, it is very difficult for a gay parent to gain custody over a child of a heterosexual marriage, and still more difficult for a same sex couple to adopt a child or become genetic parents through artificial insemination or a surrogacy arrangement. Even under European law and international human rights documents, the rights to marry or to be recognized as eligible for family rights have not been accepted by courts. The European Court of Justice in 1998 decisively rejected a claim that a refusal to accord equal employment related benefits to same sex partners as to heterosexual partners amounted to sex

---

[80] *Smith and Grady v. United Kingdom* (2000) 29 EHRR 493.
[81] Local Government Act 2000, s. 104, amending Local Government Act 1988, s. 2A.

discrimination in breach of European Community law.[82] Even more disturbingly, the European Court of Human Rights has confined the right in Article 12 of the ECHR to marry and found a family to the traditional marriage between persons of opposite sexes.[83] Although the European Commission of Human Rights has been prepared to accord privacy rights under Article 8 of the Convention to men involved in a stable homosexual relationship, it has nevertheless reiterated that such a relationship does not fall within the scope of the right to family life under the same article. This has meant, for example, that a woman could not establish that her right to family life under Article 8 had been breached when the State refused to grant her parental rights in relation to the child of her long-term lesbian partner. Her relationship with the child did not fall within the definition of 'family' and so she could not claim the protection of her right to family life.[84]

Only as the end of the millennium approached did some glimmers of hope appear. First the European Court of Human Rights held it to be a breach of the Convention for a court to refuse to give custody of the children of a marriage to a father solely on grounds of his homosexuality. This, it was held, was a breach of his right not to be discriminated against in respect of his right to family life.[85] Similarly, in a surprisingly perceptive decision, the House of Lords decided by a majority that a man who had lived in a long-standing, loving, and monogamous homosexual relationship counted as a member of the family of his partner and was therefore entitled under the Rent Act 1977 to succeed to his partner's tenancy rights.[86] Most importantly, new powers given to the EU under the Treaty of Amsterdam permit the EU to legislate against discrimination on a wide range of grounds. This has led to two new directives, one of which requires Member States to legislate to prohibit discrimination on grounds, *inter alia*, of sexual orientation.[87] This means that the UK will need to enact express legislation forbidding discrimination on grounds of sexual orientation by December 2003.

A similar host of legal disabilities has, until very recently, faced transsexuals. This time, it was the ECJ which led the way, with the ECHR

---

[82] Case C-249/96 *Grant v. South-West Trains Ltd* [1998] ECR I-621.

[83] *Rees v. United Kingdom* Series A No 106, [1986] 9 EHRR 56; *Cossey v. United Kingdom* Series A No 184, [1990] EHRR 622.

[84] *S v. United Kingdom* (1986) 47 DR 274.

[85] *Salgueiro da Silva Mouta v. Portugal* (ECHR December 21, 1999).

[86] *Fitzpatrick v. Sterling Housing* [1999] 2 WLR 1113 (HL).

[87] EC Directive 2000/78.

trailing behind. Thus in the seminal case of *P v. S*,[88] the ECJ held that discrimination against transsexuals was a species of sex discrimination. As a result, the Sex Discrimination Act was recently amended to include transsexuality as a ground of discrimination. However, other legal disabilities remain. Despite the decision of the ECJ in *P v. S*, the ECHR has recently held that there is no sufficient consensus among contracting states on the moral, social, and legal issues raised in respect of transsexuality to permit the Court to interpret Article 8 as imposing an obligation on a State to recognize the transsexual partner of a woman as the father of the children she conceived by artificial insemination.[89]

## IV DISABILITY

Disability differs from other types of discrimination in that it is a possibility which faces all members of society. The borderline between 'we' and 'they' is not only arbitrary but shifting. Nevertheless, able-bodied people tend to see disabled people as the 'Other', suppressing the knowledge, and the deep anxiety, that disability could come upon anyone at any time. Thus disabled people have always suffered from stigma, prejudice, and exclusion from society. The able-bodied norm is pervasive and exclusive: from public transport and pavements to working arrangements, to leisure and social facilities. Yet disability has only recently even gained recognition as a legitimate subject of anti-discrimination legislation. Until the last decade of the twentieth century, disability was thought to be at most an issue for national assistance through social security or, in cases in which fault could be established, tort law. In the employment field the only measure was one establishing 'special protection' for disabled people. The Disabled Persons (Employment) Act 1944 required employers of a substantial number of employees to employ a set quota of people registered as disabled, a quota which was enforced by criminal sanctions. However, compliance with the Act was negligible, partly because the conditions for registration as disabled were so severe as to exclude many genuinely disabled persons, and partly because of lack of proper enforcement. The result was that, while over 8.5 million people in the UK, or 14 per cent of the adult workforce, are disabled, only about one in ten are in employment.

It was only in 1995, and after as many as sixteen unsuccessful attempts,

---

[88] Case C-13/94 *P v. S and Cornwall County Council* [1996] ECR I-2143.
[89] *X, Y and Z v United Kingdom* Case No 75/1995/582/667 (March 20, 1997).

that the Disability Discrimination Act finally reached the statute books. It was initially characterized as establishing a framework broadly similar to statutes outlawing discrimination on grounds of race or sex.[90] Indeed, it appeared to be a weaker version for various reasons. First, it excluded employers with fewer than twenty employees (now lowered to fifteen); second, its formulation of discrimination was more limited than that in race and sex discrimination statutes; and third, it was backed up by a commission, the National Disability Council, which lacked some of the key powers of its counterparts, the Commission for Racial Equality and the Equal Opportunities Commission. However, it has become clear that the framework should be interpreted quite differently from the sex and race discrimination legislation. Of central importance is its imposition of a positive duty on employers to make reasonable adjustments. Instead of simply requiring conformity to the able-bodied norm as a precondition for protection, the Act requires some adjustment of that norm to afford genuine equality to disabled people. This has been reinforced by judicial interpretation, which has moved decisively away from an able-bodied norm in deciding whether direct discrimination has taken place.[91] The Act was also considerably strengthened by the creation of a fully fledged Disability Rights Commission to replace the National Disability Council. This Commission, which has been in place since April 2000 has an annual budget of twice that of the EOC and three quarters of that of the CRE, and has the same powers as its counterparts in other fields. Nevertheless, the Act still depends primarily on individual enforcement rather than proactive or preventive action, and is correspondingly limited in its impact.

## V AGE DISCRIMINATION

The issues raised by age discrimination differ in some important respects from those discussed so far. As a start, since we have all been young and many of us will become old, the opposition between 'Self' and 'Other' prevalent in other kinds of discrimination is not as stark with respect to age discrimination as in other sorts of discrimination. In addition, there is no clearly demarcated boundary between the group subject to discrimination and others: workers as young as thirty-five

---

[90] See generally, M. Stacey and A. Short, *Challenging Disability Discrimination at Work* (Institute of Employment Rights, 2000).

[91] *Clark v. Novacold* [1999] 2 All ER 977 (CA); see further Chapter Four below.

*Discrimination Law*

have been identified as 'older' workers, and the age brackets for those considered to be 'young workers' have varied over time. Nor is there clearly a dominant and subordinate group, a 'discrete and insular minority' defined by age. In fact, there may be clear conflicts of interest. In catering for the interests of older workers, those of younger workers may be compromised and vice versa. Indeed, 'ageism' is often justified on the grounds that older workers should in fairness be required to make space for younger people. This suggests that it is a mistake to consider age discrimination as a unitary problem. Discrimination against older workers on grounds of their age is quite a different phenomenon from that against younger workers on grounds of their youth. Not only is the nature of the discrimination facing older workers qualitatively different from that confronting younger workers. In addition, the membership of the two groups is obviously distinct, at least temporally, and as we have seen, their interests may well conflict. While young people will necessarily grow out of the group, and may therefore shake free of any discrimination attaching to their youth, older people cannot escape their age and the attached stigma and stereotyping, material disadvantage, and social exclusion. Instead, discrimination against older people has closer links with gender discrimination and disability discrimination than it has with discrimination against younger people. It is in recognition of the need to address discrimination against older people in a different framework from that against younger people that the US statute on age discrimination focuses on a 'protected group' of people aged forty or over. In this section, therefore, discrimination against older people will be dealt with separately from discrimination against younger people.

Traditionally, the question of age has been considered to be a legitimate differentiating factor between employees or others. Young workers have been subject to special protective legislation; and while similar legislation relating to women is now frequently considered discriminatory, special protection of young workers remains widely accepted. Several EC directives on young workers have recently been adopted,[92] and these generally do no more than reflect existing domestic law. While such legislation may in fact benefit young workers, there remain significant areas of negative discrimination, both in State policy and in the labour market as a whole. Thus minimum wage legislation sets a lower rate for younger workers, defined broadly to include employees under the age of

---

[92] Council Directive on the Protection of Young People at Work (94/33/EC).

twenty-six.[93] In addition, research has shown that the majority of young people believe that there is age discrimination at work, and a significant minority feel they have been discriminated against at work or when looking for work on grounds of their age.

So far as older workers are concerned, discrimination within employment has until very recently been considered entirely legitimate, with protection provided instead through the social security system; in the form of pensions and other benefits. However, several interlocking trends have pushed the issue of discrimination against older workers into the foreground. Perhaps most importantly, the cost of high unemployment and industrial restructuring over the last three decades of the twentieth century was disproportionately borne by older people. Older people were deliberately made redundant before younger people, partly because younger people were often cheaper to employ, and partly because they were considered to be more in need of the scarce available jobs. Policies encouraging early retirement were bolstered by incentives created by State social policy in favour of early exit from the workforce. The result has been a steep decline in employment rates of older workers. For men aged fifty-five to fifty-nine in the UK, employment rates slumped from 93 per cent in 1971 to 74 per cent in 1999. Although there has been an upturn since then, the proportion of economically inactive older people remained static. This mirrors a similar pattern of decline in Europe as a whole. The pattern for women has been somewhat different. As we have seen, women's employment rate has been increasing over the past two decades, and this includes older women. However, it is striking that the marginal increase in employment rates of women aged fifty-five to sixty (from 51 per cent in 1977 to 55 per cent in 1999) is much less than the increase experienced by younger women.[94]

This decline in economic activity of older people has coincided with an inexorable demographic trend towards an ageing population. Predictions for the European Union suggest that in less than 20 years the numbers of people aged fifty to sixty-four will have increased by 26 per cent; while the number of twenty to twenty-nine year olds will have decreased by 20 per cent.[95] The increasing population of older people, combined with the

---

[93] National Minimum Wage Act 1998, s. 3.

[94] All figures in this section are taken from *Memorandum from the Department for Education and Employment to Select Committee on Education and Employment* (January 2001) found at http:///www.parliament.the-stationery-office.co.uk/cgi-bin/htm.

[95] Demographic Report 1997, Employment and Social Affairs (Luxembourg: Office for Official Publications of the European Communities, 1998).

high levels of economic inactivity has been a costly brew. It has been estimated that the drop in work rates amongst people aged fifty and over has cost the economy between £16 and £26 billion per year in lost GDP; and its direct costs to the State in extra benefits and lost taxes have been £3–£5bn. The need to reverse these trends has become particularly apparent with a return to higher levels of employment, and a marked shortage of skilled labour. The new emphasis on combatting age discrimination is not, therefore, a result of a sudden appreciation of the need for fairness, but gains its chief impetus from business and macro economic imperatives. It is the business case for combatting age discrimination which is most prominent in recent policy statements. Nevertheless, the human and social costs of age discrimination, particularly when it leads to exclusion from the labour force, should not be under-estimated. Increased poverty, ill health and depression, as well as low self-esteem and social isolation, are themselves strong justifications for legal intervention.

Older workers as a group suffer from some of the central hallmarks of discrimination. Stigma and stereotyping of older workers make it more difficult for them to retain their jobs or re-enter the labour market than younger workers. A recent survey found that a fifth of older people believed they had been discriminated against in employment because of their age. This impression is born out by surveys of employers, a significant proportion of whom consider age to be an important criterion in the recruitment of staff. This is particularly evident in the fact that early retirement remains a common company policy, with many employees expected to retire at 55. Prejudice against older workers is most evident at the stage of recruitment, but it also manifests in relation to training, development opportunities, and promotion. The Labour Force Survey for Spring 2000 shows that older people are significantly less likely to receive training than younger people. Many companies overtly restrict training opportunities on the grounds that older people are perceived to be more inflexible and not worth the investment of training resources. Older people are also very likely to suffer from indirect discrimination, in the form of apparently neutral practices which in fact operate to exclude more older than younger people. This is particularly evident in respect of educational qualifications. Older workers are far less likely than younger workers to possess formal qualifications; yet many employers include specific reference to job qualifications in advertisements. Undue emphasis on formal qualifications rather than relevant experience or transferable skills disproportionately excludes older workers.

In addressing discrimination against older or younger workers, traditional anti-discrimination law may not necessarily be the most effective approach. Certainly, recent government policy has focused instead on providing training and individualized advice. Notably, such schemes specifically differentiate between age categories, offering different packages to workers over fifty, from those available to workers between eighteen and twenty-four, and again those over twenty-five. Thus there is a New Deal 50 Plus, a New Deal for Young Workers, a New Deal 25 plus, and a New Deal for Disabled People. These offer targeted training, personal advice and help with job-seeking, as well as a small cash grant to make up for loss of benefits, and in-working training grants. The government claims some success for such programmes, showing that 25,000 people aged fifty or more have been helped from benefits into work in the first eight months of the operation of New Deal 50 plus. Notably, there is no upper age limit on beneficiaries of this scheme. However, the scheme is only available to a very limited pool of persons: it does not cover the 1.5 million people classed as economically inactive, nor those who have been unemployed for less than six months. So far as private employers are concerned, the government has until now eschewed legislative provision, preferring a voluntary code of conduct, advising employers on good practice in respect of recruitment, retention, training, and promotion. Assessment of the impact of the code has been mixed. The Department of Education and Employment consider the impact has been positive; in particular, there has been a significant drop in the proportion of companies taking age into consideration when selecting the best candidate for a job. However, the Employers Forum on Age reports widespread ignorance of the Code, and even lower levels of implementation.

The preference of soft law cannot however be sustained in light of the recent EU directive requiring Member States to introduce legislation prohibiting age discrimination in employment.[96] In order to comply with the directive, the UK will by 2006 need to introduce legislation outlawing direct and indirect discrimination in employment, including recruitment, promotion, terms and conditions of employment, pay, and dismissal. The directive also requires regulation of discrimination in vocational training and membership of employers' and professional organizations. Both the public and private sectors must be included. The directive does not apply to state social security payments; and Member States may choose to

---

[96] Council Directive 2000/78/EC Establishing A General Framework for Equal Treatment in Employment and Occupation.

exclude membership of or benefits under occupational pension schemes. However, compulsory retirement ages must be prohibited unless they are objectively justified.

Anti-discrimination legislation, when introduced, needs to be carefully crafted. As a start, the purpose needs to be carefully identified. As we have seen, the emphasis in government policy documents has been on the business case for age discrimination laws. The aim, on this view, is to improve business efficiency by tapping into as wide a pool of potential workers as possible. It is the loss of expertise and experience to business from age discrimination which is stressed, rather than the desire to promote individual dignity and autonomy or well being. Stereotyping and prejudice are considered inefficient for the business rather than unfair to the individual. This means, in turn, that it is age diversity which is defined as the aim, rather than equal or proportional representation of older workers. Thus the Employers Forum on Age argue that one of the chief reasons why the code of practice has been unsuccessful is because of its focus on older workers, rather than on facilitating the choice of the best worker for the job and thereby promoting age diversity. The alternative view, that anti-discrimination legislation is necessary to protect individual dignity, would lead to a very differently formulated statute. Instead of focusing on individualized decision-making, with the aim of increasing age diversity in the workforce, such legislation would aim to enhance the inclusion of older workers for its own sake.

On a more specific level, age discrimination legislation quickly encounters one of the central problems of equality legislation: namely who is the relevant comparator? The directive defines direct discrimination as occurring when one person is treated less favourably than another is or would be, on grounds of age. Given the fluidity of the boundaries between different age groups, there are likely to be many skirmishes regarding the question of whether the person treated 'more favourably' is significantly different with respect to age. The US courts in applying the Age Discrimination in Employment Act of 1967 have made it clear that the key question is whether a person has suffered detriment on grounds of his or her age, rather than whether he or she has been less favourably treated than a person of a different age. The role of the comparator is simply to demonstrate causation, that is that the reason for the detrimental treatment was the age of the employee. This makes it possible, in the US context, to draw a comparison between two employees of significantly different ages, even if both are over forty and therefore within the 'protected category'.

But possibly the biggest challenge concerns the kinds of justification which are considered acceptable. The directive permits Member States to provide that differences of treatment on grounds of age do not constitute discrimination if they are objectively and reasonably justified by a legitimate aim, and if the means of achieving that aim are appropriate and necessary. Three examples of justifiable differences of treatment are given. First, positive action which is aimed to promote the vocational integration of young people, older workers or persons with caring responsibilities might justify differential treatment, if it involves the setting of special conditions on access to employment or training, or on such issues as dismissal and conditions of remuneration. Second, it may be justifiable to require workers to be over a given age, experience, or seniority before they are given access to employment or advantages linked to employment. Third, a maximum age for recruitment may be set if it is based on the training requirements of the employer, or the need for a reasonable period of employment before retirement.

# 3

# The Scope of Discrimination Law

A key contribution of liberal equality has been its insistence that individuals should be judged according to their personal qualities. This basic tenet is contravened if individuals are subjected to detriment on the basis only of their status, their group membership, or irrelevant physical characteristics. Distinctions on such grounds are invidious and should, on this theory, be outlawed. On the other hand, not every distinction is discriminatory. Governments classify people into groups for a wide variety of reasons and many of them are legitimate. In addition, there are many group characteristics which are a valued part of the identity of individuals. The challenge therefore is to frame laws which are sensitive enough to outlaw invidious distinctions; while permitting and even supporting positive difference.

This chapter considers the ways in which the scope of discrimination law has been delineated. There are two main dimensions of the question. The first concerns the grounds of discrimination. Which groups ought to be protected against discrimination? Although there is now general consensus that sex and race should be within the list of grounds of discrimination, even these were only achieved after struggle and controversy. It is only relatively recently that other grounds, such as disability, age, and sexual orientation have been accepted as attracting special protection. But what about other groups? Should farmers or publicans or ratepayers claim protection against discrimination? And how narrowly should the groups be defined? We know that women of Bangladeshi or Pakistani origin tend to be the most disadvantaged in society. Should they constitute a protected group, claiming equality with other women as well as men?

The second dimension of the scope of discrimination law is concerned with its reach. Does it apply to public actors or private actors? Does it apply only in specified fields such as employment, or does it apply across the board? Part I of this chapter examines the first dimension, the grounds of discrimination, while Part II considers the second dimension.

# I  GROUNDS OF DISCRIMINATION

## (I)  DEFINING THE GROUNDS OF DISCRIMINATION: WHO DECIDES AND HOW?

What sort of distinctions should be outlawed by the law as illegitimate and unacceptable? We could search for a unifying principle which explains existing grounds of discrimination and generates the answer to new questions. Or we could argue that the decision is simply a political one, reflecting the balance of opinion in society at a particular time. Shadowing this set of issues is the debate about which institution should make the decision: the courts or the legislature. It could be argued that since one of the main reasons for providing protection for particular groups is their political powerlessness, it is counterproductive to rely on the majority to enact anti-discrimination laws through the political process. On this view, the decision as to which groups should be protected is one for the judiciary. However, this assumes that there is a set of principles which guide the judges in making decisions as to whether a particular group should be protected. If there is no such set of logical principles, then a political decision or value judgement is being delegated to unelected judges. A different solution could be to create a list of protected groups at international level, enshrined in a treaty such as the International Covenant for the Protection of Civil and Political Rights. This transcends the particular balance of power in any participating State. But it runs the risk of doing no more than establishing a lowest common denominator.

It is also important to view the democratic dimension as embracing more than just legislature and courts. In fact much modern equality theory stresses that the participation of affected groups in decision-making is a central value. This is equally true for the courts, which need to be adapted to be inclusive in this way. Equally complex is the question of how a group is defined. Is it enough for a set of individuals to believe themselves to constitute a group, or is it necessary to formulate objective criteria? And how does the law deal with those who belong to more than one specified group, such as black women?

There are three types of response to these questions. The first is to frame a broad open-textured equality guarantee, stating simply that all persons are equal before the law, without specifying any particular grounds. This approach takes the decision out of the political process, and instead leaves it to judges to decide when a classification is prohibited. It is epitomized by the US Constitution, which simply states, in the Fourteenth Amendment, that no State may 'deny to any person within its jurisdiction the equal protection of the laws'. A second approach, at the other end of the spectrum, is to formulate legislation containing an exhaustive list of grounds. This contrasts with the first approach in that the choice of ground is made wholly within the political process with no discretion left to the judges. Grounds can be added or removed only legislatively and not judicially. This 'fixed category' approach is found in both UK anti-discrimination legislation and in the law of the EU. In between these two extremes is the third approach, which specifies a list of grounds of discrimination, but indicates that the list is not exhaustive. This is the approach adopted in the European Convention on Human Rights, the Canadian Charter of Rights, and the South African Constitution. Thus Article 14 of the European Convention on Human Rights states that the enjoyment of the rights and freedoms in the Convention shall be secured without discrimination 'on grounds *such as* . . . ' The Canadian Charter of Rights and Freedoms states: 'Every citizen is equal before and under the law and has the right to the equal protection and benefit of the law without discrimination *and in particular* without discrimination based on race, national or ethnic origin, colour, religion, sex, age or mental or physical disability' (italics added).[1] This approach gives judges some discretion to extend the list according to a set of judicially generated principles; but judicial discretion is bounded by the existence of enumerated grounds.

Each of these approaches is problematic in different ways. The fixed category approach, because it is based on the assumption of clearly delineated boundaries, has the effect of excluding groups only marginally outside of those boundaries. This creates great pressure on the judiciary to redraw the margins, resulting in even more complex and anomalous distinctions. These difficulties are endemic in British and EU law, and are discussed in the following section. The next section turns to some of the challenges encountered when it is left to the judiciary to formulate principles to establish new categories.

## (II) STRETCHING EXISTING CATEGORIES: SEMANTICS OR SUBSTANCE

Although the UK has sophisticated anti-discrimination legislation in some areas, its coverage is far from comprehensive and there is no general

---

[1] Canadian Charter of Rights and Freedoms, s. 15(1).

constitutional guarantee of equality. The Sex Discrimination Act prohibits discrimination on grounds of sex or being married, a list recently extended to include transsexuality.[2] The Race Relations Act prohibits discrimination on grounds of colour, race, nationality, or ethnic or national origins. Disability discrimination is prohibited by the Disability Discrimination Act. As this indicates, there are some glaring omissions. Until the very end of the twentieth century, there was no domestic legislation providing protection against discrimination on grounds of sexual orientation or age. Discrimination on grounds of religion and political opinion, although prohibited in Northern Ireland, was lawful in Great Britain.[3] The coverage of EC law has until very recently been even more limited. For most of its history, EC legislation prohibited discrimination solely on grounds of sex, marriage, or EC nationality, and recent judicial intervention led to the inclusion of transsexuality.[4]

This jagged coverage is now augmented as a result of important new initiatives at EU level. Under new powers given by the Treaty of Amsterdam, a directive 'implementing the principle of equal treatment between persons irrespective of racial or ethnic origin' was adopted in June 2000.[5] A second directive extending the principle of equal treatment to prevent discrimination on grounds of age, disability, religion and sexual orientation (the 'framework directive') was adopted five months later.[6] Member States have two years within which to implement these directives. The list is further extended by the incorporation into domestic law of the ECHR by the Human Rights Act 1998, which came into effect in October 2000. This states that the enjoyment of Convention rights must be secured without discrimination on any grounds such as sex, race, colour, language, religion, political or other opinion, national or social origin, association with a national minority, property, birth, or other status. Finally, the Northern Ireland Act 1998 includes in section 75 a long list of grounds to which public bodies must have due regard, including religion, political opinion, racial group, age, marital status, sexual orientation, gender, disability, and persons with dependants and persons without.

This looks like a considerable expansion. However, coverage remains far from complete. Even more problematic, as will be seen below, the

---

[2] Sex Discrimination (Gender Reassignment) Regulations 1999 SI 1999/1102.
[3] Race Relations Act 1976, s. 3(1); Sex Discrimination Act 1975, ss. 1–3; Fair Employment (Northern Ireland) Act 1989, s. 49; Disability Discrimination Act 1995, s. 4.
[4] *P v. S and Cornwall County Council* [1996] ECR I-2143.
[5] Council Directive 2000/43/EC of June 29, 2000 [2000] OJ L180/22.
[6] Council Directive 2000/78/EC of November 27, 2000 [2000] OJ L303/16.

extent of the coverage provided to any one group is variable. The domestic sex and race discrimination legislation is confined to employment, education, and the provision of services. The ECHR provisions only apply to the enjoyment of Convention rights, and it is not clear whether they extend beyond the public sphere. The EU provisions are particularly complex. The directive on race extends beyond employment to include education, housing, and other social protection; but the directive on sexual orientation, religion, age, and disability is limited to discrimination within employment, vocational training, and membership of workers or employers' organizations. Social security is specifically excluded. The result is a hierarchy of directives within EU law, with race and ethnic origin given the widest reach, followed by gender discrimination, which covers employment and social security, and trailed by the discrimination on grounds of age, religion, sexual orientation, and disability. Excluded altogether is discrimination on grounds of nationality, except in respect of nationals of Member States; and third country nationals are only protected if the difference of treatment is not related to provisions governing their entry or residence.

Such uneven coverage has made it inevitable that excluded groups will attempt to bring themselves within established grounds. This in turn necessitates bright line distinctions between different grounds of discrimination. For example, the omission of sexual orientation as a protected ground has led litigants to argue that sexual orientation discrimination is a species of sex discrimination. Similarly, the inclusion of 'ethnic origin' but the exclusion of religion has meant that Sikhs, Muslims, Jews, and Rastafarians have had to argue that they are groups defined by their ethnic origin and not by their religion. Yet ethnicity is intimately bound up with religion. In deciding these cases, it might be expected that the courts would have attempted to develop some principles based on the underlying purpose of the legislation. However, little attempt has been made to do so. Instead, particularly in the UK, courts have tended to decide the case on the basis of technical definitions of the statutory words themselves.

This is particularly apparent in the well known case of *Mandla v. Lee*,[7] in which the House of Lords was required to define 'ethnic origin' in a way which set it apart from 'religion'. Notably, the court did not approach the question by concentrating, as courts in other jurisdictions have done, on issues such as a history of discrimination or political powerlessness.

---

[7] [1983] 2 AC 548 (HL).

Instead, it drew on the dictionary definition of the phrase 'ethnic origin', and focused on the grammar of the statute. The essential conditions for a group to constitute an ethnic group were, according to Lord Fraser: (i) a long shared history, of which the group is conscious as distinguishing it from other groups; and (ii) a cultural tradition of its own, including family and social customs and manners, often but not necessarily associated with religious observance. Also relevant characteristics are some of the following: (i) a common geographic origin, or descent from a small number of common ancestors; (ii) a common language, not necessarily peculiar to the group; (iii) a common religion different from that of neighbouring groups or the general community; or (iv) being a minority, or an oppressed or dominant group within a larger community. Only the final factor mentioned touches on the underlying purposes of the aims of the equality guarantee, and even then dominant groups are included.

The technicality of this approach has inevitably created anomalies. In *Mandla v. Lee* itself, it was found that Sikhs were a distinctive and self conscious community, with a history going back to the fifteenth century, a written language and a common geographical origin. They were thus held to be an ethnic group. However, other groups have not succeeded in persuading the courts that they fall within the scope of discrimination law, regardless of their disadvantage or history of prejudice. This is clearly illustrated in the response to discrimination claims by Rastafarians. In *Dawkins v. Department of Environment*,[8] Dawkins, a Rastafarian, was refused a job unless he cut off his dreadlocks. He claimed that this constituted unlawful discrimination. This required an answer to the threshold question: were Rastafarians a group defined according to ethnic origin? The employment tribunal answered in the affirmative, on the grounds that Rastafarians had a long shared history and a cultural tradition of their own. They were also found to have a common geographical origin, a distinctive literature, and a sense of being an oppressed minority.[9] However, both the Employment Appeal Tribunal and the Court of Appeal came to the opposite conclusion. In the view of the EAT, the fact that the Rastafarian movement was only born sixty years ago meant that its history was not long enough to fulfil this criterion, a view which was supported by the Court of Appeal. Both the EAT and the Court of Appeal also decided that Rastafarians had not established a separate identity from the rest of the Afro-Caribbean community. They could be described as a 'religious sect, and no more'.[10] The group's own perception

---

[8] [1993] IRLR 284 (CA).     [9] [1991] ICR 583 (EAT) at 594.     [10] *ibid.*

of itself as having a distinct social identity was given no credence.[11] The result of the focus on definition rather than purpose was that discrimination against Rastafarians was held to be lawful.

Equally serious is the refusal to recognize Muslims as a group defined by their ethnic origins. Thus when a group of Muslims were disciplined for taking a day off work to celebrate Eid, their claim of direct discrimination on grounds of their ethnic origin failed. The tribunal held that since Muslims were a religious grouping, they could not be treated as an ethnic grouping and therefore did not fall within the grounds specified in the Race Relations Act.[12] Instead, they were required to prove that they had been subjected to indirect discrimination on grounds of their race. In other words, since most of the Asians working at the factory in question were Muslim, the requirement to work on Eid excluded substantially more Asians than whites. Although the complainants were successful in this case, there are two important disadvantages to an indirect discrimination claim. First, it requires a showing that considerably more Asians in the workforce were Muslim than whites; and second, it left the employer the option of justifying the disparity on business grounds. A direct discrimination claim requires neither of these obstacles to be surmounted.

The failure of the legislature to include transsexuality and sexual orientation as explicit grounds for protection against discrimination has led to similar pressure through the courts to include these as types of sex discrimination. By contrast with the stance of the House of Lords in *Mandla v. Lee*, there were signs that the European Court of Justice was developing a set of teleological principles to decide these cases. In the ground-breaking case of *P v. S*,[13] the ECJ held that discrimination against transsexuals was a species of sex discrimination. Crucially, this decision was not made on simply technical grounds. In what appeared to be the development of a much wider equality right, more akin to the US Constitutional guarantee, the ECJ stated the Equal Treatment Directive was 'simply the expression, in the relevant field, of the principle of equality, which is one of the fundamental principles of Community law'. To tolerate discrimination against a transsexual would be tantamount to a failure to respect the dignity and freedom to which he or she is entitled. As a result of *P v. S*, the Sex Discrimination Act was explicitly amended to include transsexuality as a prohibited ground of discrimination.

---

[11] Compare *King-Ansell v. Police* [1979] 2 NZLR 53; and see S. Poulter, *Ethnicity, Law and Human Rights: The English Experience* (Oxford: Clarendon Press, 1998), pp. 353–354.

[12] *J.H. Walker v. Hussain* [1996] IRLR 11 (EAT).

[13] See above n. 4.

However, the ECJ quickly retracted from the position that equality is a fundamental dignity right. In particular, it has refused to hold that sexual orientation discrimination is included in the prohibition on sex discrimination in the Equal Treatment Directive. Instead, it held that discrimination could only be established if the complainant had been treated less favourably than a person of the opposite sex on grounds of sex (not sexual orientation). As will be seen in Chapter Four, everything then depends on who is chosen as the comparator. If a gay woman is compared with a heterosexual man, there may well be discrimination. But if a gay woman is compared with a gay man, the opposite conclusion can be reached. In *Grant v. South West Trains*,[14] the ECJ held that the relevant comparator was not a heterosexual, but a homosexual man. Since a man living with a male partner was treated in the same way (i.e. equally badly) as the woman living with a woman partner, she could not complain that she had been treated less favourably than a similarly situated man. It was therefore held that there was no discrimination on grounds of sex.[15]

By contrast, the European Court of Human Rights has held that sexual orientation *is* included in the prohibition against discrimination on grounds of sex, as set out in Article 14 of the European Convention on Human Rights. In the 1999 case of *Salgueiro da Silva Mouta v. Portugal*,[16] the Court held that the refusal to grant custody of a child to her gay father on grounds only of his sexual orientation amounted to a denial of his right to family life which was discriminatory on grounds of sex contrary to Article 14 of the ECHR. Indeed, the inclusion of sexual orientation is now considered so well established that the drafters of the new Protocol 12 to the ECHR, which expands the equality right contained in Article 14, expressly decided that it was unnecessary to amend the list of enumerated grounds to include an explicit reference to sexual orientation.[17]

From a strategic point of view, it is possible to stretch the concept of sex discrimination in order to argue that discrimination on grounds of sexual orientation falls within this category.[18] However, the very fact that

---

[14] Case C-249/96 *Grant v. South-West Trains Ltd* [1998] ECR I-621.

[15] See too *Secretary of State for Defence v. MacDonald* [2001] IRLR 431 (Court of Session). Contrast *Oncale v. Sundowner Offshore Services Inc* (1998) 523 US 75, 118 S Ct 998, in which the US Supreme Court held that harassment of a male employee by a male supervisor was discrimination on grounds of sex.

[16] *Salgueiro da Silva Mouta v. Portugal* (unreported; ECHR December 21, 1999).

[17] See explanatory memorandum.

[18] See generally R. Wintemute, 'Sexual Orientation Discrimination' in C. McCrudden and G. Chambers (eds.), *Individual Rights and the Law in Britain* (Clarendon, 1994).

the comparison can be manipulated to achieve the desired result is indicative of the absence of principled decision-making. In fact, of course, the scope for manipulation arises because the real reason for the difference of treatment is not sex but sexual orientation. Far more appropriate would be the explicit inclusion of sexual orientation into the list of prohibited grounds, as has now been done in the new framework directive. Indeed, the ECJ in *Grant* was clearly influenced by the fact that if it extended sex discrimination to include sexual orientation discrimination, it would be pre-empting new legislative powers to deal explicitly with sexual orientation.

The inclusion of age, religion, and sexual orientation into the test as a result of EU law certainly represents an important step forward and relieves the pressure on existing categories. Even so, the approach remains one of fixed categories. This in turn depends on a particular assumption about the nature of a group. Groups on this view are characterized as mutually exclusive, defined according to objective and static characteristics, and operating in opposition to one another. Each individual is considered to be wholly determined by his or her membership of a particular group, as defined by the contrast with other groups. The problematic nature of such fixed boundaries is demonstrated by the contrasting decisions of *Mandla* and *Dawkins*. In *Mandla*, Sikhs were considered a group defined by their ethnic origin because they were distinct from groups around them, whereas in *Dawkins*, Rastafarians were not considered a group because they were held not to have established a sufficiently distinct boundary between themselves and other Afro-Caribbeans.

Bright line distinctions are also problematic in respect of cumulative or 'intersectional' discrimination. Some individuals experience discrimination based on more than one ground. Thus black women are subject to racism and sexism; as well as bearing the 'third burden', namely the burden of discrimination against black men. Such discrimination is not fully described by simply adding two kinds of discrimination together. Black women share some experiences in common with both white women and black men, but they also differ in important respects. Thus while white women may be the victims of sex discrimination, they may also be the beneficiaries and even the perpetrators of racism. The relationship of dominance between white 'madams' and black 'maids' is a well-known example. Conversely, black men may experience racism but be the beneficiaries and perpetrators of sexism. Nor is it accurate to generalize about 'black' women: this category fragments under the pressure of cultural diversity. We have already seen that the experience of women of Afro-Caribbean origin is quite different from that of women of Pakistani and Bangladeshi origin, not least in respect of religious differences. The existing legal framework contains no mechanism for dealing with these cross currents. Notably, the two new EU directives make an unusually explicit acknowledgement of the reality of cumulative discrimination, stating in the preamble that in implementing the principle of equal treatment the Community should aim to 'promote equality between men and women, especially since women are often the victims of multiple discrimination'.[19] But no concrete links are made as between the directives, and cumulative discrimination on other grounds, such as disability and sexual orientation, is not dealt with. Equally problematic is the absence of recognition of the possibility of conflict between the differing grounds. Gender equality may well conflict with religious or ethnic equality.

Progress beyond such a fixed categorical approach entails revising the meaning of group identity. The above analysis characterizes a group on the basis of apparently fixed attributes. Yet, as Young argues, a group is better described in terms of a sense of affinity between individuals, and a social process of interaction. Moreover, groups intersect, so that different groups share some common experiences and even have some common membership. This in turn entails a reconceptualization of the notion of difference itself. Instead of difference connoting 'absolute otherness', or deviance from a single norm, difference is about relationships between and within groups. This allows groups to define themselves, rather than being subject to a devalued essence imposed from outside.[20] Such an approach can only be captured legally by a single harmonized statute which includes all the relevant grounds of discrimination, and does not necessitate harsh distinctions between different grounds. It is true that some grounds require specific treatment: disability may require special measures. But the applicability of the special measures should be based on an understanding of group membership as one with fluid boundaries, not dependent on a rigid definition of the group itself.

---

[19] Directive 2000/43, preamble, para. 14; Directive 2000/78, preamble, para. 4.
[20] I. M. Young, *Justice and the Politics of Difference* (Princeton University Press, 1990), pp. 168–172.

## (III) GENERATING PROTECTED GROUNDS:
## JUDICIAL PRINCIPLES

The alternative to the approach based on legislatively predetermined categories is one which gives judges discretion to develop categories, either from an open-textured equality guarantee, or from a non-exhaustive list of protected grounds. This approach will now become necessary even in British domestic law, because the equality guarantee of the European Convention on Human Rights, now incorporated into domestic law, contains a non-exhaustive list. It is instructive therefore to consider the ways in which courts in other jurisdictions have dealt with such questions.

As we have seen, the US Constitution simply states, in the Fourteenth Amendment, that no State may 'deny to any person within its jurisdiction the equal protection of the laws'. The US Supreme Court is therefore left with the full responsibility for deciding when a classification constitutes a breach of the Constitution. This is a particularly sensitive task, given that any classification whatsoever may be challenged, be it a welfare law providing specific protection to vulnerable members of society or one that unduly burdens a group for reasons of pure prejudice. The extent of the power thus given to judges to strike down legitimate policy decisions in the socio-economic sphere was demonstrated in the early years of the century when the Court unrelentingly struck down social policy legislation such as minimum wage laws, maximum hour, and child labour regulations. It was only after 1937 that the Court began to recognize the need for judicial deference to democratic decision-making in certain areas. At the same time, it was necessary to retain control over invidious prejudice. In order to distinguish between these two spheres, the Court developed its well-known double standard of scrutiny. Most classifications need only be rational, in the sense of being rationally related to a legitimate State interest. However, in some cases, a heightened degree of judicial scrutiny may be necessary. It should be noted that this approach means that the determination of grounds for discrimination is inevitably closely linked to the question of whether discrimination has taken place at all. In principle, a classification could even survive strict scrutiny.

How to decide which level of scrutiny was applicable was the next major challenge. The first and most pressing question was whether racial classifications should be subject to strict scrutiny. Despite the persistence of a variety of pernicious forms of racism well after the abolition of slavery, the US Supreme Court initially answered this question in the negative. In the notorious case of *Plessy v. Ferguson*,[21] the US Supreme Court found that laws segregating blacks and whites did not breach the equality guarantee. According to the leading judgment, a State had every right to use classifications, as long as the classification was not capricious, arbitrary, or unreasonable. The fact that the classification was based on race did not attract any particularly intensive judicial scrutiny. Indeed, although the segregation (in this case of train carriages) was clearly part of a widespread set of laws aimed at reinforcing the superiority of whites and stigmatizing blacks as inferior, the Court held that the government had done its duty by securing equal rights to all of its citizens. 'If one race be inferior to the other socially, the Constitution of the United States cannot put them upon the same plane'.

It was thus of enormous historical significance when the Court eventually recognized the perniciousness of racial classifications. It did this by formulating a particularly intensive standard of judicial scrutiny of racial classifications as compared to other sorts of classifications. 'Legal restrictions which curtail the civil rights of a single racial group are immediately suspect . . . Courts must subject them to the most rigid scrutiny'.[22] Strict scrutiny means first that, in order to justify a racial classification, it must be shown to further not just a legitimate but a compelling State interest. Second, the racial classification must be more than rationally related to that interest: it must be narrowly tailored to achieve that interest. Although this, in principle, leaves open the possibility of justification of a racial classification, in practice the strict scrutiny test has almost invariably led to the Court striking down racial classifications operating to the detriment of blacks.[23]

The decision that 'race' was a suspect category did not in itself generate principles for determining which classifications should be subject to heightened scrutiny. The first major statement of a set of principles for deciding this question was found in one of the most famous footnotes in history, footnote four of the *Carolene Products* case.[24] According to Stone J, 'more searching judicial inquiry' may be required for statutes directed at particular religious or national or racial minorities, or where 'prejudice against discrete and insular minorities . . . tends seriously to curtail the operation of those political processes ordinarily to be relied upon to

---

[21] *Plessy v. Ferguson* (1896) 163 US 537, 16 S Ct 1138.
[22] *Korematsu v. United States* (1944) 323 US 214, 65 S Ct 193.
[23] See, e.g. *McLaughlin v. Florida* (1964) 379 US 184, 85 S Ct 283; (1967) *Loving v. Virginia* 388 US 1, 87 S Ct 1817.
[24] *United States v. Carolene Products Co* (1938) 304 US 144, 58 S Ct 778.

protect minorities'.[25] Later case-law has elaborated on these basic criteria: a class is 'suspect' if it has been 'saddled with such disabilities, or subjected to such a history of purposeful unequal treatment, or relegated to such a position of political powerlessness as to command extraordinary protection from the majoritarian political process'.[26] In addition, a classification is suspect if it is particularly stigmatic, or is based on an immutable characteristic, which prevents the individual from being judged on the basis of personal merit.

It is noteworthy that remarkably similar criteria have been articulated by the Canadian Supreme Court in deciding whether a group not specifically mentioned in the Canadian Charter should be protected by the equality guarantee. These include the fact that the targeted group has suffered historical disadvantage; that it constitutes a 'discrete and insular minority'; that the distinction is made on the basis of a characteristic attributed to the individual, not on his or her merit, but on the basis of association with a group; or that the distinction is based on an immutable characteristic.[27]

In some cases, the application of these indicia has led to clear and principled results. Thus the US Federal Court of Appeals, faced with a challenge by a gay man of the constitutionality of army regulations banning homosexuals from service in the military, applied all the main indicia for a suspect classification. Had the group suffered from a history of discrimination? Was the class defined by an immutable trait that bears no relation to the ability of members to perform the job in question? Had the class been discriminated against because of prejudicial stereotypes? And was the group a discrete and insular minority which lacks the political power necessary to obtain political redress? Having answered all these questions in the affirmative, the Court was able to hold that it was. The application of the strict scrutiny test therefore led to the conclusion that the regulations breached the constitutional equality guarantee.[28] Similarly, in the Canadian case of *Law Society of British Columbia v. Andrews*,[29] the complainant had been refused admission to the British Columbia Bar because he was not a Canadian citizen. A British subject permanently resident in Canada, he met all the other requirements of the Bar except

---

[25] *United States v. Carolene Products Co* (1938) at 152.

[26] *San Antonio Independent School District v. Rodriguez* (1973) 411 US 1, 93 S Ct 1278 (*per* Powell J).

[27] See *Miron v. Trudel* [1995] 2 SCR 418 at 496–497 (*per* McLachlan J).

[28] *Watkins v. United States Army* (1988) 837 F 2d 1428 (US Ct of Apps (9th Cir)).

[29] [1989] 1 SCR 143.

for citizenship. Were 'non-citizens permanently resident in Canada' protected by the equality guarantee, although not expressly mentioned? The Court held that they were. The test to be applied, according to Wilson J, was whether this group was a 'discrete and insular minority' as specified in the *Carolene Products* case. Non-citizens lacked in political power relative to citizens, and were therefore vulnerable in that their interests were liable to be overlooked by elected representatives. In that sense, they were held to be analogous to the groups specifically enumerated in the Charter. Moreover, citizenship is typically not within the control of the individual and is, at least temporarily, a characteristic of personhood which is not alterable by conscious action and which in some cases is not alterable except on the basis of unacceptable costs. At the same time, judges have stressed that these indicators are not rigid preconditions. The range of discrete and insular minorities has changed and will continue to do so; requiring a sensitive and balanced approach.

While there may be agreement on the criteria to be used, their application to particular issues diverges widely. Indeed, on closer examination, it can be seen that none of these indices produces cut-and-dried results. For example, what is an 'immutable characteristic'? The paradigm category of race is not easily generalizable to other groups. The question whether sexual orientation is an immutable characteristic leads into a debate which is itself saturated with prejudice, and seems irrelevant to the social reality of protection against discrimination. Similarly, the question of whether one's religious convictions are characterized as a matter of choice or not yields many different responses, but none of them is particularly relevant to the question of whether religious discrimination should be tolerated. Even the apparent immutability of race and sex could on closer inspection be doubted. Indeed, many recent cases have concerned discrimination against transsexuals: here it is the very mutability of their sex that has triggered the discrimination. Race too is now recognized as a question of social context rather than physiology. Notably, in the *Andrews* case quoted above, the question of immutability was rephrased in the context of citizenship in terms of whether or not the characteristic was within the control of the individual, alterable by conscious action, or not alterable except on the basis of unacceptable costs. Similarly, the clear outlines of other indicia blur under closer scrutiny. Why does a history of past disadvantage not apply to poverty or social class? Courts in most jurisdictions have been concerned to prevent the equality guarantee from reaching to the basis of the capitalist society—namely inequalities of wealth. For example, in a US case, the system of funding local schools by local property taxes was challenged on the grounds that this discriminated against poor districts, whose property taxes were not of the standard of richer areas, and therefore whose schools were correspondingly less well resourced. The US Supreme Court held that none of the traditional indicia of suspect-ness applied: there was no history of purposeful unequal treatment or political powerlessness. It is difficult to see why this is the case.

The difficulty in applying the criteria is particularly well demonstrated in the approach of the US Supreme Court to sex discrimination. Did the standard of strict scrutiny applied in race cases also apply to discrimination against women? In earlier cases, such as the exclusion of women from compulsory jury service, it was held that there was no parallel between sex and race discrimination. This meant that strict scrutiny did not apply: as long as any 'basis in reason' could be conceived for the discrimination, there was no violation of equal protection.[30] The reasons given for this conclusion simply show up the continuing prejudices of the judiciary. Thus it was stated that sex discrimination differed from race discrimination because there was no history of prejudice against women.[31] A good enough reason for differentiating, according to Harlan J, was that women were the centre of home and family life. It was only in the 1970s that the US Supreme Court decisions began to recognize that women had been subject to a long history of discrimination; that they had been under-represented on legislative bodies; and that sex was an immutable characteristic, bearing no relationship to the capacity to perform a job or contribute to society.[32] In 1971, for the first time, the US Supreme Court ruled in favour of a woman who complained that her State had denied her the equal protection of its laws.[33] Nevertheless, the Court has consistently refused to regard gender classifications as suspect. Instead of requiring the most intense scrutiny, as applied to race, an 'intermediate' test is applied.[34] As reformulated in 1996, this test requires the State to produce a justification which is 'exceedingly persuasive'.[35] This means that the State must show that the discriminatory classification is substantially related to the achievement of important governmental objectives.

---

[30] See, e.g. *Goesart v. Cleary* (1948) 335 US 464, 69 S Ct 198.

[31] *Hoyt v. Florida* (1961) 368 US 57, 82 S Ct 159.

[32] *Frontiero v. Richardson* (1973) 411 US 677, 93 S Ct 1764; *Reed v. Reed* (1971) 404 US 71, 92 S Ct 251.

[33] *Reed v. Reed* (1971) 404 US 71, 92 S Ct 251.

[34] *Craig v. Boren* (1976) 429 US 190, 97 S Ct 451; (1979) *Orr v. Orr* 440 US 268, 99 S Ct 1102; *Michael M v. Superior Court* (1981) 450 US 464, 101 S Ct 1200.

[35] *United States v. Virginia* (1996) 116 S Ct 2264.

Why then the difference between the levels of scrutiny imposed for race and sex? Until recently, this was because sex discrimination was seen as somehow less pernicious than race discrimination. A new and more positive perspective was provided in 1996 by one of the two women justices on the US Supreme Court, Ginsburg J, who saw the lesser standard as providing an opportunity to frame legislation which positively promoted equal opportunities for women, while striking down legislation based on over-broad generalizations about different talents, capacities, or preferences of men and women. As we shall see in Chapter Five, the US Supreme Court has recently taken a strictly symmetrical approach to discrimination on grounds of race, holding that both invidious discrimination and discrimination designed to compensate for past disadvantage should be subject to strict scrutiny. Ginsburg J, however, made it clear that sex classifications can be used to compensate women for particular economic disabilities or to develop their talents and capacities fully. But they cannot be used to perpetuate the legal, social, and economic inferiority of women. Whereas supposed inherent differences are no longer accepted as a ground for race classifications, ' "inherent differences" between men and women, we have come to appreciate, remain cause for celebration, but not for denigration of the members of either sex or for artificial constraints on an individual's opportunity'.[36]

More recently, courts in both the US and Canada have recognized the indeterminacy of the indicia of 'suspectness'. This is particularly apparent in relation to sexual orientation. Some cases appeared to have little difficulty applying the criteria. In a more recent case, the US Supreme Court left the indicia behind and resorted to more fundamental principles. The litigation in question concerned an amendment to the Constitution of Colorado which prohibited the enactment of any legislation outlawing discrimination on grounds of sexual orientation.[37] This was challenged as a breach of the Equal Protection Clause. In upholding the challenge, Kennedy J for the majority based his opinion on the fundamental principle that the Constitution 'neither knows nor tolerates classes among citizens'. The Supreme Court found it unnecessary to rely on the specific ground upheld in the lower court, namely that the amendment would have infringed the right of gays and lesbians to participate in the political process. Instead, it was held that the Equal Protection Clause was breached for two fundamental reasons: it imposed

---

[36] *ibid.*, text to footnotes 6 and 7.
[37] *Romer v. Evans* (1996) 517 US 620, 116 S Ct 1620.

a broad and undifferentiated disability on a single named group, and secondly, that it raised the inevitable inference that the measure was borne of animosity towards the class of persons affected. 'A State cannot so deem a class of persons a stranger to its laws'.[38]

Possibly the most rigorous and principled approach is that of the Canadian Supreme Court. Although sexual orientation is not expressly mentioned in the Canadian Charter, the Canadian Supreme Court has had no difficulty in accepting it as an analogous ground. In the words of La Forest J: 'I have no difficulty accepting the appellants contention that whether or not sexual orientation is based on biological or physiological factors, which may be a matter of some controversy, it is a deeply personal characteristic that is either unchangeable or changeable only at unacceptable personal costs, and so falls within the ambit of s. 15 protection as being analogous to the enumerated grounds'.[39] Other members of the Canadian Supreme Court have openly expressed doubts as to the usefulness of particular indicia. Thus, according to L'Hureux-Dube J, the focus on particular indicia, such as the immutability of a characteristic, is too narrow and formalistic. Instead of focusing on the characteristics of the individual or group at issue, she argues, the Court should consider whether the law in question breaches the primary mission of the equality guarantee, namely, 'the promotion of a society in which all are secure in the knowledge that they are recognized at law as human beings equally deserving of concern, respect and consideration'.[40] On this view, a person or group has been discriminated against when a legislative distinction makes them feel that they are less worthy of recognition or value as human beings, as members of society.[41]

## II SCOPE OF DISCRIMINATION LAW

Many of the constitutional documents examined so far have contained an all-embracing equality provision, guaranteeing equality before the law without specifying its scope. The Universal Declaration of Human Rights provides that 'all are equal before the law and are entitled without any discrimination to equal protection of the law'.[42] As we have seen, the

---

[38] *Romer v. Evans* (1996) at 623, 1623 (*per* Kennedy J).

[39] *Egan v. Canada* [1995] 2 SCR 513 at 528.

[40] *Andrews v. Law Society of British Columbia* [1989] 1 SCR 143 at 171.

[41] *Egan v. Canada* at 545 (para. 39); *Vriend v. Alberta* [1998] 4 BHRC 140 at 185 (para. 182).

[42] Universal Declaration of Human Rights (1948), art. 7.

US Constitution declares simply that 'no State shall deny to any person within its jurisdiction the equal protection of the laws'.[43] British law, by contrast, contains no general equality guarantee, but only a set of specific statutes, augmented by EU law and the ECHR, now incorporated by the Human Rights Act 1998. Even when all these fragments are put together, the result is not comprehensive. Some provisions apply solely to education, employment, and the provision of services; others only to the application of fundamental human rights. Some bind public bodies only, while others contain exceptions for acts of public bodies or carried out with statutory authority. This section briefly describes this patchwork protection, considers the reforms which are already in the pipeline, and argues that a more comprehensive equality provision is now sorely needed.

## (I) SEX, RACE, AND DISABILITY DISCRIMINATION LEGISLATION

Existing race and sex discrimination laws apply only to education, employment, and the provision of services. Acts done by public bodies and acts done by or on behalf of the Crown are included,[44] but only so far as they relate to employment, education, or the provision of services. The Disability Discrimination Act is similarly limited to specific areas, namely employment, the provision of goods, facilities and services, premises, education, and transport. Discrimination outside of the specified areas is not outlawed by these statutes. Even within these fields, there are significant exceptions. Thus the Sex Discrimination Act does not prevent organized religions from limiting employment to one sex so as to comply with the doctrines of the religion or avoid offending the religious susceptibilities of a significant number of its followers.[45] Charities may confer benefits on persons of one sex,[46] and it is permissible to limit participation in sport to one or other sex. Similarly, differentiation on grounds of sex by reference to actuarial or other reasonably reliable data is permissible for insurance purposes.[47] Also of importance is the exception for discriminatory acts done for 'for the purpose of ensuring the combat effectiveness of the armed forces'.[48] Thus the Royal Marines have a policy of excluding women from all positions in the service, on the grounds

---

[43] US Constitution 14th Amendment.
[44] Sex Discrimination Act 1975, s. 85(1); Disability Discrimination Act 1995, s. 64(1) (excluding fire services, and naval, military, or air forces of the Crown: s. 64(6), (7)); Race Relations Act 1976, s. 75.
[45] Sex Discrimination Act 1975, s. 19.    [46] Contrast Race Relations Act 1976, s. 34.
[47] Sex Discrimination Act 1975, ss. 43–5.    [48] *ibid.*, s. 85(4).

that all members, including chefs, should be capable of fighting in a commando unit. This meant that it was not discriminatory to refuse to transfer a woman chef to the Royal Marines on her redundancy from the Royal Artillery.[49] A range of exceptions applies too to the Disability Discrimination Act, including a particularly invidious exception for small businesses[50] and the exclusion of education provided in colleges and universities. Nor is the set of exceptions harmonious. Both the Race Relations Act and the Sex Discrimination Act include exceptions for a list of 'genuine occupational qualifications',[51] but the list in each case differs. The RRA contains an exception for partnerships of fewer than six, whereas the SDA applies to all partnerships.[52] The RRA provisions in relation to sport[53] and charities are different from those in the SDA.

It is in the area of race relations that the gaps in coverage of the legislation have recently proved to be particularly problematic. In particular, it was held that the RRA did not apply to immigration control[54] nor to police when pursuing and arresting or charging alleged criminals.[55] In addition, chief officers of police were insulated from vicarious liability for the discriminatory acts of their officers on the technical ground that police officers are office holders, not employees. Yet these are areas in which the individual is most vulnerable to racial discrimination, as was brutally demonstrated by the reaction of the police and other authorities to the racist murder of a young black man, Stephen Lawrence. The MacPherson Inquiry, established to examine the response to the murder, found unequivocally that institutional racism was rife in the Metropolitan Police Service, in other police services and in other institutions countrywide.[56] Yet, under existing race discrimination legislation, it was entirely lawful. Also problematic was the exemption for acts done for the purposes of safeguarding national security if so certified by a Minister.[57]

The exposure by the MacPherson Inquiry of such extensive gaps in the coverage of race discrimination legislation has prompted the enactment of new and significant amendments to the Race Relations Act. First, the new provisions will make it unlawful for a public authority to

---

[49] Upheld by the ECJ in Case C-273/97 *Sirdar Army Board* [1999] ECR I-7403.
[50] Disability Discrimination Act 1995, s. 7.
[51] Race Relations Act 1976, s. 5; Sex Discrimination Act 1975, s. 7.
[52] Race Relations Act 1976, s. 10; cf. Sex Discrimination Act 1975, s. 11.
[53] Race Relations Act 1976, s. 39.
[54] *R v. Entry Clearance officer (Bombay), ex p Amin* [1983] 2 AC 818 (HL).
[55] *Farah v. Commissioner for Police for the Metropolis* [1998] QB 65 (CA).
[56] Home Office 'Report of the MacPherson Inquiry' Cmd. 4262 February 24, 1999, 6.39.
[57] Sex Discrimination Act 1975, ss. 51–52.

discriminate against or victimize a person on racial grounds in carrying out any of its functions. Crucially, this is not confined to employment, education, and services, but applies to all functions of specified public authorities. Law enforcement, whether by the police, local authorities, or tax inspectors, will for the first time be subject to anti-discrimination laws, as will the core functions of the prison and probation service, the implementation of the government's economic and social policies, certain public appointments, and the activities of immigration and nationality staff when they exceed what is expressly authorized by statute or Ministers. Second, chief officers of police are for the first time made vicariously liable for acts of discrimination. Third, more safeguards are provided against the power of a minister to issue a conclusive certificate that an act of racial discrimination is not unlawful if it is done for the purposes of safeguarding national security. This was necessary because the European Court of Human Rights had recently found that the power to issue such conclusive certificates is incompatible with the right to a fair trial under Article 6 of the European Convention on Human Rights. It will therefore no longer constitute a complete defence to a claim of race discrimination to show that an act was done for the purposes of national security. Finally, and perhaps most importantly, a positive statutory duty to promote race equality and provide for its enforcement will be imposed on public authorities. This last provision is discussed in more detail in Chapter Six.

## (II) THE HUMAN RIGHTS ACT 1998, INCORPORATING THE ECHR

We have seen that the grounds for discrimination under Article 14 of the ECHR are wider than those under domestic legislation. Nor is Article 14 limited to employment, education, and services. Equality in the enjoyment of rights such as privacy and family life, freedom of expression, and the right to a fair trial will therefore be guaranteed for the first time. But Article 14 still falls short of a comprehensive equality guarantee. As will be recalled, this Article states only that 'the enjoyment of the rights and freedoms set forth in this Convention shall be secured without discrimination . . . '. This means that it is a derivative equality provision: only the rights and freedoms set forth in the Convention must be secured without discrimination. The result is that no claims can be made of unequal treatment except in conjunction with one of the specified rights. This limitation is somewhat softened by the fact that it has been held not to be necessary to show an actual breach of one of the substantive rights. For example, a right may justifiably be restricted under one of the specified headings, but this would amount to a breach of Article 14 if the restriction is applied in a discriminatory manner.[58] Nevertheless, there is still no right to equality outside of these fields.

The limitations of this dependent nature of Article 14 have finally been acknowledged and a more general equality guarantee, in the form of Protocol 12, was opened for signature on November 4, 2000. Article 1(1) provides that 'the enjoyment of any right set forth by law shall be secured without discrimination' on any of the specified grounds, while Article 1(2) states that 'no-one shall be discriminated against by any public authority' on one of the specified grounds. Thus there can be no discrimination, not just in the enjoyment of Convention rights, but also in the enjoyment of any right specifically granted to an individual under national law. The equality right arises even if the right has not been specifically granted, but inferred from a duty imposed upon a public authority. For example, the statutory duty to provide education for school-age children, or to house the unintentionally homeless, while not necessarily creating rights in individuals, would attract the duty not to discriminate. The duty also arises in the exercise by a public authority of discretionary powers, for example the granting of certain subsidies, as well as in respect of any other act or omission of a public authority. This would cover, for example, the behaviour of law enforcement officers when controlling a riot.[59] It is noteworthy that this extension of the equality duty closely resembles the extended coverage of the Race Relations Act, which, as has been seen above, will, once amended, place a duty not to discriminate on public authorities in all their functions. However, the RRA duty only extends to discrimination on grounds of race, ethnic or national origins, nationality, or colour. Protocol 12, by contrast, imposes the obligation in respect of the whole list of prohibited grounds, including sex, language, religion, political or other opinion, national or social origin, etc.

As things stand, however, it is Article 14 rather than Protocol 12 which has been incorporated by the Human Rights Act. Its location in the HRA sets Article 14 apart from existing anti-discrimination legislation in that the primary target of the human rights legislation is the State. According to the Human Rights Act 1998, it is only public authorities whose actions must be compatible with the Convention rights.[60] To take account of the

---

[58] *Belgian Linguistic Case* Series A No. 6, (1968) 1 EHRR 252.

[59] See para. 22 of the explanatory report appended to Draft Protocol No. 12 as transmitted by the Steering Committee for Human Rights CCDH 99(10), June 25, 1999.

[60] Human Rights Act 1998, s. 6.

shifting boundary between public and private in the modern State, 'public authority' is defined widely to include 'private persons or bodies when they are exercising functions of a public nature'.[61] There is no direct application to private persons in exercising private functions. However, there are two ways in which the HRA affects private actions indirectly. First, it could be argued that the government has a duty to organize its institutional apparatus so that it is capable of ensuring free and full enjoyment of human rights.[62] The second results from the fact that the courts are required to act in a way that is compatible with human rights. This means that the court must ensure that the common law is developed and interpreted in a manner which protects human rights, even when it regulates private persons only.

In some respects, this focus on State action is a source of strength. As we have seen, prior to the Race Relations (Amendment) Act 2000, public bodies were only regulated by anti-discrimination legislation in their role as employers or providers of education and services.[63] By contrast, under the Human Rights Act, the courts have powers to declare primary legislation incompatible with Convention rights. Even more powerfully, the courts may strike down secondary legislation, the use of discretionary powers, and other types of executive action. This creates a standard much higher than that under existing law, which allows for no challenge of primary legislation, and only vague and deferential grounds for review of secondary legislation or uses of discretion. Its importance for discrimination law is clearly illustrated by the 'gay rights in the military' cases, in which three gay men and a lesbian woman challenged the policy of excluding and dismissing anyone who was gay or lesbian from the military. They had no claim under domestic discrimination law because of the absence of a discrete ground of sexual orientation; and the claim that sexual orientation discrimination fell within the prohibition for sex discrimination failed as a result of the ECJ's decision in *Grant*, discussed above. As the HRA had not yet come into effect, their only claim in the domestic courts was that the public authorities had acted in a way which was so unreasonable that no reasonable authority could have done so, the so-called *Wednesbury* standard of review. The extremely deferential nature of this standard and its contrast with the standards to be applied

---

[61] *ibid.*, s. 6(3)(c).

[62] See C. N. Chinkin, 'Women's Rights as Human Rights under International Law' in C. Gearty and A. Tomkins (eds.), *Understanding Human Rights* (Mansell, 1996), p. 564.

[63] A duty to promote racial equality has been introduced by the Race Relations (Amendment) Act 2000. See further Chapter Six.

under Convention rights were highlighted in all the proceedings. Thus Simon Brown LJ in the Divisional Court stated that 'only if [the minister's] purported justification outrageously defies logic or accepted moral standards can the court, in exercising its secondary judgment, properly strike it down'.[64] The position, in his view, would be markedly different were the Convention part of our law. 'If the Convention were part of our law, and we were accordingly entitled to ask whether the restriction on human rights involved can be shown proportionate to its benefits, then clearly the primary judgment . . . would be for us: the constitutional balance would shift'.[65] Indeed, when the case reached the European Court of Human Rights,[66] the government's purported justifications were found to fall short of the required standard of necessity and the policy was therefore held to be in breach of the Convention. It is this more piercing standard which domestic courts will need to apply to public authorities' actions now that the HRA is in force.

It will be recalled that one of the most important innovations of the amended Race Relations Act is the imposition of positive duties on public authorities to promote equality. Does the new Protocol 12 create positive duties? In particular, does it oblige the Parties to take measures to prevent discrimination, even where it occurs between private persons? The explanatory report attached to the Protocol insists that although Article 1 requires a State to 'secure the enjoyment of a right without discrimination, the Article does not intend to impose a general positive obligation to take measures to prevent or remedy all instances of discrimination in relations between private persons'.[67] Nevertheless, and somewhat paradoxically, the report declares that the duty to 'secure' might entail positive obligations, for example if there is a clear lacuna in domestic law protection from discrimination. In particular, a failure to provide protection from discrimination in relations between private persons might, it is suggested, be sufficiently serious and clear-cut to bring it within the scope of Article 1. However, such a breach is only likely to fall within this exception where relations between private persons are in the public sphere and normally regulated by law. The examples given in the memorandum include arbitrary denial of access to restaurants and employment contracts. This last is particularly notable given the preference of the

---

[64] *R v. Ministry of Defence, ex p Smith* [1995] 4 All ER 427 at 447.
[65] *ibid.*, at 448.
[66] *Smith and Grady v. United Kingdom* (2000) 29 EHRR 493.
[67] Explanatory memorandum para. 25.

domestic courts to treat employment matters as questions of private contract.[68]

## (III) EU LAW

The third source of discrimination law, EU law, is similarly restricted in its application, but again in different ways and for different reasons. EU anti-discrimination law has been shaped by the basic imperatives behind the formation of the European Community, namely the creation of a common market in Europe. From the inception of the Community, therefore, equality as a principle was only relevant in so far as it was needed in the creation of a European-wide labour market.[69] There was only one area within traditional discrimination law that was considered relevant to the creation of a common market: pay discrimination between men and women. Member States which permitted lower wages for women than men doing the same work would, it was argued, enjoyed a competitive advantage over those with equal pay laws.[70] Article 119 (now known as Article 141) of the Treaty of Rome therefore created a right to equal pay for equal work for men and women, a right which was to grow into a powerful equality tool. In addition, free movement of labour required a legal prohibition of discrimination by one Member State against nationals of other Member States. But the elimination of race discrimination was simply not considered necessary to the project of creating a common market in labour, and indeed raised awkward questions in relation to discrimination against non-EU nationals. As a result, the right not to be discriminated against on grounds of race was conspicuously absent, apart from several soft law initiatives.[71]

During the 1970s, the expansion of Community competence into multifarious areas affecting the lives of individuals made it essential to pay greater attention to social rights. A social tint was therefore added to the market colouring of the equality principle in the form of the introduction of the right to equal pay for work of equal value[72] and the right to equal treatment for men and women in employment related areas apart

---

[68] *R v. East Berkshire Health Authority, ex p Walsh* [1985] QB 152 (CA).

[69] See, e.g. W. Streeck, 'From Market Making to State Building' in S. Leibfried and P. Pierson (eds.), *European Social Policy: Between Fragmentation and Integration* (Brookings Institution, 1995), p. 397.

[70] ILO, 'Social Aspects of European Economic Co-operation' (1956) 74 *International Labour Review* 107.

[71] See, e.g. Joint Declaration on Fundamental Rights, April 5, 1977 (OJ C 103/1); Action Plan on the Fight against Racism COM (1998) 183 final of March 25, 1998.

[72] Council Directive (EEC) 75/117 Equal Pay Directive [1975] OJ L45/19.

from pay.[73] It was not, however, until the late 1990s that the limited prohibitions on sex discrimination and discrimination against nationals of a Member State were transformed into a broadly based non-discrimination principle. Articles 2 and 3 of the Treaty of Amsterdam elevated equality between men and women to the status of one of the central tasks of the Community. Equally importantly, Article 13 of the Treaty enabled the Council to take appropriate action to combat discrimination based on sex, racial or ethnic origin, religion or belief, disability, age, or sexual orientation. As we have seen, this power was swiftly used to pass two directives: one on race discrimination; the other on age, disability, sexual orientation, and religion.[74] The Race Discrimination Directive is of particular importance because its reach is wider than the employment and social security field, to which all the other discrimination directives are confined. As well as conditions for access to employment and terms and conditions of employment, the directive also refers to social protection, including social security and health care; social advantages; education, and access to and supply of goods and services which are available to the public, including housing.[75] Notably, the preamble continues to stress market-based goals. Discrimination based on racial or ethnic origin, it is declared, may undermine the achievement of the objectives of the EC Treaty, in particular, the attainment of a high level of employment and of social protection. At the same time, the preamble stresses equity and justice as goals. 'To ensure the development of democratic and tolerant societies which allow the participation of all persons irrespective of racial or ethnic origin, . . . [it is necessary to] go beyond access to employed and self-employed activities and cover areas such as education, social protection, social advantages and access to and supply of goods and services'.

## III CONCLUSION

This chapter has considered the scope of discrimination legislation. The grounds for discrimination can be seen to be largely politically determined. Courts in other jurisdictions have attempted to develop

---

[73] Council Directive (EEC) 76/207 Equal Treatment Directive [1976] OJ L39/40.

[74] Council Directive 2000/43/EC of June 29, 2000 [2000] OJ L180/22 (implementing the principle of equal treatment between persons irrespective of racial or ethnic origin); Council Directive 2000/78/EC of November 27, 2000 [2000] OJ L303/16 (establishing a general framework for equal treatment in employment and occupation). General reference: http:// europa.eu.int/comm/employment_social/fundamri/eu_racism/publications.htm.

[75] Directive 2000/43, Art. 3(1).

generalizable principles to decide when discrimination law ought to be extended to an unenumerated group, and many of these make sense in relation to the aims of discrimination law more generally. A history of disadvantage, political powerlessness, and the irrelevance of certain personal characteristics are all relevant factors, and domestic courts will need to draw on them in the application of the new discrimination provisions under the Human Rights Act. However, their precise applicability to a particular situation nevertheless requires a judicial value judgement.

The reach of discrimination law has been shown to be similarly jagged, its coverage depending on whether it arises from domestic law, the ECHR or EU law. Although some important reforms are in hand, there remains a pressing need for a harmonized statute. An influential new report reviewing UK anti discrimination legislation (the 'Hepple Report') has argued forcefully that the complex structure of existing discrimination law makes it impossible to ensure effective enforcement. A single Equality Act would both remove inconsistencies and encourage the active promotion of equality, rather than dependence on external enforcement of the existing tangle of rules. Such a framework, according to the Report, should be based on clear, consistent, and easily intelligible standards, and be effective, efficient, and equitable, aimed at encouraging individual responsibility and self-generating efforts to promote equality.[76] Although there have been conflicting statements from different sources, the government has committed itself to harmonizing at least the provisions of the SDA, RRA and DDA.[77] As this chapter has demonstrated, there is clearly a need to go further and create a single, clear, and consistent framework.

[76] B. Hepple, M. Coussey, and T. Choudhury, *Equality: A New Framework* Report of the Independent Review of the Enforcement of UK Anti-Discrimination Legislation (Hart, 2000), paras 2.8–2.16.
[77] Cabinet Office, Equality Statement (November 30, 1999).

# 4

# Legal Concepts: Direct, Indirect Discrimination, and Beyond

We have seen that anti-discrimination legislation has grown rapidly, in both scope and complexity. Yet true equality remains elusive. Women, ethnic minorities, and people with disabilities are still disproportionately disadvantaged. Gay men, lesbian women, and bisexuals are still subject to specific legal impediments, and those discriminated against on grounds of religion or political opinion still have only partial protection against discriminatory treatment. This prompts a closer examination of the different concepts of equality used in anti-discrimination law. Is the limited effect explained by flaws in the ways in which the equality principle is transposed into legal forms? Or are we expecting equality to achieve something of which it is incapable? It is to these difficult questions which we now turn.

Legal definitions of equality have been developed as increasingly sophisticated responses to the challenges of discrimination. The most basic principle is that of equality before the law, which requires the removal of specific legal impediments. While significant progress has been made for some groups, there remain groups for whom even juridical equality remains elusive. At the same time, it has quickly become evident that equality before the law is insufficient on its own. For women, equal voting and property rights did not eliminate pay structures in which women were explicitly paid less than men doing the same work; women were still dismissed from paid employment on marriage or pregnancy; and women remained segregated into low paid, low status jobs. Similarly, the basic right to citizenship for ethnic minorities did not prevent racism, nor exclusion on grounds of colour from jobs or housing, nor institutionalized hostility from police forces and other service providers.

To tackle these phenomena, a more developed notion of equality was needed. Instead of simply removing juridical impediments, it was necessary to prohibit prejudiced behaviour and discrimination by public and private actors. It was well into the 1960s before this second and crucial step was taken. The Race Relations Acts of 1965 and 1968 constituted a belated recognition by the legislature of the reality of a multi-ethnic Britain, but their significance was largely symbolic. More important were the statutes of the 1970s: the Equal Pay Act 1970, the Sex Discrimination Act 1975 and the Race Relations Act 1976, augmented, in the sex discrimination field, by EU law. A more recent addition has been the Disability Discrimination Act 1995. Since 2000, there has been a further flurry of activity. The equality guarantee in Article 14 of the European Convention on Human Rights became part of the domestic law from October 2000, and a far reaching amendment to the Race Relations Act 1976 was adopted.[1] In addition, two new EU directives adopted during 2000 require further legislation to be introduced. Northern Ireland has seen the development of even more sophisticated statutes.[2]

However, there is no uniform approach to the definition of discrimination. Instead, we are faced with a bewildering array of differing statutory formulae. At least five basic legal approaches can be discerned: direct discrimination; indirect discrimination; equality as proportionality; equality as dignity; and a positive duty to promote equality. The aim of this chapter is to develop an understanding of these foundational concepts, focusing particularly on direct and indirect discrimination. Drawing on the analysis developed in Chapter One, four main themes will be addressed. First, is the concept based on consistency or substantive equality? Second, is it a comparative concept, requiring the identification of a similarly situated comparator? Third, how does it deal with competing priorities, such as macro or micro economic concerns? Finally, what are its aims? Does it aim at equality as an end in itself, or does it aspire to a deeper aim, such as the amelioration of existing disadvantage, or the promotion of dignity?

## I TREAT LIKES ALIKE: EQUAL PAY AND DIRECT DISCRIMINATION

The bedrock principle that likes should be treated alike is found in all the major statutes. Its most basic formulation is in the Equal Pay Act 1970 which gives a woman a right to equal pay with a man doing like work or work of equal value (and vice versa). A more sophisticated definition is

[1] Race Relations (Amendment) Act 2000.
[2] Fair Employment and Treatment (Northern Ireland) Order 1998 (FETO) SI 1998/ 3162 (NI 21); Northern Ireland Act 1998, s.75.

found in the Sex Discrimination Act and Race Relations Act. Thus, SDA 1975 defines direct discrimination as follows:

A person discriminates against a woman if . . . on the ground of her sex he treats her less favourably than he treats or would treat a man.[3]

Similar definitions are found in the RRA and the DDA.

The concept of direct discrimination at EC level was first developed judicially and only defined in legislation recently. Article 141 of the EC Treaty states simply that Member States must ensure that 'the principle of equal pay for male and female workers for equal work or work of equal value is applied'. The various directives on sex equality apart from pay adopt a similarly general approach, referring to a principle of equal treatment, defined to mean that 'there shall be no discrimination what-soever on grounds of sex either directly or indirectly'.[4] It was from these sources that the ECJ fashioned a concept of 'less favourable treatment'. This has now been reflected in statutory definitions. The directive on race now specifically defines direct discrimination as occurring when 'one person is treated less favourably than another is, or would be treated in a comparable situation on grounds of racial or ethnic origin'[5] and a similar definition is found in the framework directive.

How then does direct discrimination as a principle answer the four questions dealt with above? Each will be dealt with in turn.

### (I) CONSISTENCY RATHER THAN SUBSTANCE

Direct discrimination, with its emphasis on 'less favourable treatment', is clearly based on the concept of equality as consistency formulated in Chapter One. As such, it is primarily a relative concept. It is not the treatment per se that is at issue, but the fact that one person is treated less favourably than another of the opposite sex or race. As long as there is consistency, the outcome is irrelevant. Equality is achieved if both parties have been equally well treated; but it is also achieved if they have been equally badly treated. There is nothing to suggest that the first is more desirable than the second. For example, it has been stated that if a bisexual employer harasses both men and women, then there is no

---

[3] Sex Discrimination Act 1975, s. 1(1)(a).

[4] Council Directive (EEC) 76/207 Equal Treatment Directive [1976] OJ L39/40, Art. 2(1).

[5] Council Directive 2000/43 on equal treatment between persons irrespective of racial or ethnic origin, Art. 2(1)(a); Council Directive 2000/78/EC of November 27, 2000 [2000] OJ L303/16 establishing a general framework for equal treatment in employment and occupation.

discrimination on grounds of sex because they are both treated equally badly.[6] In a recent case, it was held that an employer who took no action to prevent continuing sexual harassment of a woman was not discriminating against her, because he would have taken no action in respect of a claim by a man of sexual harassment.[7]

A more serious implication of the focus on consistency rather than substance is that equality is fulfilled whether a benefit is removed from the advantaged group or extended to the disadvantaged group. This is clearly illustrated in the fraught area of protective legislation, which provided for 'special' protection for women, by, for example, prohibiting night work or underground work in mines. In recent decades, there has been a general consensus that such legislation breaches the equality principle. However, this led to two quite contradictory responses. The UK government, with few exceptions, simply repealed the protective legislation; thereby withdrawing protection from women without achieving any corresponding benefits to either men or women.[8] By contrast, the European Commission declared specifically that 'equality should not be made the occasion for a disimprovement of working conditions for one sex'.[9] Even more problematic were the results of a series of cases in which men who were pensionable at sixty-five claimed that they were being treated less favourably than women, who were pensionable at sixty. The ECJ held that equality had indeed been breached. But it went on to find that it was not necessary to drop men's pensionable age to achieve equality. The breach could just as well be remedied by raising women's pensionable age to sixty-five, thus removing the extra benefit to women.[10] The result was stark. Equality was achieved, but the position of women was worsened, while men were no better off.

## (II) EQUALITY AS CONFORMITY: THE NEED FOR A COMPARATOR

A further major drawback of equality as consistency, identified in Chapter One, is the need to find a similarly situated individual of the opposite race or sex as a comparator. The definitions of direct

[6] *Barnes v. Castle* (1997) 561 F 2d 983 (US Ct of Apps (DC Cir)) at 990, n.55.

[7] *Balgobin v. Tower Hamlets* [1987] IRLR 397 (EAT).

[8] S. Fredman, *Women and the Law* (Clarendon Press, 1997), p.306, and see S. Kenney, *For Whose Protection?* (University of Michigan Press, 1992).

[9] Commission Communication, *Protective Legislation for Women in the Member States of the EC*, COM (87) 105 final.

[10] See Fredman, above n.10, p.350; see, e.g. *Smith v. Advel* Case C-408/92 [1994] IRLR 602 (ECJ).

discrimination above show that a comparison is at the core of the legal formula. The right to equal pay depends on demonstrating that a woman's pay is less than that of a man doing equal work. Direct discrimination as defined in the Sex Discrimination Act requires proof that a woman has been treated less favourably than a man would have been; and the race discrimination provisions require proof that one person has been treated less favourably on racial grounds that another person would have been. The need for a comparator has been one of the most problematic and limiting aspects of direct discrimination. So much so that, as will be seen below, there have been important attempts to reformulate the notion so as to free it of the shackles of the comparator.

The role of the comparator is at its most concrete in the Equal Pay Act. Not only must the complainant find a man doing the same work or work of equal value as she is, her comparator must also be employed by the same employer; and be working in the same establishment or in an establishment with common terms and conditions. Yet, as we have seen, one of the chief causes of low pay among women is the fact that so many women work in segregated workplaces, either doing 'women's work' or in the lower grades of mixed professions. A woman working in a segregated workplace or a segregated grade within a mixed workplace is unlikely to find a male comparator doing like work or work of equal value. Even if there are a handful of men doing 'women's work', they are likely to be equally badly paid. Men may be willing to work at a 'woman's' rate because they are ill, or, like students, only casually attached to the workforce or are using a job as a route to promotion.[11]

Nor can the comparison be extended to other establishments of the same employer, unless it can be shown that the complainant and her comparator are employed at establishments with 'common terms and conditions'. Yet this limited extension of the scope of comparison has only raised further obstacles in the path of a complainant wishing to establish equal pay. This was clearly demonstrated in a recent attempt to challenge the deeply gendered structure of employment in the coal-mining industry which had, until 1975, maintained separate pay scales for men and women, and which continues to operate an intense system of job segregation between low paid women workers and higher paid men. Women canteen workers and cleaners found themselves at different establishments from the better paid male clerical workers and surface

---

[11] J. Rubery, *The Economics of Equal Value* Research Discussion Series, No. 3 (Equal Opportunities Commission, 1992), p.50.

mineworkers who, they claimed were doing work of equal value. It took the applicants eleven years and a trip to the House of Lords to do no more than establish that they were entitled to draw the comparison, on the basis that the men and women worked at establishments with common terms and conditions.[12] Many of the women are retired and some will have even died before their claim is adjudicated on the merits.

The limits resulting from the need to find a comparator employed by the same employer are particularly starkly demonstrated when work is out-sourced or contracted out. In the public sector during the 1980s and the 1990s in Britain, authorities were under statutory obligations to put services previously provided by directly employed workers out to tender, and award the contract to the lowest bidder. The services which were put out to tender in this way were primarily in the area of cleaning and catering, and therefore were predominantly female. Because of the tradition of collective bargaining in the public services, women employed by local authorities were likely to be better paid than those employed by private contractors: indeed, it was their ability to offer lower pay that gave private contractors the advantage in the tendering process. Yet the Equal Pay Act has no mechanism for comparing the pay of cleaners working for a private contractor with those working for the authority.

The comparison in Article 141 is somewhat wider. The ECJ in the early case of *Defrenne* firmly set its face against allowing inter-industry comparisons, but it has more recently held that a woman could compare her pay with a man doing the same work who was not employed by the same employer but worked in the same service.[13] The domestic courts have refused to extend the notion of 'service' to allow contracted out workers to compare their pay with employees of their former employers. But a test case[14] has now been referred to the ECJ to determine the question of whether contracted out workers can compare themselves with previous employees.

The need for a comparator is less harsh in the Sex Discrimination, Race Relations and Disability Discrimination Acts than that in the equal pay legislation. These provisions continue to rely on the basic principle that likes should be treated alike. But while the Equal Pay Act requires the woman to compare herself with a man actually employed at her establishment, the direct discrimination provisions permit a

---

[12] *British Coal Corporation v. Smith* [1996] All ER 97 (HL).
[13] *Scullard v. Knowles* [1996] IRLR 344 (EAT).
[14] *Lawrence v. Regent Office Care Ltd* [2000] IRLR 608 (CA).

'hypothetical' comparison, based not on how a man is treated, but how he would be. The same is true for the RRA. Nevertheless, this has presented its own difficulties. At least three problems have been evident in the case-law. First, as was seen in Chapter One, the need for a norm of comparison, be it male, white or able-bodied, has created powerful conformist pressures. Most problematic, in the context of race, has been the assimilationist tendency. This is demonstrated well in the case of *Ahmad v. ILEA*,[15] in which a devout Muslim resigned his teaching post after his employer, a Local Education Authority, refused to allow him time off from his teaching duties to attend a nearby mosque for Friday prayers. He claimed that this was a breach of his rights under the European Convention on Human Rights. The Commission declared the application inadmissible on the basis of a particularly narrow conception of equality. Relying on the proposition that since all minorities had to conform to the norms of the majority religion, the Commission found that the applicant had not proved 'less favourable treatment'. Instead of requiring some accommodation of difference, it deemed it sufficient to observe that in 'in most countries, only the religious holidays of the majority of the population are celebrated as public holidays'.[16]

Second, the choice of comparator itself requires a complex value judgement as to which of the myriad differences between any two individuals are relevant and which are irrelevant. The choice of relevant characteristics is often itself determinative of the outcome. This has been particularly evident in the context of discrimination on grounds of homosexuality. Since there was, until recently, no express right not to be discriminated against on grounds of sexual orientation, the relevant comparator must be constructed so that only his or her sex differs from that of the complainant. It has been held that a male homosexual can only complain of discrimination under the Sex Discrimination Act if he can show that he has been treated less favourably than a lesbian woman but not a heterosexual man.[17] This means, of course, that homophobic treatment directed at both lesbian women and homosexual men does not count as sex discrimination. For example, in the *Grant* case, the ECJ stated: 'Travel concessions are refused to a male worker if he is living with a person of the same sex, just as they are to a female worker if she is living with a person of the same sex. Since the condition . . . applies in the same way to female and male workers, it cannot be regarded as

[15] *Ahmad v. ILEA*, Application 8160/78 [1981] 4 EHRR 127 (European Commission).
[16] *ibid.*, at para. 28.
[17] *Smith v. Gardner Merchant* [1998] 3 All ER 852 (CA).

constituting discrimination directly based on sex'.[18] Similarly, it has been held that a woman teacher who was forced out of her employment by homophobic taunts directed specifically at her lesbianism could not succeed in a claim unless she was treated less favourably than a man subject to taunts about his homosexuality.[19] Equally problematic, the comparator can be constructed in different ways, leading to entirely different outcomes. Thus in the *Grant*[20] case, the applicant argued that the comparison was not between a woman living with another woman and a man living with another man, but between a woman with a female partner, and a man with a female partner. If this comparison was chosen, the gay woman would certainly have been successful in her claim.

Third, there are important situations in which there is simply no appropriate comparator. The problem is at its most glaring in relation to pregnancy discrimination.[21] Indeed, this difficulty has been sufficiently acute to prompt a reformulation of the equality principle liberating it from the need for a comparator. In the early pregnancy cases, it was held that since there was no appropriate male comparator to a pregnant woman, pregnancy was simply excluded from the protection of the sex discrimination legislation. 'In order to see if she has been treated less favourably than a man ... you must compare like with like and you cannot. When she is pregnant a woman is no longer just a woman. She is a woman ... with child and there is no masculine equivalent'.[22] The result was to dismiss claims of sex discrimination by women who were dismissed or subjected to other detriment on grounds of their pregnancy.[23] Later cases took a more sophisticated view of the male comparator. Courts were now prepared to consider an ill man as the appropriate comparator, since the effects of illness on the capacity to work could be similar. 'To postulate a pregnant man is an absurdity, but I see no difficulty in comparing a pregnant woman with a man who has a medical condition which will require him to be absent for the same period of time and at the same time as does the pregnant woman'.[24] A similar

---

[18] *ibid.*

[19] *Pearce v. Governing Body of Mayfield Secondary School* [2000] IRLR 548 (EAT).

[20] Case C-249/96 *Grant v. South-West Trains Ltd* [1998] ECR I-621.

[21] For a more detailed discussion, see Fredman, above n.10, pp. 184–192; S. Fredman, 'A Difference with Distinction: Pregnancy and Parenthood Reassessed' (1994) 110 LQR 106.

[22] *Turley v. Allders Stores Ltd* [1980] ICR 66 (EAT) at 70D (*per* Bristow J).

[23] A similar route was followed in the US: see *Geduldig v. Aiello* (1974) 417 US 484, 94 S Ct 2485 and *General Electric Co v Gilbert* (1976) 429 US 125, 97 S Ct 401.

[24] *Webb v. EMO* [1992] 2 All ER 43 (CA) at 52g (*per* Glidewell LJ). The case later went to the House of Lords and the ECJ.

progression from a refusal to find an appropriate male comparator to a focus on the job-related effects of a condition is evident in the US.[25] This development at least gave pregnant women the opportunity to claim protection from sex discrimination laws. But it did so at a cost. Pregnancy is not an illness and should not be stigmatized as 'unhealthy'. In addition, it assumes that the only dimension of pregnancy with which discrimination law should be concerned is its effect on an employee's ability to work. It thereby ignores the positive medical and social reasons for leave, such as the need to breast-feed and develop a relationship with the child.

It was the clear inappropriateness of a comparative approach which finally led courts in different jurisdictions to attempt to formulate a notion of equality which moved beyond the comparative approach. In a series of important cases, the ECJ emphatically scotched the notion that a comparison should be drawn between a pregnant woman and a man who was incapable of working for medical or other reasons. Indeed, there was no need for a comparator of any sort. Instead, the Court has held that discrimination on grounds of pregnancy contravenes the equal treatment principle because only women can be treated badly for this reason.[26] Similarly, the Canadian Supreme Court has held that discrimination on grounds of pregnancy is necessarily discrimination on grounds of sex, because only women have the capacity to become pregnant.[27] The US Supreme Court has achieved a similar result by recasting the way in which the comparison is drawn. Women could only be treated equally if they could participate fully and equally in the workforce. This could only be achieved by ensuring that women, like men, could have families without losing their jobs. The answer to the claim that maternity rights amounted to preferential treatment for women lay in extending the same rights to men, not in removing them from women. In other words, men should have parental leave just like women.[28] Thus the seeds of a female rather than a male norm are sown.

The move away from the comparator has not, however, been complete, even in the pregnancy field. Indeed, the ill male comparator has proved remarkably tenacious. Thus the ECJ has held that where pregnancy-related illness continues after the expiry of maternity leave, however short, a woman will only be able to prove a breach of the equality

---

[25] See Pregnancy Discrimination Act 1978.
[26] Case C-177/88 *Dekker* [1990] ECR I-394; Case C-32/93 *Webb* [1994] ECR I-3567.
[27] *Brookes v. Canada Safeway Ltd* (1989) 1 SCR 1219.
[28] *California Federal Savings and Loan Association v. Guerra* (1987) 479 US 272, 107 S Ct 683.

principle if she can show that she was treated less favourably than an ill man would have been treated.[29] The ill male comparator even haunts the operation of statutory rights to maternity leave and pay. The Pregnant Workers Directive was intended to give women specific rights to protection in the event of pregnancy, thus moving away from the need for a comparator at all. Nevertheless, the directive provides that pay during maternity leave is adequate if it is equivalent to sickness pay.[30] This in turn, has led to the use of the equality principle, not to enhance pregnant workers' rights, but to defeat claims by women for full pay while on maternity leave. Instead, such a claim is construed as a demand for preferential treatment. Thus in *Gillespie*[31] a claim by women that they should receive full pay while on maternity leave was dismissed on the grounds that benefits received by ill employees were far less. Yet there are many countries in Europe which have recognized that maternity is not comparable to illness and have therefore been prepared to see maternity pay as a full substitute for earnings.[32]

In disability discrimination cases, similar difficulties in finding an appropriate comparator have been experienced, leading to a move away from a comparative approach. Under the Disability Discrimination Act 1995, an employer discriminates against a disabled person if 'for a reason which relates to the disabled person's disability, he treats him less favourably than he treats or would treat others to whom that reason does not or would not apply . . . '.[33] Who then is the appropriate comparator, an able-bodied person at work, or a person unable to do the work for a different reason, such as illness? To take a recent example, an employee was dismissed after a long period of absence caused by his disability. Should he compare his position with another employee who had also been absent for a long period because of illness rather than disability? On this approach, the comparator is similarly situated, but better treated; the implication being that the employer is simply hostile to disabled people. Thus the only cases which would succeed under the DDA would be those where the dismissal was due to prejudice on the part of the employer against

---

[29] C-179/88 *Hertz* [1990] ECR I-3979. Illness during pregnancy or maternity leave still attracts protection without the need for a comparator; Case C-394/96 *Brown v. Rentokill* [1998] ECR I-4185, [1998] IRLR 445.

[30] Council Directive (EEC) 92/85 on the protection of the safety and health at work of pregnant and breastfeeding workers [1992] OJ L348/1, Art. 11(3).

[31] Case C-342/93 *Gillespie* [1996] ECR I-475.

[32] Women on maternity leave are paid in full in Austria, Belgium (for the first four weeks), Finland, Greece, Luxembourg, the Netherlands, Norway, Portugal, and Spain.

[33] And the treatment cannot be justified: Disability Discrimination Act 1995, s.5(1)(a).

disabled people. Alternatively, should he or she compare his or her position with the treatment of an able-bodied person who is able to do the work? 'Less favourable treatment' is established simply by showing that the disabled person had been subjected to a detriment because of her disability. The burden then passes quickly to the employer to establish justification. It was this, second sense, which was adopted by the Court of Appeal in the seminal case of *Clark v. Novacold*.[34] Mummery LJ noted the 'futile attempts of the . . . courts to find and identify the characteristics of a hypothetical non-pregnant male comparator for a pregnant woman in sex discrimination cases'.[35] He therefore deliberately distanced himself from the difficulties experienced under the race and sex discrimination legislation in identifying the characteristics of a hypothetical comparator. Instead, he interpreted the provisions according to the aim of the legislation, drawing specifically on statements in Parliament during the passage of the bill and examples given in the relevant code of practice. This indicated that the appropriate comparison was with an able-bodied person at work. This is certainly a welcome development and provides appropriate protection for disabled people. However, as in the case of pregnancy, it does so by minimizing the role of the comparator to almost vanishing point.

### (III) COMPETING PRIORITIES: JUSTIFYING DISCRIMINATION AND MARKET CONSTRAINTS

The third question to be addressed in relation to direct discrimination concerns its relationship to other social priorities, such as economic or social policy factors. If a finding of direct discrimination has been made, can it nevertheless be justified on the basis that the difference in treatment serves other ends, such as the business interests of the employer or the social policies of the State? Can it be argued that it is too difficult or costly to correct? The value placed by society on equality is reflected both in the decision as to whether it is permissible to raise such a defence, and in the weight given to the defence relative to the discriminatory act.

The principle of direct discrimination in the SDA and RRA stands out in that it is not subject to justification of any sort. Nor is there a defence to a claim of direct discrimination in EC law, although there has been much pressure to permit one. It is particularly significant that the definition of direct discrimination in the newly adopted race discrimination directive does not include a justification defence. In this respect, the right

---

[34] [1999] 2 All ER 977 (CA).      [35] *ibid.*, para. 63.

to equality, in its slenderest form of equality as consistency, is given greater legal weight than any competing claims.

However, other manifestations of the principle that likes should be treated alike are not absolute in this respect. The equal pay legislation, both domestic and EU, includes a clear mandate for employers to justify differential pay, provided the justification is not itself based on sex. The question then arises as to whether the employer can assert his or her own business interests as a legitimate factor outweighing the right to equal pay for work of equal value; and, if so, how much weight should be given to each of these competing values. The courts in the equal pay context have permitted business needs to be used by employers to justify unequal pay for equal work.[36] This in itself reflects the courts' and legislature's unwillingness to see equality as a trump over other rights. It has been mitigated somewhat by establishing two sorts of control. First, the justification must be objective in that the employer cannot simply assert that he or she is of the opinion that the difference in pay serves his or her business interests. Second, and primarily under the influence of the ECJ, a strict test of proportionality has been developed, according to which the employer must show that the means chosen serve a real business need, that they are appropriate to achieve that objective and are necessary to that end.[37] This test has been developed in similar terms for indirect discrimination, and is dealt with in more detail below. For the present, it suffices to note that the equality value is clearly seen as open to subordination by the competing self interest of the employer, subject to a high level of proof that inequality is indeed necessary to serve those ends.

Of even greater concern has been the role of justification under the disability discrimination legislation. Unlike the direct discrimination provisions in the SDA and RRA, the DDA specifically allows an employer to justify treating disabled people less favourably.[38] In cases in which the employer does not have a duty to make adjustments, the standard of justification has been held to be very low. As long as the reason relates to the individual circumstances in question and is not just trivial or minor, direct discrimination against a disabled person can be justified.[39] A

---

[36] Case 96/80 *Jenkins v. Kingsgate* [1981] ECR 911.

[37] Case 170/84 *Bilka-Kaufhaus v von Hartz* [1986] ECR 1607.

[38] Disability Discrimination Act 1995, ss.5 and 6. Where the employer has a duty to make reasonable adjustments, because his or her arrangements or premises place the disabled person at a substantial disadvantage, then a further barrier is required: see below. See also framework directive, above n.5.

[39] *Clark v. Novacold*, above n.34; *Heinz v. Kenrick* [2000] IRLR 144 (EAT).

wider survey of what is reasonable is not required; nor is there any need
for the reason to be objective. Although the EAT has regretted the ease
with which this barrier can be surmounted, it has held to be an inevitable
result of the wording of the statute. As Lindsay P put it, 'This is a
conclusion which we do not reach with enthusiasm, . . . but the remedy
for the lowness of the threshold, if any is required, lies in the hands of the
legislature and not the courts'.[40] This does not mean that a justification
will always exist. It was held in a recent case that an employer's dismissal
of an employee suffering from chronic fatigue syndrome was not justified
because the employer had not considered the possibility of offering a
part-time alternative.[41] Nevertheless, there seems little reason for the
marked disparity between the standard of justification in this legislation
and that in the Equal Pay Act and EU law. It has been argued that, unlike
sex or race, disability might be a good reason for treating a person differently,[42] not because he or she is less worthy of respect, but because he or
she cannot perform the essential functions of the job. However, this is
better reflected by removing the open-ended opportunity to justify less
favourable treatment; and instead providing a statutory list of rational
grounds upon which less favourable treatment might be defended. Such a
list might include cases where such treatment is necessary to prevent
danger to the health and safety of the disabled person or other employees;
where the disabled person is genuinely unable to perform the essentials of
the job, even with reasonable adjustments; or where necessary to prevent
undue hardship, including unreasonable costs, to the employer. As the
Hepple Review concluded, such a framework would create greater cer-
tainty by giving specific guidance to employers;[43] as well as reasserting the
basic equality value, namely that disabled people are worthy of equal
concern and respect in all circumstances.

## (IV) THE AIMS OF DIRECT DISCRIMINATION: SYMMETRY

Direct discrimination, based as it is on a concept of equality as consistency, treats equality as an end in itself, rather than as a means to a
different end, such as the alleviation of disadvantage or the enhancement
of individual dignity. An important reflection of this underlying aim is

---

[40] *Heinz* at p.146, para. 16.       [41] *ibid.*

[42] B. Doyle, 'Reform of the DDA' Working Paper No. 4 *Independent Review of the
Enforcement of UK Anti-Discrimination Legislation* November 1999, p.4.

[43] B. Hepple, M. Coussey, and T. Choudhury, *Equality: A New Framework* Report of the
Independent Review of the Enforcement of UK Anti-Discrimination Legislation (Hart,
2000), para. 2.45.

the fact that direct discrimination is a symmetrical concept. Discrimination is treated as wrongful whether it is directed against a member of a group which is disadvantaged or one which is relatively privileged. Discrimination against a man is as invidious as discrimination against a woman; discrimination against a white is prohibited to the same measure as discrimination against a black.

This result was clearly established by the House of Lords in the case of *James v. Eastleigh BC*,[44] in which it was held that the test for establishing direct discrimination consisted of applying what was termed the 'but for' test. If it is established that a person would not have been denied a benefit 'but for' his or her sex, then direct discrimination had been established. This test holds true regardless of whether the treatment is aimed at alleviating or entrenching disadvantage. The result can be seen by considering the facts of the case itself. In *James*, a male pensioner claimed he had been subjected to sex discrimination because he was not eligible for pensioner's benefits until sixty-five, his pensionable age. A comparable woman pensioner, he argued, was treated more favourably because she was eligible for the same benefits at sixty, women's pensionable age. Thus at the age of sixty-two, he argued, he was treated less favourably than a woman of sixty-two. The authority defended the policy by arguing that it aimed at alleviating disadvantage. The true reason for the concession was not the person's sex, but the fact that he or she had passed pensionable age, whatever that might be, the object being to give concessions to those who experienced a drop in income following pensionable age. However, the majority of the House of Lords found that the reason why the policy was adopted could not alter the fact that the man would have received the benefits 'but for' his sex. The fact that he was, in principle, in a better position between sixty and sixty-five than a woman because he was not yet a pensioner was held to be irrelevant. Equal treatment was seen as an end in itself, regardless of the background conditions within which it operated. This can be contrasted with the substantive view expressed in his dissenting judgment by Lord Griffiths: 'What I do not accept is that an attempt to redress the result of that unfair act of discrimination by offering free facilities to those disadvantaged by the earlier act of discrimination is, itself necessarily discriminatory on the grounds of sex'. The implications of symmetry for reverse discrimination are explored in detail in Chapter Five.

[44] [1990] 2 AC 751 (HL).

## II INDIRECT DISCRIMINATION

We have seen that equal treatment is not in itself sufficient to address inequality in society. Equal treatment may well lead to unequal results; treating people in the same way regardless of their differing backgrounds frequently entrenches difference. Thus selection criteria based on educational qualifications, although equally applicable to all, will exclude those who have been deprived of proper schooling; jobs which require full-time working and mobility will exclude those with primary responsibility for child-care. It is in recognition of this that the concept of indirect discrimination was shaped, in the pioneering US case of *Griggs v. Duke Power*.[45] In this case, the US Supreme Court was presented with a clear demonstration of the way in which apparently neutral criteria sustain and reinforce the disadvantaged position of blacks in the US. The employer had maintained an explicit policy of exclusion of black workers until the Civil Rights Act 1964, which prohibited such practices. The employer abandoned the express policy, but instead instituted literacy tests for all applicants, even for unskilled jobs where such qualifications were not necessary. The same test was applied to all candidates, but the ongoing effects of discrimination against blacks in the education system meant that a disproportionate number failed to achieve the required standard. Thus the workforce remained almost entirely white. The Court responded by expanding the principle of equality: equal treatment was held to be discriminatory if the result was that fewer blacks could comply, unless the requirement was necessary for the proper execution of the job in hand.

This concept rapidly made its way across the Atlantic, first to Britain, then to Europe. Its transposition in the UK was in the form of a tight statutory definition, in line with the British style of legislative drafting. Thus the SDA provides that a person discriminates against a woman if:

(b) he applies to her a requirement or condition which he applies or would apply equally to a man but—

(i)  which is such that the proportion of women who can comply with it is considerably smaller than the proportion of men who can comply with it, and

(ii) which he cannot show to be justifiable irrespective of the sex of the person to whom it is applied, and

---

[45] 401 US 424, 91 S Ct 849.

(iii)  which is to her detriment because she cannot comply with it.[46]

An identical formulation is found in the context of race discrimination.[47] While this formulation presented a substantial advance, its tight wording led the courts towards an unduly restrictive interpretation. In particular, the courts held that to be a 'requirement or condition' for the purposes of the statute, a criterion must constitute an absolute barrier. A more informal practice, or a set of factors to be weighed up, would not fall foul of the provision whatever its impact. For example, in *Perera*,[48] an applicant was excluded because of his nationality; but nationality was only one of several factors, and a non-national could, in principle, be acceptable if other factors were of sufficient weight. The Court held that the requirement of nationality did not fall within the statutory definition of a 'requirement or condition'. It is striking too that the Disability Discrimination Act 1995 does not contain an indirect discrimination provision, nor do recently enacted provisions guaranteeing equal treatment to part-time and fixed term workers.

At the level of the EU, it was initially the ECJ which introduced a notion of indirect discrimination, through its interpretation of the open-textured equal treatment principle. There was no statutory underpinning until 1997, when a definition of indirect sex discrimination was included in the Burden of Proof Directive.[49] This directive defines indirect discrimination as:

an apparently neutral provision, criterion or practice [which] disadvantages a substantially higher proportion of the members of one sex unless that provision, criterion or practice is appropriate and necessary and can be justified by objective factors unrelated to sex.[50]

An even more refined definition is found in the newly passed race equality directive. Here indirect discrimination is:

taken to occur where an apparently neutral provision, criterion or practice would put persons of a racial or ethnic origin at a particular disadvantage compared with other persons, unless that provision, criterion or practice is objectively justified by a legitimate aim and the means of achieving that aim are appropriate or necessary.

The most important advance represented in these definitions is the

---

[46] Sex Discrimination Act 1975, s.1(1)(b).     [47] Race Relations Act 1976 s.1(1)(b).
[48] *Perera v. Civil Service Commission (No 2)* [1983] IRLR 166 (CA).
[49] Directive (EC) 97/80/EC on the burden of proof in cases of discrimination based on sex ('Burden of Proof Directive').
[50] *ibid.*, Art. 2(2).

inclusion of 'practices' as well as provisions or criteria. This makes it
clear that it is not necessary to prove an absolute bar, but that a looser
practice or provision will suffice. The Burden of Proof Directive also
clarifies the test to be applied when establishing justification. This aspect
is discussed in more detail below.

The European Court of Human Rights has been less confident than
the ECJ about importing a concept of indirect discrimination into the
open-ended equality guarantee in Article 14 of the ECHR. Indeed, in the
immigration case of *Abdulaziz*,[51] the European Court of Human Rights
took a narrow formal view of discrimination, holding that Article 14 only
prohibited regulations which expressly differentiated on grounds of race
or ethnic origin. Implicitly rejecting the concept of indirect discrimination, the Court declared that the UK's immigration rules were not
unlawful simply because of the fact that 'the mass immigration against
which the rules were directed consisted mainly of would-be immigrants
from the New Commonwealth and Pakistan, and that as a result they
affected at the material time fewer white people than others'. Yet, as has
been seen above, this was exactly the point at which a searching concept
of equality was needed. The incorporation of Article 14 into domestic law
by the Human Rights Act 1998, however, opens up the possibility that
domestic courts might be more robust in developing the concept of
indirect discrimination in this context.

How then does indirect discrimination fare in respect of the four issues
identified above? Each will be examined in turn.

## (I) SUBSTANCE OR CONSISTENCY

It is in the move beyond consistency to substance that the chief strength
of the indirect discrimination concept lies. It has been particularly effective in dealing with criteria which specifically disadvantage women with
child-care responsibilities. Thus a maximum age limit of twenty-eight for
new entrants to the civil service has been held to be a condition with
which fewer women than men can comply because many women spend
their twenties having babies and caring for them.[52] Similarly, the fact that
women continue to bear primary responsibility for childcare means that
considerably more women than men work part-time. A condition which
makes full time working a prerequisite for access to a range of
employment related benefits, such as pensions, protection against unfair

---

[51] *Abdulaziz, Cabales and Balkandali v. United Kingdom* Series A No. 42, (1985) 7 EHRR
471.
[52] *Price v. Civil Service Commission* [1977] IRLR 291 (EAT).

dismissal, and equal hourly pay has thus been held to be indirectly discriminatory. Indirect discrimination has also made some progress towards fashioning a notion of equality which can accommodate diversity. By examining the impact of apparently neutral practices and criteria, indirect discrimination reveals the extent to which the dominant culture or religion is favoured. Thus in the landmark case of *Mandla v. Lee*[53] the House of Lords held that a school had unlawfully discriminated against a Sikh boy by excluding him from the school when he refused to take off his turban in order to comply with a school rule requiring boys to come bare-headed to school. An apparently neutral rule, applying equally to all pupils, was recognized as in practice requiring conformity to a Christian way of dressing and therefore creating unacceptable barriers to those of different cultures or religions.

### (II) THE ROLE OF THE COMPARATOR

The move beyond consistent treatment has not, however, eliminated the need to find a comparator, albeit on a group rather than individual level. Thus it is necessary to establish that the condition or requirement is such that considerably fewer of one group *than the other* can comply. The choice of comparator has in practice been highly contested; indeed, the need for a comparable group rather than an individual comparator has aggravated the difficulty. As many cases have shown, the figures might differ substantially depending on which statistics are chosen. Should the number of women who can comply be taken as a proportion of the appropriately qualified workforce, or of the number of women in the particular establishment, or of the number of women in the workforce as a whole? Moreover, as in the case of direct discrimination, the very choice of comparator might reinforce discrimination. In the race discrimination field, this result was strikingly illustrated in the US Supreme Court case of *Wards Cove*.[54] This concerned a workforce which was almost wholly segregated, with Filipino and other ethnic minority workers doing all the unskilled work, and whites doing the skilled work. The lower court held that this level of segregation on its own was evidence of discrimination. But the US Supreme Court disagreed, holding that it was not appropriate to compare the number of unskilled Filipinos with the number of whites. Instead, only Filipinos with the requisite qualifications needed to be considered. This of course ignores the contribution of past

---

[53] [1983] 2 AC 548 (HL).
[54] *Wards Cove v. Atonio* (1989) 490 US 642, 109 S Ct 2115.

discrimination in preventing Filipinos from obtaining the necessary skills. Moreover, the absence of relevantly qualified Filipinos was held to defeat the claim, when it should have given rise to obligations to train or otherwise equip them for the job.

Even if agreement can be reached as to which statistics are relevant, it may be difficult to decide whether the difference is 'considerably smaller'. This was well illustrated by the long-running litigation in the recent case of *R v. Secretary of State, ex p Seymour Smith and Perez.*[55] The case challenged existing legislation which limited the right to complain of unfair dismissal to employees who had been employed for more than two years at the date of dismissal. The applicants argued that the proportion of women who could comply with the two year eligibility requirement was considerably smaller than the proportion of men, thus raising a prima facie case of indirect discrimination. The figures showed that over the period from 1985 to 1991, the proportion of men who had two or more years of service ranged from 72 per cent to 77.4 per cent; while the proportion of women in this category was consistently lower, ranging from 63.8 per cent to 68.9 per cent. This meant that the ratio of qualified men to qualified women was roughly 10:9 over the relevant period. It was accepted that the difference in the impact of the requirement was statistically significant, in that it could be said with confidence that it was due to social factors rather than to chance. But was the proportion of women who could comply 'considerably smaller' as required by the legislation? The case was aired before four different courts, and all came to different conclusions. The Divisional Court found that the proportion was not considerably smaller; while the Court of Appeal found a considerable and persistent difference. The ECJ held that it was for the national court to decide this question. Nevertheless it took the view that the statistics for 1985 did not appear to show that a considerably smaller percentage of women than men were able to fulfil the requirement. At the same time, it suggested that a difference which was 'lesser' than 'considerably smaller' may yet be evidence of indirect discrimination if it was 'persistent and relatively constant'. It was still difficult to reach consensus when the House of Lords finally decided the issue, six years after the first hearing. The majority judgment is notable for finally taking a perceptive and common sense view of the matter. Most importantly, it was stated that, given that the context was the achievement of equality of pay or

---

[55] (No 1) [1994] IRLR 448 (DC); [1995] IRLR 464 (CA); [1997] IRLR 315 (HL); [1999] IRLR 253 (ECJ); (No 2) [2000] IRLR 263 (HL).

treatment, the latitude afforded by the word 'considerably' should not be exaggerated.[56] The obligation was to avoid applying unjustifiable requirements which have a considerable disparity of impact. Although the impact was relatively small, that fact that it was persistent and constant meant that it should not 'be brushed aside and dismissed as insignificant or inconsiderable'. Thus the majority held that the difference was considerable. Notably, however, they went on to find it justifiable (see below).

Some attempt is made to clarify this issue in the formulations of indirect discrimination in the recent EC directives. The Burden of Proof Directive states that indirect discrimination exists where a provision 'disadvantages a substantially higher proportion of members of one sex'. The race discrimination directive requires proof that a provision 'would put persons of a racial or ethnic origin at a particular disadvantage compared with other persons' (in both cases subject to a justification defence, discussed below). Both formulae make it unnecessary to show that the difference is between those 'who can comply' and those who cannot. This suggests that, instead having to demarcate a pool of comparison on the basis of those who can comply with the condition, the comparison is simply between proportions of women and men; or those of racial or ethnic origin and others. However, it is notable that the Burden of Proof Directive requires a determination that the proportion is 'substantially higher'. This still raises the question of whether something more than statistical significance is required, and if so by how much. In referring to 'particular disadvantage' the race discrimination legislation attempts to escape the need for any comparison of proportions of groups. However, it is still necessary to show that the practice puts persons of racial or ethnic origin at a particular disadvantage *compared with other persons*. It has been argued that this simply allows a comparison with another individual, avoiding the difficulty of delineating a group. But this in turn undermines the group aspect which is the essence of indirect discrimination. Instead, the conundrum can only be overcome if it is accepted that a difference between the groups (widely defined by gender or race) which is statistically significant is sufficient to establish a prima facie case of indirect discrimination. The burden of proof of justification would then pass quickly onto the employer.

---

[56] [2000] IRLR 263 at 270, para 57 (*per* Lord Nicholls).

## (III) COMPETING PRIORITIES

The third problematic issue in respect of indirect discrimination concerns the way in which the balance is drawn between equality and
other social priorities, particularly the business interests of the
employer or state policy. Indirect discrimination has always been structured in such a way as to permit a prima facie case of discrimination to
be rebutted by a justification, provided that latter is not itself grounded
in sex or race discrimination. In other words, indirectly discriminatory
barriers need only be dismantled if they cannot be justified on gender
or race neutral grounds. Yet many such exclusionary barriers can
indeed be so justified. Criteria which are job-related remain
legitimate—yet disadvantaged groups, by virtue of their disadvantage,
might find it impossible to comply. This is particularly problematic in
situations in which qualifications are necessary for a job, but the
absence of qualifications is due to past or ongoing discrimination. Thus
in one British case, training places for management jobs were only
available to applicants with previous work experience in Britain. This
made it impossible for those, who due to prejudice in the labour market, or because they were recent arrivals, had no such experience.[57]
This means that the ability of indirect discrimination to achieve its
redistributive goals is limited.

The strength of the equality principle as manifested in indirect discrimination is thus dependent on the relative weights given to equality
versus other competing interests. As Browne-Wilkinson J (as he then was)
noted in an early sex discrimination case, there is no generally accepted
view of the relative priorities to be given to the elimination of discriminatory practices on the one hand and the profitability of a business on the
other.[58] The seminal US case of *Griggs* set the value of equality high,
requiring proof that the exclusionary practice was necessary for the business of the employer or that it was essential to effective job performance.
Even if the employer could prove business necessity and job relatedness,
it remained open for the plaintiff to argue that there was a less discriminatory alternative which would also serve the employer's business interest.[59]
A similar set of priorities was evidenced in the earliest UK cases, requiring the employer to show both that the requirement was necessary and

---

[57] *Ojutiku v. Manpower Services Commission* [1982] IRLR 418 (CA).
[58] *Clarke v. Eley Kynoch* [1982] IRLR 482 (EAT).
[59] *Griggs v. Duke Power Co* (1971) 401 US 424, 91 S Ct 849; *Albermarle v. Moody*
(1975) 422 US 405, 95 S Ct 2362.

that no non-discriminatory alternative was available.[60] However, the extent to which the tribunals and courts were prepared to prioritize equality issues soon waned, and the standard of justification progressively slipped. A particularly low point was reached in the race discrimination case of *Ojutiku v. Manpower Services Commission*,[61] in which the Court of Appeal held that an act was justified merely if the reasons for doing it were such that they would be acceptable to right thinking persons as sound and tolerable reasons for so doing. A similar decline in the standard of justification in the US[62] was only partially arrested by legislation.[63]

The signals from the ECJ have been particularly complex. The standard of justification was significantly tightened in the seminal case of *Bilka*.[64] In this case, it was held that for employment related discrimination, the employer must show that the means chosen serve a real business need, that they are appropriate to achieve that objective and are necessary to that end. Where legislation or social policy has a discriminatory impact, the State can only justify its continuation if the means correspond to an objective which is necessary for social policy, and which is appropriate and necessary to achieve that end.[65] This standard has exerted a powerful influence on the UK courts. Indeed, in *ex p EOC*[66] the House of Lords felt able to use that test to strike down a central part of the Thatcher government's deregulatory policies, namely the exclusion of part-timers from job security rights for the first five years of employment. The government had argued that the exclusion was necessary to reduce unemployment among flexible workers. In a highly significant decision, the House of Lords rejected this justification, holding that the empirical evidence for the government's claim was not available.

However, no sooner had the UK courts been persuaded to insist on a strict standard of justification, than the ECJ began to dilute that standard. Thus in *Nolte*[67] the Court held that Member States retained a broad discretion in social policy. Indirectly discriminatory legislation or social policy, under this test, need not be adopted for a necessary social policy reason—one which is legitimate will suffice, provided it is unrelated to any discrimination based on sex. In addition, the means need not be

---

[60] *Steel v. UPW* [1978] ICR 181 (EAT).    [61] Above n.56.
[62] *Wards Cove v. Atonio*, above n.53.
[63] Civil Rights Act 1991, s.105; and see (1992) 105 *Harvard Law Review* 913; (1993) 106 *Harvard Law Review* 1621.
[64] *Bilka-Kaufhaus*, above n.36.
[65] Case 171/88 *Rinner-Kuhn* [1989] ECR 2743.
[66] *R v. Secretary of State for Employment, ex p EOC* [1995] 1 AC 1 (HL).
[67] Case 371/93 *Nolte* [1995] ECR I-4625.

objectively necessary to achieve the ends. Instead, it is sufficient if the Member State could reasonably consider that the means were suitable for attaining that aim. This test, which was extended to employment related policies in *Seymour Smith*,[68] was immediately injected into UK law by the House of Lords. Stressing that the burden placed on the government in this type of case was not as heavy as previously thought, the House of Lords held that the insistence in the lower courts on objective justification was therefore too stringent. Instead, a relatively wide margin of appreciation is to be given to governments. 'Governments must be able to govern. They adopt general policies, and implement measures to carry out their policies. Governments must be able to take into account a wide range of social, economic and political factors . . . National courts, acting with hindsight, are not to impose an impracticable burden on governments which are proceeding in good faith'. Indeed, it seems that only generalized assumptions, lacking any factual foundation, would be rejected as insufficient justification. Thus in *Seymour Smith*, the government argued that the two year qualification period was adopted in order to reduce the reluctance of employers to take on more employees. Lord Nicholls acknowledged that government evidence amounted to no more than the citation of reports indicating that various small percentages of employers considered that the unfair dismissal legislation might inhibit the recruitment of employees. But since the test was merely whether the Secretary of State was reasonably entitled to consider that the longer qualifying period might help reduce the reluctance of employers to take on more people, the House of Lords held that this evidence was sufficient to discharge the burden of justification.[69] The House of Lords did impose a small constraint by requiring that, if a government measure has a disparately adverse effect on women, it is under a duty to take reasonable steps to monitor the working of the measure. The greater the disparity of impact, the greater the diligence which can reasonably be expected of the government. However, the application of this test showed that it too left considerable latitude to government discretion. The statistics only related to six years, and six years was held to be too short a period within which to expect a final determination of whether a measure had achieved its purpose and if necessary to introduce changes. On the facts of the case, the government had therefore discharged the burden of justification.

---

[68] Above n.54.        [69] *(No 2)*, above n.54.

## (IV) AIMS OF INDIRECT DISCRIMINATION

The aims of the concept of indirect discrimination are ambiguous. The principle clearly intends to reach beyond equal treatment towards equality of results. But its goals are not necessarily the achievement of equality of results. A disparate impact is not itself discriminatory. Unequal results are legitimate if no exclusionary barrier can be identified, or if the inequality can be justified by reference to business needs or State social policy. Even if all these factors are made out, the remedy may well be just individual compensation, rather than a duty to take action to remove the offending requirement. Equality of results is therefore not the end to be achieved. Instead, the results are part of the process of diagnosis of discrimination. Under-representation of a group makes it likely that an exclusionary criterion is operating; but then, the applicant must go further and find a practice, requirement, or condition which leads to this effect and which cannot be justified.

If indirect discrimination is only partially about equality of results, is it instead about equality of opportunity, in that it aims to equalize the starting point? Again, this is only partially true.

A finding of indirect discrimination renders some barriers unlawful and therefore requires them to be removed. But not all barriers need to be removed—only those which are not justifiable on business or social policy grounds. Criteria which are job-related will generally remain legitimate. Yet disadvantaged groups, by virtue of their disadvantage, might find it impossible to comply. There is no obligation to ensure that applicants are equipped for a job or other benefit; and thereby to create genuine equality of opportunity. This is clearly evident in respect to part-time work. The indirect discrimination provisions have made significant progress in the removal of specific detriments attached to part-time work. But they do nothing to change the underlying division of power within the family which leaves women with the primary responsibility for child-care. The result is that women part-time workers might find their position at work improved as a result of the prohibition of indirect discrimination. But the fact that the vast majority of women are part-time workers remains unchanged. Nor does a successful claim in itself oblige the employer to remove the discriminatory barrier. Although many employers may in fact do so to avoid further proceedings, the only legal requirement is to compensate the individual victim.

## III  EQUALITY AS PROPORTIONALITY

In many jurisdictions, instead of a statutory definition of discrimination, there is a more general equality guarantee, stipulating that all persons are equal before the law. Equality on its own is, however, too indeterminate, in that not all distinctions are discriminatory. The challenge has therefore been to evolve principles which distinguish between invidious discrimination and appropriate differentiation. To do this, many jurisdictions have evolved a proportionality test. This requires a respondent (usually the State) to show that it has instituted differential treatment for legitimate aims and that the differentiation is appropriate to achieve that aim. But proportionality is an elastic concept. It leaves open both the question of which aims are legitimate, and how closely the means need to fit the ends. One way of understanding proportionality is to assert that it is disproportionate to use a sledge-hammer to crack a nut. But assuming that nut-cracking is a legitimate government aim, what would be appropriate? Anything smaller than a sledge-hammer, or only a nut-cracker? The extent of legitimate discrimination is wholly dependent on answers to questions of this sort.

It has been a proportionality approach, rather than one based on direct or indirect discrimination, which has been central to the equality jurisprudence of the European Court of Human Rights, which is directly relevant to UK law as a result of incorporation. The European Court of Human Rights has consistently held that not all differences of treatment are discriminatory, even if based on one of the specified grounds for discrimination. A difference is only discriminatory, according to the Court, if it has 'no objective and reasonable justification', that is, if it does not pursue a legitimate aim, or if there is not a 'reasonable relationship of proportionality between the means employed and the aim sought to be realized'.[70] It is argued that the fact that not every distinction is discriminatory makes it unnecessary to include a separate defence or restriction: distinctions for which an objective and reasonable justification exists simply do not constitute discrimination.[71] The elasticity of a proportionality test such as this is immediately evident in its differential application to different grounds of discrimination. The advancement of equality

---

[70] *Belgian Linguistic Case (No 2)* Series A No. 6, (1968) 1 EHRR 252 at para. 10; *Marckx v. Belgium* Series A No 31, (1979) 2 EHRR 330 at para. 33; *Abdulaziz v. United Kingdom,* above n.50 at para. 72.
[71] Draft Protocol 12, Explanatory Report, paras. 18 and 19.

between men and women is a major goal of the Council of Europe. 'Very weighty reasons' must therefore be advanced before a difference of treatment on grounds of sex is regarded as compatible with the Convention.[72] Thus far, however, it appears that no more than the ordinary 'reasonable relationship' is required in the case of differentiation on grounds of race, religion, or ethnicity.

The operation of the proportionality standard is demonstrated well by the case of *Abdulaziz*,[73] in which the European Court of Human Rights held that the UK's 1980 Immigration Rules were discriminatory on the grounds of sex, but not of race. Under the Rules, husbands settled in Britain could gain permission for their wives to enter the country; but wives could not gain permission for their husbands. The argument centred on whether the aim was legitimate and the means were proportional. The UK government attempted to justify the decision by asserting that husbands of settled wives were more likely to seek employment and therefore to exacerbate the UK's unemployment problems. The Court accepted that protection of the domestic labour market by excluding foreign labour was a legitimate aim. By comparison, the reasons given for excluding husbands but not wives did not meet the high standard required. However, the exclusion of particular groups on grounds of nationality was held to be a legitimate means of achieving the legitimate aims of immigration policy, even though such exclusion had a disparate impact on black and Asian people.

The approach of the European Court of Human Rights can be contrasted with the way in which the US Supreme Court has applied the Equal Protection Clause of the US Constitution. As we have seen, that Court has responded to the need to permit some degree of classification by creating a sliding scale of review, depending on the subject matter of the classification. Where a classification involves a 'suspect category', the most important of which is race, the legislation in question is subject to 'strict scrutiny'. This is the strictest proportionality test. It requires the State to do more than merely assert a legitimate objective: it must advance a compelling governmental interest in the classification. Nor is it enough to show that the differentiation is reasonable and appropriate to achieve that end; the classification must be narrowly tailored to achieve the purpose.[74] By contrast, when the classification does not involve a suspect

---

[72] *Abdulaziz v. United Kingdom*, above n.50 at para. 78.

[73] *Abdulaziz v. United Kingdom*, above n.50.

[74] *United States v. Carolene Products Co* (1938) 304 US 144, 58 S Ct 778, footnote 4; *Korematsu v. United States* (1994) 323 US 214, 65 S Ct 193.

category, the government need only advance a substantial interest, and show that the means chosen are rationally related to the end. This second test is a deeply deferential one, easily satisfied. In between is the 'inter- mediate' test[75] which requires the State to produce a justification which is 'exceedingly persuasive'.[76] This means that the State must show that the discriminatory classification is substantially related to the achievement of important governmental objectives. It is noteworthy that a different hier- archy operates here: whereas the ECHR puts sex discrimination at the top of the hierarchy, the US Supreme Court puts race. It is arguable that to distinguish in this way between different grounds of discrimination is itself invidious.

How then does proportionality relate to direct and indirect discrimin- ation in respect to the four themes outlined above? Central to proportion- ality is its movement beyond the notion of a comparator. Instead of requiring that likes be treated alike, it permits treatment to differ accord- ing to the degree of difference in the subjects. However, this does not mean that it is based on a substantive notion of equality. Proportionality, in prescribing a notion of equality as rationality, is itself a sophisticated form of consistency, namely that difference should be treated according to its degree of difference. This means that disparate impact may well be beyond its reach. A facially neutral criterion does not appear to be a classification, and therefore does not require justification. This was clearly evident in the European Court of Human Rights' approach to race discrimination in the *Abdulaziz* case. Stressing that the regulations did not openly distinguish between different racial groups, it was held that there was no relevant classification even to justify. It is evident too in the US, where the Supreme Court has held that a disparate impact claim cannot be brought in a Constitutional claim under the Equal Protection Clause,[77] even though it is sustainable under Title VII of the Civil Rights Act.

A proportionality approach also stands apart in that the tension between competing interests is at its core, rather than functioning as a defence at the second stage. Since proportionality inevitably requires two interests to be weighed against each other, it is more difficult for the equality interest to function as a trump. Everything hangs then on which factors are acceptable as potentially outweighing the equality interest and

---

[75] *Craig v. Boren* (1976) 429 US 190, 97 S Ct 451; *Orr v. Orr* (1979) 440 US 268, 99 S Ct 1102; *Michael M v. Superior Court* (1981) 450 US 464, 101 S Ct 1200.

[76] *United States v. Virginia* (1996) 116 S Ct 2264.

[77] *Washington v. Davis* (1976) 426 US 229, 96 S.Ct 2040.

what weights are ascribed to each side of the balance. Will community interests suffice, or must the countervailing interest be another individual's right? And will the two sets of factors simply be balanced against each other, or must it be established that the countervailing interest is necessary? If a mere assertion by the State of a community interest will suffice, then the proportionality principle yields a very weak equality doctrine. This is illustrated in the *Belgian Linguistics* case, in which French speaking parents living in areas designated as Dutch uni-lingual areas claimed the right to French education in their local school. The European Court of Human Rights held that Article 14 did not prohibit distinctions which, 'being based on the public interest, struck a fair balance between the protection of the interests of the community and freedoms safeguarded by the Convention'. However, a stronger equality principle emerges if the proportionality principle required gives greater weight to equality than to countervailing factors. A particularly interesting approach is that found in the new South African Constitution, which distinguishes between fair and unfair discrimination, with a presumption that all discrimination is unfair unless proved fair. Even unfair discrimination can be justified if the limitation is reasonable and justifiable in an open and democratic society based on human dignity, equality, and freedom, taking into account all relevant factors including the nature of the right; the importance of the purpose of the limitation; the relation between the limitation and its purpose; and less restrictive means to achieve the purpose.[78] However, even the most sophisticated tests depend on judicial application, and it is not always the case that a sufficiently nuanced test has been developed.

## IV  EQUALITY AS DIGNITY

It was argued in Chapter One that a commitment to the underlying value of human dignity can provide a valuable underpinning to the concept of equality. To what extent has this permeated the legal definitions of discrimination? At its most general level, dignity can operate as a guiding principle, permeating all decisions on equality. This has been its role in the text and judicial development of the South African Constitution. In one of the first equality cases to be decided, the South African Constitutional Court declared: 'At the heart of the prohibition of unfair discrimination lies a recognition that the purpose of our new constitutional

---

[78] The Constitution of South Africa, s.36(1).

and democratic order is the establishment of a society in which all human beings will be accorded equal dignity and respect regardless of their membership of particular groups. The achievement of such a society in the context of our deeply inegalitarian past will not be easy, but that that is the goal of the Constitution should not be forgotten or overlooked'.[79] Similarly, the Canadian Supreme Court has used dignity as a fundamental principle in deciding to whom the equality guarantee should apply. Thus, the Court stated: 'Equality means that our society cannot tolerate legislative distinctions that treat certain people as second-class citizens, that demean them, that treat them as less capable for no good reason, or that otherwise offend fundamental human dignity'.[80]

In its application to more specific areas, dignity has also played a role. Possibly the clearest arena for development has been that of sexual harassment. Canadian jurisprudence has been most explicit in recognizing sexual harassment as a demeaning practice, constituting a profound affront to the dignity and self-respect of the victim both as an employee and a human being.[81] In the UK, dignity has been the crucial additional ingredient in transforming the principle of direct discrimination to encompass a prohibition on sexual harassment. Thus, in the first UK case to recognize harassment as a species of sex discrimination, Lord Elmslie had no difficulty in finding it to be 'a particularly unacceptable form of treatment which it must be taken to have been the intention of Parliament to restrain'.[82] Indeed, in the field of harassment, the stress on dignity has facilitated a transformation of direct discrimination from a principle based entirely on consistency, to one embedded in substantive values. In particular, the comparison with treatment of a person of the opposite sex or race is no longer centre stage. Thus the EC directive on race discrimination simply defines harassment as unwanted conduct related to racial or ethnic origin [which] 'takes place with the purpose or effect of violating the dignity of a person and of creating an intimidating, hostile, degrading, humiliating or offensive environment'.[83] Such conduct is deemed to be discriminatory. Similarly, the new draft directive on sex discrimination defines sexual harassment as 'unwanted conduct related to sex . . . with the purposes or effect of affecting the dignity of a person

---

[79] *President of the Republic of South Africa v. Hugo* CCT 11/96 (April 18, 1997), 1997 (4) SA 1 (CC), para. 41.

[80] *Egan v. Canada* (1995) 29 CRR (2d) 79 at 104–5.

[81] *Janzen v. Platy Enterprises Ltd* [1989] 1 SCR 1252, 59 DLR (4th) 352.

[82] *Strathclyde Regional Council v. Porcelli* [1986] IRLR 135 (CS).

[83] Directive 2000/43, above n.5. Art.2(3).

and/or creating an intimidating, hostile, offensive or disturbing environment, in particular if . . . rejection of or submission to such conduct is used as a basis for a decision which affects that person'. Put together, all these developments can be seen as deepening the notion of equality beyond consistency into a substantive concept, based on the fundamental values of dignity and respect for the individual.

A similar stress on dignity led the European Commission on Human Rights to accept that racism can constitute a breach of the right not to be subjected to cruel and unusual treatment. The boldest decision in this area was that in the *East African Asians* case,[84] which concerned the explicit exclusion from Britain of East African Asians who were being forced out of Uganda and Tanzania. The Commission held that discrimination based on race could, in certain circumstances, amount to degrading treatment contrary to Article 3 of the Convention, which states that 'no-one shall be subjected to torture or to inhuman or degrading treatment or punishment'. In the case in hand, the Commission found that the UK legislation in question was racially motivated and destined to harm a specific racial group. However, the Commission was careful to stress that it was not faced with a general question of whether racial discrimination in immigration constituted degrading treatment as such. Instead it was specifically concerned with the Commonwealth Immigrants Act 1968 which explicitly subjected Asians in Tanzania and Uganda to particularly restrictive immigration control.[85] The classification of immigration controls as explicitly racist and therefore constituting inhuman and degrading treatment is therefore unlikely to function as the primary source of challenge of immigration rules.

## V BEYOND INDIRECT DISCRIMINATION: EQUAL OPPORTUNITIES AND POSITIVE DUTIES

The recognition of the limits of both direct discrimination and indirect discrimination has led law-makers to strike out in a new direction, namely the imposition of positive duties to promote equality, rather than just the negative requirement to refrain from discriminating. Such a duty has taken diverse forms, beginning in the US with the imposition of positive duties on government contractors to increase the representation of

---

[84] *East African Asians v. United Kingdom* (1981) 3 EHRR 76.
[85] *ibid.*, at para. 196; the Committee of Ministers held, however, that there had been no violation, largely because of measures taken by the UK to meet the Commission's objections.

minorities and of women in the workforce.[86] More recently, increasingly sophisticated duties have been imposed both on public authorities and private employers to develop positive plans to dismantle institutional racism and sexism.

Such 'fourth generation'[87] anti-discrimination provisions address some of the serious weaknesses in the existing structure of equality legislation. Most importantly, this approach moves beyond the fault-based model of existing discrimination law. As we have seen, under existing direct discrimination provisions, only an individual who can be shown to have treated the complainant less favourably on grounds of his or her sex can be held to be legally liable; and then the remedy is usually simply an obligation to compensate the individual victim. Even indirect discrimination requires proof that an individual employer has imposed a practice or condition which excludes disproportionate numbers of women or blacks. At the root of the positive duty, by contrast, is a recognition that societal discrimination extends well beyond individual acts of racist prejudice. This has important implications for both the content of the duty and the identification of the duty bearer. The duty becomes that, not just of compensating identified victims, but of restructuring institutions. Correspondingly, the duty-bearer is identified as the body in the best position to perform this duty. Even though not responsible for creating the problem in the first place, such duty bearers become responsible for participating in its eradication. This reformulation of the basis of the anti-discrimination law then has effects which ripple out through the whole remedial structure. The new duty avoids the need for proof of individual prejudice, or of unjustifiable disparate impact as a result of a practice or condition. Instead, the positive duty is triggered as a result of evidence of structural discrimination. Thus the duty is triggered by chronic under-representation in particular types of work or positions of power; inequitable access to the benefits of employment or State provision of services; or the imposition of inordinate costs on those who attempt to maintain religious or cultural preferences which conflict with those of the dominant group. The duty itself is not simply one of providing compensation for an individual victim. Instead, positive action is

---

[86] Executive Order 10925, introduced by President Kennedy in 1961. The current Order 11246 issued by President Johnson in 1964 and amended in 1967 to cover sex and religion, covers about 300,000 federal contractors, employing about 40 per cent of the working population. (See Hepple, Coussey, and Choudhury, above n.42, para 3.23.)

[87] Hepple, Coussey, and Choudhury, above n.42.

required to achieve change, whether by encouragement, accommodation, or structural change.

A particularly important dimension of fourth generation equality laws is their potential to encourage participation by affected groups in the decision-making process itself. Because the duty is prospective, and can be fashioned to fit the problem at hand, it is not a static duty, but requires a continuing process of diagnosing the problem, working out possible responses, monitoring the effectiveness of strategies, and modifying those strategies as required. If participation is built in as a central aspect of such duties, not only is it likely that strategies will be more successful, but the very process of achieving equality becomes a democratic one. Participation rights are particularly important in the context of rights for religious, ethnic, and cultural minorities. It has been argued above that ethnicity should not be regarded as a static notion, but as one that is part of an ongoing dynamic interaction both between those who regard themselves as within the group and between the group and the dominant culture. Thus any attempt to encapsulate the content of minority rights without active participation of the groups in questions will be patronizing, erroneous, and unlikely to succeed.

'Fourth generation' equality laws, based on a positive duty to promote equality, rather than simply to refrain from discriminating, are considered in detail in Chapter Six. At this stage, it is important to stress that the proactive nature of positive duties changes the structure of equality law, but is not itself enough. Positive duties are only meaningful if they are targeted towards particular aims. It is therefore still important to focus on what we are trying to achieve by means of positive action. Is the aim to achieve the removal of prejudice and harassment; or to redistribute resources; or to accommodate diversity? And which principle of equality is being utilized: formal, equality of results, equality of opportunity, or some other substantive value? Many positive duties appear to be furthering a redistributive aim, in that they are formulated in terms of improving the representation of minorities or women in a given sector. However, a change in representation might not in itself be sufficient. As was argued above, an increase in the proportions of previously underrepresented groups may do no more than reflect a greater tendency of members of those groups to conform to existing structures. Positive duties to be truly effective must also be used to effect changes in underlying discriminatory structures. This in turn requires substantive improvements not just in the availability of opportunities; but the ability to use them. It demands more than changes in the colour or gender make-up of existing structures, but also an attempt to reshape those structures to accommodate diversity.

# 5

# Symmetry or Substance: Reverse Discrimination

The previous chapter showed clearly that, in order to be effective, anti-discrimination policies must reach beyond legal prohibitions and incorporate positive measures. But is it permissible to go beyond promotion and encouragement, and institute policies which openly discriminate in favour of the disadvantaged group? Official support for reverse discrimination is growing among Member States of the EU; and the US has a long tradition of positive discrimination in the allocation of federal contracts, employment, and other areas. Yet such programmes appear to offend against basic principles of equality. Much of the century has been spent convincing judges and legislators that race and gender are irrelevant and their use in the allocation of benefits or rights is invidious. How then can it be legitimate to permit such use for purportedly remedial purposes? The answer to this question differs according to different conceptions of equality. According to a conception of formal equality, or equality as consistency, reverse discrimination must inevitably constitute a breach of the equality principle. By contrast, reverse discrimination may well be compatible with a substantive view of equality, particularly a notion of equality which aims at the alleviation of disadvantage. A notion of equality of opportunity, on the other hand, produces an equivocal response to reverse discrimination. But the theoretical debate is only part of the issue. Even if its legitimacy is established, it is still necessary to justify reverse discrimination on a strategic level. The mere presence of a handful of women or blacks in positions of power is not necessarily of assistance in reversing discrimination against women or blacks in society in general. For example, the position of many women declined during the premiership of Margaret Thatcher. Thus it is crucial to ask of any particular programme: What are its aims? Is it effective in achieving those aims? And are the costs fairly spread?

The first part of this chapter will explore the influence on the legitimacy of reverse discrimination of these different conceptions of equality. In the second part, a range of legal responses in different jurisdictions will be examined. The third part considers more closely some of the strategic issues involved.

## I CONCEPTS OF EQUALITY AND REVERSE DISCRIMINATION

Affirmative action denotes the deliberate use of race- or gender-conscious criteria for the specific purpose of benefiting a group which has previously been disadvantaged or excluded on grounds of race or gender. Its aims range from providing a specific remedy for invidious race or sex discrimination, to the more general purpose of increasing the participation of groups which are visibly under-represented in important public spheres such as education, politics, or employment. In its strongest form of reverse discrimination, it requires that individual members of the disadvantaged group be actively preferred over others (who may be equally or even better qualified), in the allocation of jobs, promotion, training, university places, and other similar benefits.

Given its deliberate use of race- or sex-conscious criteria, it is not surprising that the legitimacy of reverse discrimination is highly problematic. However, a closer look shows that its acceptability or otherwise depends entirely on which conception of equality is utilized. This section explores the implications for reverse discrimination of the three main conceptions of equality considered in Chapter One: formal equality or equality as consistency; substantive equality; and equality of opportunity.

### (I) FORMAL EQUALITY: SYMMETRY AND STATE NEUTRALITY

The arguments presented by opponents of reverse discrimination appear at first sight to be unassailable. If equality is the goal, how can it be possible to justify policies requiring unequal treatment on the grounds of sex or race? This argument, however, only appears irrefutable because it is based on a particular formal conception of equality. There are three salient characteristics of formal equality which make it inevitable that reverse discrimination will constitute an illegitimate breach. First, formal equality presupposes that justice is an abstract, universal notion, and cannot vary to reflect different patterns of benefit and disadvantage in a particular society. If discrimination on grounds of gender or race is unjust, it must be unjust whether it creates extra burdens on a group already disadvantaged, or whether it redistributes those burdens to a

previously privileged group. Equality mu
metrical; applying with equal strength regard
against or in favour of a disadvantaged group. .
Justice Powell declared in the famous case of *L*
equal protection cannot mean one thing when ap.
and something else when applied to an individual o.
this view, there is a moral and constitutional equiva          .aws
designed to subjugate a race and those that distribute b.        .s another
Supreme Court Justice, Thomas J put it in a later ca.c, government-
sponsored racial discrimination based on benign prejudice should be considered to be just as noxious as discrimination motivated by malicious
prejudice.[2] Other judicial statements have made it clear that the aim is not
the alleviation of disadvantage: discrimination on grounds of race is considered to be odious even if directed against a group that has never been
the subject of governmental discrimination.[3]

The second premise of formal equality which makes reverse discrimination internally contradictory is its individualism. Group characteristics such as sex or race should always be disregarded in distributing
benefits or allocating jobs or promotion; instead, individuals must be
rewarded only on the basis of individual merit. To revert to other criteria
is not only unfair but also inefficient: reverse discrimination simply permits the appointment of people less well qualified and therefore less able
to do the job properly.[4] Conversely, burdens should only be allocated on
the basis of individual responsibility. Thus individuals may only be
treated as responsible for their own actions; they should not be held
accountable for more general societal wrongs. This means in particular
that an individual man or white person should not be required to compensate for historical or institutional sex or race discrimination by being
excluded from a job or promotion for which he is well qualified. There
can, on this view, be no 'creditor or debtor race'.[5]

Third, formal equality entails equality before the law. The State should
be neutral as between its citizens, favouring no one above any other.
'Without doing violence to the principles of equality before the law and
neutral decision-making, we simply cannot interpret our laws to support

---

[1] *Regents of University of California v. Bakke* (1978) 438 US 265, 98 S Ct 2733.

[2] *Adarand v. Pena* (1995) 515 US 200, 115 S Ct 2097 at 241, 2119 (*per* Thomas J).

[3] *Wygant v. Jackson Board of Education* (1986) 476 US 267, 106 S Ct 1842.

[4] M. Abram 'Affirmative Action: Fair Shakers and Social Engineers' [1986] 99 *Harvard Law Review* 1312 at 1322.

[5] *Adarand v. Pena*, above n. 2, at 239, 2118 (*per* Scalia J).

ur-blindness for some citizens and colour-consciousness for
rs'.[6] The proposition that a group should be favoured on account of
gender or race, even in a remedial sense, is therefore anathema. Moreover,
argues Abram, any attempt to move from the individual to the group is
bound to degenerate into a 'crude political struggle between groups seeking favoured status'.[7] State neutrality also entails a State which inter-
venes as little as possible in the 'free market'. In its revived neo-liberal
form, this version of State neutrality is used to oppose the use by the
State or other public bodies of their contractual powers within the market
to pursue public policies such as the elimination of discrimination. This
necessarily outlaws the use of contract compliance or 'set-asides' of State
funds for the purpose of aiding minorities or women.

## (II) SUBSTANTIVE EQUALITY

Reliance on substantive rather than formal equality gives rise to a very
different analysis of reverse discrimination. The substantive approach to
reverse discrimination rejects an abstract view of justice and instead
insists that justice is only meaningful in its interaction with society. The
unfortunate reality is that it is women rather than men who have suffered
cumulative disadvantage due to sex discrimination; blacks rather than
whites who have suffered from racism. Once this is accepted, it becomes
clear that to adopt a symmetrical approach, whereby unequal treatment
of men is regarded as morally identical to discrimination against women,
is to empty the equality principle of real social meaning. As Dworkin puts
it: 'The difference between a general racial classification that causes
further disadvantage to those who have suffered from prejudice, and a
classification framed to help them, is morally significant'.[8]

Similarly, the substantive approach rejects as misleading the aspirations of individualism. It is true that the merit principle has played a
valuable role in advancing equality of opportunity by displacing nepotism
and class bias in the allocation of jobs or benefits. However, in the context
of sex or race, the uncritical use of merit as a criterion for employment or
promotion could perpetuate disadvantage. This is because, despite the
appearance of scientific objectivity, the choice of criteria for deciding
merit may well reinforce existing societal discrimination or incorporate
implicit discriminatory assumptions. Thus the adoption of literacy or
other educational tests for selection for jobs can perpetuate inequality if

---

[6] Abram, above n. 4, at 1319.      [7] *ibid.*, at 1321.
[8] R. Dworkin, *A Matter of Principle* (Harvard University Press, 1985), p. 314.

there is discrimination in schools; a stress on formal qualifications and work experience rather than acquired knowledge or informal experience is likely to undervalue women's skills. Equally misleading is the reliance on a notion of individual fault, which generates an image of an 'innocent' third party who is deprived of a job or other opportunity because he is white or male. A substantive view of equality suggests that the responsibility for correcting disadvantage should not be seen to rest merely with those to whom 'fault' can be attributed. Instead, all who benefit from the existing structure of disadvantage should be expected to bear part of the cost of remedy. A community structured on racial or gender discrimination has conferred benefits on the dominant group as a whole. Each member of the community should, therefore, be required to bear part of the costs of correction, provided these costs are not disproportionate for the individual.

Finally, the substantive approach rejects the possibility of a neutral State which is separate from society with its current set of power relations. The State is no more than an emanation of the democratic process, the aim of which is to function as a conduit for or resolution of the cross-currents of social power. The modern State plays a central role in distributing benefits in society. It cannot therefore be truly neutral: if it refuses to take an active role in reducing disadvantage, it is in fact supporting the existing dominant groups in maintaining their position of superiority over groups which have suffered from discrimination and prejudice. A substantive view of equality would view the State as having a duty to act positively to correct the results of such discrimination. On all these counts, then, reverse discrimination could be entirely legitimate if a substantive view of equality is accepted.

## (III) EQUAL OPPORTUNITIES

The approach based on 'equal opportunities' yields a more equivocal view of the legitimacy of reverse discrimination. As will be recalled, the equal opportunities conception is similar to substantive equality in that it recognizes the shallowness of the notion of formal justice, and acknowledges the extent to which an individual's life chances are distorted by structural discrimination based on group membership. Equality cannot be achieved if individuals begin the race from different starting points. Thus it is part of the function of equality to equalize the starting point, even if this might necessitate special measures for the disadvantaged group. It is, however, at this point that the primacy of the individual and the stress on individual merit reassert themselves. Once individuals enjoy equality of opportunity, it is argued, the problem of institutional discrimination has been overcome, and fairness demands that they be treated on the basis of their individual qualities, without regard to sex or race. This model there-fore specifically rejects reverse discrimination if it aims to achieve equal-ity of outcome by treating individuals purely on the basis of their sex or colour.

We have seen, however, that the metaphor of equalizing starting points is misleading. The removal of specific barriers to women, blacks or others open up more opportunities to women or minorities, but they do not guarantee that more women or minorities will in fact be in a position to take advantage of those opportunities. Those who lack the requisite qualifications as a result of past discrimination will still be unable to meet job-related criteria; women with child-care responsi-bilities will not find it easier to take on paid work. An equal opportun-ities approach could indeed be radical, provided it went beyond the removal of barriers and gave disadvantaged groups the means to bene-fit from the available opportunities. Such a programme would require substantial resource input from the State, including education and training programmes, investment in child-care facilities, and guarantees of flexible working opportunities available both to the mother and the father.

## II  REVERSE DISCRIMINATION AND THE LAW: CONTRASTING JURISDICTIONS

The arguments rehearsed above have been part of a lively debate in various jurisdictions about the legality of reverse discrimination. But the dominant model has differed widely as between countries, with the UK (except in Northern Ireland) relying largely on formal equality, the EU on equal opportunities, and the US displaying a fierce debate between proponents of substantive equality and those endorsing formal equality. Each of these will be examined in turn.

### (I)  THE UK: THE DOMINANCE OF FORMAL EQUALITY

The anti-discrimination legislation in the UK leaves little room for reverse discrimination of any kind. The dominant characteristic is one of symmetry. The legislation explicitly provides that the provisions are applicable equally to the treatment of men and women;[9] and to all races or

---

[9] Sex Discrimination Act 1975, s. 2(1).

ethnic groups. This is reinforced by judicial interpretation. In the case of *James v. Eastleigh Borough Council*,[10] the House of Lords held that the simple question to be considered was whether the complainant would have received the same treatment from the defendant 'but for' his or her sex. This line of reasoning is explicitly symmetrical, relying on a formal notion of justice which is abstracted from the social power relations within which it operates. Thus Lord Ackner declared, 'the reason why the policy was adopted can in no way affect or alter the fact that . . . men were to be treated less favourably than women, and were to be so treated on the ground of, because of their sex'.[11] This can be contrasted with the substantive notion of justice expressed in the dissenting judgment of Lord Griffiths. On his view, it could not be discriminatory to attempt to redress the result of an unfair act of discrimination by offering free facilities to those disadvantaged by the earlier act of discrimination.[12] It is notable too that similar words in the comparable US legislation[13] have been found to be capable of bearing a far wider meaning. In *United Steelworkers v. Weber*,[14] for example, it was argued that the prohibition in Title VII of the Civil Rights Act 1964 of discrimination on racial grounds made it inevitable that remedial reverse discrimination was unlawful. The Supreme Court by a majority rejected this argument. Instead it held that the prohibition against discrimination on grounds of race must be interpreted within the spirit of the Act, which is to ameliorate the problems caused by racism against black people. Using this approach, it was held that Title VII did not condemn all private race-conscious plans aimed at ameliorating high black unemployment.

One of the most significant obstacles presented by the symmetrical principle relates to attempts to redress the serious under-representation of women in positions of power within the decision-making process, particularly in Parliament. Other jurisdictions have responded to this by permitting a certain proportion of women to be given priority over men in the process of selection of candidates.[15] At European level, the Commission has adopted a Council recommendation which aims to promote more balanced participation of women in decision-making bodies of all

---

[10] [1990] 2 AC 751 (HL).     [11] *ibid.*, at 769.

[12] *James v. Eastleigh Borough Council*, above n. 10, at 768.

[13] Civil Rights Act, Title VII, ss. 703(a) and (d).

[14] *United Steelworkers v. Weber* (1979) 443 US 193, 99 S Ct 2721.

[15] In Israel, for example, which uses a proportional representation system, both major parties reserve seats for women in their lists of Parliamentary candidates.

kinds.[16] In Britain, the Labour Party introduced all-women short-lists in a limited number of constituencies[17] in 1993. This policy was a major factor in almost trebling the number of women Labour Party MPs returned to Parliament after the 1997 election.[18] However, the symmetrical approach soon stifled this strategy. On a complaint by two men who wished to be considered as candidates in three such constituencies, an employment tribunal struck down the policy as unlawful sex discrimination.[19] The case is notable for the absence of any of the sophisticated arguments on reverse discrimination found in other jurisdictions. The tribunal regarded the matter as conclusively decided by the 'simple' answer to the 'simple' test of whether the complainant would have received the same treatment but for his sex. 'It is obvious direct discrimination on grounds of sex'.[20]

The stress on an abstract, formal notion of justice in the UK is complemented by an equivalent emphasis on individualism and State neutrality. This has led British courts to a restrictive interpretation of one of the few statutory openings for reverse discrimination, namely the exception for 'genuine occupational qualifications'. The Race Relations Act provides that it is not unlawful to discriminate on grounds of race where race is a 'genuine occupational qualification', in that the 'holder of that job provides persons of that racial group with personal services promoting their welfare and those services can most effectively be provided by a person of that racial group'.[21] In an early case,[22] the EAT was prepared to accept that being of Afro-Caribbean origin was a genuine occupational qualification for a job at a nursery with Afro-Caribbean children, since this would help in maintaining the cultural awareness of the children and provide a link with their parents. The Court of Appeal has, however, taken a far more restrictive view, holding in a subsequent case that a local authority had discriminated unlawfully by reserving two managerial posts within its housing benefits department for employees of Asian or

---

[16] Council Recommendation 694/96 EC of December 2, 1996 on the balanced participation of women and men in the decision-making process (OJ L319, December, 10, 1996 P. 0011–0015).

[17] 50 per cent of the constituencies were either (i) marginal; (ii) new, or (iii) the sitting Labour MP was not standing at the next election.

[18] See M. Eagle and J. Lovenduski, *High Time or High Tide for Labour Women* Fabian Pamphlet 585 (Fabian Society, 1998).

[19] *Jepson v. The Labour Party* [1996] IRLR 116 (IT).

[20] *ibid.*, at 117.

[21] Race Relations Act 1976, s. 5(2)(d); a similar exception applies in the case of sex: see Sex Discrimination Act 1975, s. 7(2)(e).

[22] *Tottenham Green Under Fives' Centre v. Marshall* [1989] IRLR 147 (EAT).

Afro-Caribbean origin.[23] The Council argued that being Afro-Caribbean or Asian was a 'genuine occupational qualification' as required by the statute, because over half of the tenants in its area were of Afro-Caribbean or Asian origin, and the housing benefits system would be more sensitive to the needs and experience of black people if the services were provided by an Afro-Caribbean or Asian person. This argument is strongly reminiscent of Dworkin's redefinition of the merit principle. If a black skin will, as a matter of regrettable fact, enable a doctor to do a medical job better than a white skin, he argues, then that black skin is by the same token 'merit' as well.[24] In the Court of Appeal, however, Balcombe LJ unequivocally dismissed the view that one of the main purposes of the Race Relations Act was to promote positive action to benefit racial groups. Apart from the specific provisions permitting discriminatory training (see below), the purpose of the Act was solely to render acts of racial discrimination unlawful.

The final characteristic of the symmetrical model, the assertion of the neutrality of the State, is most apparent in the context of the controversy over the use by public bodies of their financial and contractual powers to further equal opportunities for women and blacks. 'Contract compliance' is a strategy whereby private contractors who enter into contracts with public bodies are required, as a condition of the contract, to institute equal opportunities or other social policies among their workforce. This can be a highly effective strategy since the penalties, both legal and social, for breach of a public contract can be financially far more damaging than a compensation award from a court or tribunal. In fact it has been used very successfully in the US in the race discrimination field. In the UK, contract compliance was used in a different field: under a series of Parliamentary resolutions, government contractors were required to institute fair wages and promote freedom of association as a condition of their contracts.[25] In the early 1980s, several London local authorities began using contract compliance to promote equal opportunities for women and blacks. The strategy was relatively effective: the Equal Opportunities Unit of the Greater London Council persuaded 77 out of 106 companies to institute equal opportunities action programmes in its first years of operation.

However, the Conservative governments in power from 1979 to 1997

---

[23] *Lambeth LBC v. CRE* [1990] IRLR 231 (CA).

[24] Dworkin, above n. 8, p. 299.

[25] For a detailed discussion see S. Fredman and G. Morris, *The State as Employer: Labour Law in the Public Services* (Mansell, 1989), pp. 454–74.

were openly hostile to contract compliance strategies. Relying on a premise of State neutrality, it was argued that the State should not use its contractual powers to advance social policies in favour of particular groups, even if those groups have been systematically disadvantaged because of their race or sex. The Fair Wages Resolutions were repealed as soon as the Conservatives came to power. In addition, provisions were included in the 1988 Local Government Act which were expressly 'designed to prevent abuses of the contractual process'.[26] Among these was a specific proscription of attempts to promote equal opportunities for women by inclusion of relevant terms in local authority contracts,[27] with only a limited exception permitting the furtherance of equal opportunities on racial grounds.[28] Local authorities were not even permitted to use their contractual powers to enforce the law: only the remedies specified in the Act itself are permitted, however weak. Thus in an early case,[29] the Divisional Court struck down as unlawful a clause in the model contract issued by Islington specifying that any contractor should comply with the Sex Discrimination Act 1975.[30] This contrasts vividly with the endorsement by the US Supreme Court of the right of public bodies to use their powers remedially in the race and sex discrimination field. It is also striking that contract compliance strategies are a centre-piece of Northern Ireland legislation prohibiting discrimination on grounds of religion.

This approach has now changed with legislation introduced by the Labour government elected in 1997; but the approach is markedly cautious. The guiding principle behind the new legislation is the achievement of 'best value'. New provisions[31] permit local authorities to take into account the employment practices of potential contractors only if they are directly relevant to the delivery of the service in question. Significantly, the legislation still firmly sets its face against using contractual specifications to achieve a balanced workforce. Best value and quality of service, it is argued, are not guaranteed by any particular composition of the workforce. However, if the service involves regular contact with the

---

[26] Nicholas Ridley, Secretary of State for the Environment, Hansard HC vol. 119, col. 86 (July 6, 1987).

[27] Local Government Act 1988, s. 17(5)(a).          [28] *ibid.*, s. 18(2).

[29] *R v. London Borough of Islington, ex p Building Employers Confederation* [1989] IRLR 382.

[30] '[The contractor] shall at all times comply with s. 6(1)(a) and (c) [no discrimination in selection for employment] and (2)(b) [dismissal or other detriment] of the SDA 1975'.

[31] Local Government Best Value (Exclusion of Non-commercial Considerations) Order 2001 SI 2001/909, promulgated under Local Government Act 1999, s.19; and see statutory guidance.

community, then the authority may include requirements as to how the bidder could meet the needs of a particular group. In addition, the local authority may require the contractor to abide by equal opportunities policies while the work is being carried out. The race relations provisions remain unchanged.

UK legislation does include one instance of a substantive approach. The Sex Discrimination Act expressly permits trade unions and employers or professional organizations to reserve seats on an elected executive for persons of one sex where this is necessary to secure a 'reasonable lower limit to the number of members of that sex serving on the body'.[32] This provision was enacted in recognition of the fact that women were vastly under-represented in decision-making in trade unions. UK statutes also give some credence to the advancement of equal opportunities, by permitting a degree of sex- or race-conscious remedial action in training. If there are comparatively few or no members of one sex or racial group doing a particular type of work, it is not unlawful to reserve access to training facilities to members of that group to help equip them for that work. Similarly, measures encouraging an under-represented group to take advantage of opportunities for doing that work are declared to be lawful.[33] Finally, it is not unlawful to give specific training facilities to those who are in special need of training because they have been fully engaged in family responsibilities.[34] Although these provisions provide a welcome break from the symmetrical approach, they also demonstrate the narrowness of the notion of equality of opportunity they espouse. As a start, the permission to use positive action does not extend to the actual offer of a job or promotion. A woman who has participated in a women's only training scheme declared lawful by the Act stands no better chance of being offered the employment for which she has been trained than anyone else. Nor is it permissible to offer gender-conscious training to existing employees.[35] Moreover, the measures are merely permissive rather than mandatory, and carry no commitment to government resourcing. Thus without the political will on the part of public employers, or a favourable cost-benefit analysis on the part of employers in the private sector, it is unlikely that such programmes will be mounted.

---

[32] Sex Discrimination Act 1975, s. 49.

[33] *ibid.*, ss. 47–48 (as amended by Sex Discrimination Act 1986, s. 4.); Race Relations Act 1976, ss. 37–38.

[34] Sex Discrimination Act 1975, s. 47(3).     [35] *ibid.*, s. 47(4).

## (II) EC LAW: EQUAL OPPORTUNITIES

EC law differs from that of the UK by explicitly dealing with the relationship between discrimination and positive measures to promote equality. It does so, however, in terms which put it firmly on an equal opportunities foundation. For many years, this issue was governed entirely by Article 2(4) of the Equal Treatment Directive[36] which states that the directive 'shall be without prejudice to measures to promote equal opportunity for men and women, in particular by removing existing inequalities which affect women's opportunities'. This is backed up by the recognition that 'existing legal provisions on equal treatment, which are designed to afford rights to individuals, are inadequate for the elimination of all existing inequalities unless parallel action is taken by governments, both sides of industry and other bodies concerned, to counteract the prejudicial effect on women in employment which arise from social attitudes, behaviour and structures'.[37] The proviso in Article 2(4) was modernized and expanded by the Treaty of Amsterdam. Article 141(4) of the amended Treaty now sets out the relationship between positive action and discrimination in more detail. This provides as follows:

with a view to ensuring full equality in practice between men and women in working life, the principle of equal treatment shall not prevent any Member States from maintaining or adopting measures providing for specific advantages in order to make it easier for the under-represented sex to pursue a vocational activity or to prevent or compensate for disadvantages in professional careers.

Is this then based on a substantive view of equality, or does it remain within the bounds of an equal opportunities approach? It has been left to the ECJ to answer this question, in response to a series of increasingly challenging cases. In the four major cases which have been decided within a period of four years, the ECJ has found it difficult to articulate a consistent set of values. Although all are couched in terms of equal opportunities, all are closer to an individualist than a substantive notion of equality, with the concessions to positive discrimination being formulated within the narrow compass of equivalent merit or qualifications. The following paragraphs deal with these cases in more detail.

The first three major cases challenging an affirmative action policy

---

[36] Directive (EEC) 76/207 on the implementation of the principle of equal treatment for men and women as regards access to employment, vocational training and promotion, and working conditions [1976] OJ L39/40.

[37] Recommendation 84/635/EEC of December 13, 1984 [1984] OJ 1984 L331, preamble, third recital.

concerned one of the mildest forms of preferential treatment, namely, the 'tie break' policy. According to such policies, preferential treatment can be used to redress under-representation of women in particular grades or occupations, but only in situations in which a man and a woman had the same qualifications. Even such a limited form of reverse discrimination was, however, initially struck down by the ECJ in the first major affirmative action case, *Kalanke*.[38] Taking its cue from Article 2(4) of the Equal Treatment Directive,[39] the ECJ situated Community law within the equal opportunities model. Thus the Court recognized that formal equality could well perpetuate disadvantage: equal treatment of two individuals may yield results which simply reflect their different starting points. It therefore accepted the legitimacy of measures which give an advantage to women with a view to improving their ability to compete equally with men in the labour market. However, it coupled this recognition of the limits of formal equality with a strong emphasis on the primacy of the individual and individual merit. 'National rules which guarantee women absolute and unconditional priority for appointment or promotion go beyond promoting equal opportunities and overstep the limits of the exception in Article 2(4) of the Directive'.[40] Advocate General Tesauro made this even more explicit, emphasizing that the individual's right not to be discriminated against on grounds of sex could not yield to the rights of the disadvantaged group to compensate for the discrimination suffered by that group in the past.[41] Also central to the decision in *Kalanke* is the attempt to draw a bright line between equality of opportunity, which is acceptable, and equality of results, which is not. Thus, stated the Court: 'In so far as it seeks to achieve equal representation of men and women in all grades and levels within a department, such a system substitutes for equality of opportunity as envisaged in Article 2(4) the equality of result which is only to be arrived at by providing such equality of opportunity'. In any event, according to Tesauro, equality of results will remain illusory unless it is a natural consequence of equal opportunity measures.

*Kalanke* is problematic in that its stress on individual merit in fact fails to solve the problem before it. Since both parties competing for the particular job had, by definition, equal merit, it is hard to see why the male applicant had any greater right on the assumed facts to be selected than the woman. There was thus no question of an 'innocent' person

---

[38] Case C-450/93 *Kalanke v. Freie Hansestadt Bremen* [1995] ECR I-3051, [1995] IRLR 660.

[39] Directive 76/207, above n. 36.     [40] *Kalanke*, above n. 38, at para. 22.

[41] *ibid.*, at 662.     [42] *ibid.*, at para. 23.

suffering detriment on the grounds of his sex. Given that there was no difference in merit, the Court's decision that gender cannot be used to tip the balance, even if the aim is to increase the participation of women in an under-represented area, implies that only a random selection, such as spinning a coin, would be acceptable. In addition, the Court omitted to examine what an 'equal opportunities' strategy would entail.

The result in *Kalanke* clearly flew in the face of a widening consensus on the usefulness of affirmative action policies, particularly in the public sector. The European Commission itself was faced with the need to salvage its affirmative action strategies. It did so by arguing that the Court in *Kalanke* had not rejected all preference-based policies, but only those which were automatic and left no scope for consideration of individual circumstances. The individualist concerns of the Court could be met, it suggested, by an affirmative action policy which permitted exceptions for individual men. It was this approach which was tested within two years in a second affirmative action case, *Marschall*.[43] *Marschall* differed from *Kalanke* only in that the requirement that equally qualified women be preferred to men was softened by a proviso allowing exceptions if 'reasons specific to another candidate predominate'. Despite the strong opinion of the Attorney General, who argued that there was no relevant distinction between this policy and that in *Kalanke*, the Court upheld the plan. Thus the Court held, Article 2(4) permitted a rule which gave priority to the promotion of female candidates where there were fewer women than men in the relevant post and both female and male candidates for the post were equally qualified, as long as the priority accorded to female candidates could in principle be overridden where an objectively assessed individual criterion tilted the balance in favour of the male candidate.[44]

This conclusion, like that in *Kalanke*, attempts to combine a substantive notion of equality with a continuing commitment to the primacy of the individual. Thus the Court focuses specifically on the mandate given in Article 2(4) to move beyond formal equality to a substantive notion, reiterating its view that 'Article 2(4) is specifically and exclusively designed to authorize measures which, although discriminatory in appearance, are in fact intended to eliminate or reduce actual instance of inequality which may exist in the reality of social life'.[45] Indeed it goes

---

[43] Case C-409/95 *Marschall v. Land Nordrhein Westfalen* [1997] ECR I-6363.

[44] *ibid.*, at para 35.

[45] *ibid.* at para 26; and see Case 312/86 *EC Commission v. France* [1988] ECR 6315 at para. 15 and *Kalanke*, above n. 38, at para. 18.

beyond *Kalanke* in its refusal to accept at face value the objectivity of the merit principle itself. Instead, it recognizes that an apparently objective merit based system can incorporate prejudicial assumptions:

> Even where male and female candidates are equally qualified, male candidates tend to be promoted in preference to female candidates particularly because of prejudices and stereotypes concerning the role and capacities of women in working life and the fear, for example, that women will interrupt their careers more frequently, that owing to household and family duties they will be less flexible in their working hours, or that they will be absent from work more frequently because of pregnancy, childbirth and breast-feeding;.[46]

Thus a measure giving preference to women candidates where men and women are equally qualified may fall within Article 2(4) if, subject to a savings clause, such a rule 'may counteract the prejudicial effects on female candidates of the attitudes and behaviour described above and thus reduce actual instances of inequality which may exist in the real world'.[47] However, despite this apparently robust notion of substantive equality, the Court will not give up the adherence to individuality which it evidenced so strongly in *Kalanke*. In a statement which is almost entirely devoid of reasoned support, the Court declares that a measure which guarantees absolute and unconditional priority to women goes beyond the limits of Article 2(4). By contrast, a rule which provides a guarantee of individual assessment which could override the presumption of priority to women remains within the scope of that provision.

There are two difficulties with the *Marschall* case, both necessitating further litigation for clarification. The first concerns the content of the savings clause. Under what circumstances would an equally qualified male candidate be able to rely on individual circumstances in order to justify defeating a claim by a woman for appointment to a grade in which women are under-represented? A male applicant could not claim to be more meritorious than the woman competitor, since by definition, merit is equal. Nor could he rely on age, seniority, or breadwinner status since, as the Court recognized, this would simply be reintroducing exclusionary or indirectly discriminatory criteria. It is possible that an alternative source of discrimination, such as race or disability, might rebut the presumption, but some further guidance would be needed to assist a court or decision-maker to balance the claims of a woman against those of other victims of discrimination.

The second difficulty with *Marschall* is that its justification is limited

---

[46] *Marschall*, above n. 43, at para. 29.    [47] *ibid.*, at para. 31.

to tie-break measures. It gives no guidance to the ECJ as to how to deal with measures which are not premised on equal qualification, but instead require quotas for jobs or membership of decision-making bodies. Yet it is precisely here that future challenges lie. Statistical objectives or quotas are a central part of the Commission's strategy to achieve balanced participation for men and women in decision-making.[48] Gender specific programmes to achieve a higher level of representation of women in public bodies are already in use, particularly in Germany,[49] where, in the State of Schleswig-Holstein, for example, the general rule states that, where only one seat can be nominated or delegated, alternating preferences should be given to men and women. Similarly, explicit measures have been instituted to ensure that women are represented on works' and personnel councils. As we have seen above, even in Britain, in which a symmetrical approach to affirmative action is predominant, 'women-only' training programmes are permitted where it can be shown that women are under-represented in a trade or profession. The same is true for training schemes set aside for black or other minority workers.

Both these difficulties have rapidly presented themselves to the ECJ for resolution. The extent to which claims of an individual can defeat the social policy of advancing women was central to the policy in the case of *Badeck*.[50] The case concerned a particularly far-reaching and sophisticated programme to remedy the under-representation of women in public offices, which included setting aside half of the posts in sectors in which women were under-represented for qualified women; allocating at least half of available training places to women in trained occupations in which women were under-represented, and providing that at least half the members of public bodies such as commissions and boards of directors should be women. The Hesse provisions were particularly sophisticated in their approach to the merit principle. The capabilities and experience acquired by looking after children or other persons requiring care had to be taken into account in so far as they were of importance for the suitability of applicants. On the other hand, the family status or income of the partner should not be taken into account; nor should

---

[48] Medium Term Community Action programme on equal opportunities for women and men: see EC *Equal Opportunities Magazine* No. 2 July 1997; Council Recommendation (EC) 96/694 on the balanced participation of men and women in the decision-making process [1996] OJ L319/11.

[49] All the examples of German measures are taken from N. Colneric, 'Making Equality Law More Effective: Lessons From The German Experience' [1996] 3 *Cardozo Women's Law Journal* 229 at 239 ff.

[50] Case C-158/97 *Badeck's Application, Re* [2000] All ER (EC) 289.

part-time work, leave, or delays in completing training as a result of looking after children or dependants. Seniority, age, and the date of last promotion could be considered only in so far as they were of importance for the suitability, performance, and capability of applicants. Most importantly, the savings clause went further than a simple reference to individual characteristics of the applicant. Instead, it specified five cases in which the rule of advancement of women may be overridden. The first two placed actual parenting responsibilities ahead of gender preference, whether the input is from a man or a woman. Thus priority should be given to individuals who had taken time out of work or worked on a part-time basis in order to look after children or other dependants. The fourth and fifth gave similar recognition to other social priorities, allowing the preferential treatment rule to be overridden in order to promote disabled persons or to end a period of long-term unemployment. It was the preference given to those who served longer than the compulsory period of military service, which could potentially be indirectly discriminatory.

The challenge to the Hesse provisions confronted the ECJ with two of the main issues of principle it had established in *Kalanke*: the primacy of the individual, and the difference between equality of opportunity and equality of results. Thus, the applicants argued, the Hesse statute contravened the merit principle by choosing candidates not because of their merits, but their sex. Moreover, it breached the right of all individuals to equal opportunities at the start, by attempting to ensure results which were advantageous to a specific category of persons. The ECJ, however, side-stepped these principled arguments in favour of a formulaic approach. Having rehearsed the findings in *Kalanke* and *Marschall*, it distilled a two-part formula which it proceeded to apply to each of the elements of the case before it. The formula, representing in large part the approach in *Marschall* rather than *Kalanke*, would make a measure giving priority to women in under-represented sectors of the public service compatible with Community law if (i) it does not automatically and unconditionally give priority to women when women and men are equally qualified; and (ii) the candidatures are the subject of an objective assessment which takes into account the specific personal situations of all candidates.[51] Applying the formula, the ECJ held the scheme as a whole to be compatible with the Equal Treatment Directive and *a fortiori* with the new Article 141(4), as introduced by the Treaty of Amsterdam. In doing so, however, it made little attempt to advance the law beyond that in

---

[51] *ibid.*, at para. 23.

*Marschall.* The ECJ did accept the legitimacy of the redefinition of merit in the Hesse provisions, stating that it was permissible to take into account criteria which although neutral on their face in general favour women. However, apart from accepting the validity of the particular savings clause in the Hesse statute, no further guidance was given on the type of individual circumstances which could defeat a claim for preferential treatment.

This formulaic approach differs markedly from that of Advocate General Saggio, whose opinion attempts to develop some of the principles in the previous cases, and in particular reiterates the dual emphasis on substantive equality and the primacy of the individual. The reconciliation of the two, he argues, lies in the development of a proportionality criterion. Equal treatment, or formal equality, comes into conflict with substantive equality only if the remedial measure, in this case positive action in favour of women, is disproportionate, either in that it demands excessive sacrifices from those who do not belong to the group, or when the social reality does not justify it. Positive action could therefore be lawful provided it is proportionate in this sense. However, individual merit, in his view, remains the governing principle behind the reconciliation of equality with reverse discrimination. Provided an appointment or promotion is made on the basis of an individual's suitability and qualifications for the job, it is permissible to use sex as a secondary criterion, tilting the balance in favour of women in order to remedy an under-representation of women in a particular grade or occupation. It is only therefore permissible to institute automatic preferences for women to redress under-representation if there is an objective examination of the professional and personal profile of each candidate and there is no bar on the selection of a man if he is more suitable for the job. This in turn requires merit to be purified of discriminatory assumptions, and thereafter insists that merit is the only basis of equality in selection.

Such arguments are, however, conspicuously absent in the ECJ's judgment in *Badeck*. Their absence makes it particularly difficult to deal with the second problem left open by *Marschall*, namely policies which move beyond a tie-break, and require the selection of a woman even if she is not equally qualified with a man in order to improve the proportion of women in a particular grade or career. This question was immediately raised before the ECJ in the most recent affirmative action case, *Abrahamsson.*[52] This case arose from the perception by the Swedish government

---

[52] Case C-407/98 *Abrahamsson v. Fogelqvist* [2000] IRLR 732.

that progress towards a fairer allocation of teaching posts as between women and men in higher education had been particularly slow, requiring an extraordinary effort in the short term to ensure a significant increase in the number of women professors. Thus a regulation was promulgated requiring preference to be granted to a candidate of the under-represented sex provided she possessed sufficient qualifications; even if these were less than a candidate from the opposite sex, unless the difference between the candidates' qualifications was so great as to give rise to a breach of the requirement of objectivity in the making of appointments. The case concerned a challenge to the appointment of a woman to the post of Professor of Hydrospheric Sciences, even though her male competitor had been judged by the selection committee to be clearly better qualified in the scientific field.

In its judgment, the Court made it clear that its support for substantive equality was subordinate to the primacy of the individual. The selection of candidates under the Swedish provisions was 'ultimately based on the mere fact of belonging to the under-represented sex, and this is so even if the merits of the candidates so selected are inferior to those of a candidate of the opposite sex'. This combined with the fact that candidates were not subjected to an objective assessment taking account of the their specific personal situations, meant that the method of selection was not permitted by Article 2(4) of the Directive. Nor was it permitted by the somewhat wider provisions of Article 141(4). This was because, although Article 141(4) permitted measures providing for special advantages intended to compensate for disadvantage, 'it cannot be inferred form this that it allows a selection method .... which [is] .... disproportionate to the aim pursued'. The reasons for these conclusions are not elaborated, least of all the final cryptic reference to proportionality. No indication is given of what aims are acceptable, or how closely the means should fit the ends. Nor did the ECJ comment on the approach to proportionality set out in the opinion of Advocate General Saggio in *Badeck*. Yet proportionality could well be the most sensitive measure for the legitimacy of affirmative action. It has certainly been central to the jurisprudence of the US (see section (iv) below).

## (III) FAIR EMPLOYMENT AND NORTHERN IRELAND: EQUAL OPPORTUNITY OR SUBSTANTIVE JUSTICE

Unlike its counterparts in sex and race discrimination, legislation promoting fair employment in Northern Ireland departs in crucial respects from the basic tenets of the principle of formal equality. The aim of the

Northern Ireland fair employment legislation, FETO,[53] is openly substantive: to reduce the striking differences in unemployment levels between Catholic and Protestants in Northern Ireland.[54] The legislation therefore expressly aims to secure 'fair participation in employment',[55] a term which, although 'remarkably indeterminate'[56] and nowhere defined in the statute itself, has clear substantive connotations. This is reinforced by the express provision that 'anything lawfully done in pursuance of affirmative action' does not breach the principle of equality of opportunity.[57] Similarly, there are important deviations from the individualism of the first approach, most conspicuously in departing from the fault principle. The employer is made responsible for promoting fair participation simply where disparities are apparent even though there is no proof that the employer was guilty of unlawful discrimination. It is clear from these provisions that fair participation is to be measured in terms of groups rather than particular individuals. This is reinforced by the fact that fair participation is not available as a right of any individual, but only to members of the Protestant and Catholic communities.[58] Finally, the statute deviates from the notion of a neutral State. In marked contrast to the aversion to contract compliance as a remedial measure for race and sex discrimination, the legislation explicitly provides that public authorities refrain from contracting with employers who are found to be in default of various provisions under the legislation.[59]

Given that the legislation has clearly moved beyond formal equality, does it fall within the substantive or the equal opportunities approaches? There are some visible gestures in the direction of a substantive approach: in particular, its aim is to secure fair participation in employment. But closer examination places the legislation squarely within the equal opportunities model. Indeed, the legislation explicitly declares itself as having the aim of promoting equal opportunity[60] where equality of opportunity too is

---

[53] Fair Employment and Treatment (Northern Ireland) Order 1998 (FETO) SI 1998/3162 (NI 21).

[54] Catholics were more than twice as likely to be unemployed as Protestants with the same educational qualifications in 1991 (Fair Employment Commission *The Key Facts: Religion and Community Background in Northern Ireland* (1995)).

[55] FETO art. 4.

[56] C. McCrudden, 'Affirmative Action and Fair Participation: Interpreting the Fair Employment Act 1989' [1992] 21 ILJ 170 at 176.

[57] FETO, art 5(3).    [58] McCrudden, above n. 56, p. 181.    [59] FETO, art. 64.

[60] This aim is consistent with that recommended by the Standing Advisory Commission on Human Rights *Religious Discrimination and Equality of Opportunity in Northern Ireland, Report on Fair Employment* Cm. 237 (HMSO, 1987).

defined primarily procedurally.[61] Most importantly, although affirmative action is given a central role, reverse discrimination is not permitted. Instead, affirmative action denotes such strategies as the adoption of practices encouraging participation, or the modification or abandonment of practices restricting or discouraging such participation. This is underscored by the clear priority given to the merit principle: in all cases, due allowance must be made for any material difference in suitability. As Hepple perceptively comments: 'We know . . . that there is a connection between lack of educational and skill qualifications and belonging to the Catholic community. The appeal to "merit" must appear disingenuous to members of the disadvantaged community who are rejected as "unsuitable"'.[62]

Despite this relatively narrow vision of equal opportunities, the legislation goes significantly further than EC law in actively promoting equal opportunity. Its regulatory scheme, requiring proactive steps to be taken by employers to correct imbalances in the workforce, has the potential to yield more substantive results than a simple exhortation to provide equal opportunities coupled with sanctions limited to proven acts of discrimination. Its emphasis on outreach measures and encouragement of applicants from different communities is particularly appropriate in the context of the social problem it is aimed at: namely, substantial segregation of working places, reinforced by high levels of sectarian harassment[63] and a 'chill' factor deterring potential applicants from applying for jobs in establishments known to be dominated by members of a different religious community. These issues will be explored in more detail in Chapter Seven.

## (IV) SYMMETRY V. SUBSTANCE: THE US SUPREME COURT

The US Supreme Court has been the arena of fierce struggle between judicial proponents of a formal, symmetrical view of equality and those who advocate a more substantive position. The use of affirmative action policies began in the US as a court-ordered remedy in cases of proved past discrimination.[64] This approach was upheld by the Supreme Court,[65] and indeed extended to cases under the Equal Protection Clause of the US Constitution. The Court in these cases, having signalled a clear

---

[61] FETO art. 5(4).
[62] Hepple, 'Discrimination and Equality of Opportunity—Northern Irish Lessons' [1990] 10 OJLS 408, p. 413.
[63] (1996) 70 EOR 11.      [64] Mandated by Title VII of the Civil Rights Act 1964.
[65] *Franks v. Bowman Transportation Co.* (1975) 424 US 747, 96 S Ct 1251.

departure from an abstract, formal view of justice, soon began to move beyond both individualism and the idea of a neutral State. As a start, it has been accepted that court-ordered reverse discrimination need not be restricted to the victim. Non-victims may also be beneficiaries provided they are members of a group previously suffering from invidious discrimination.[66] In addition, the emphasis on both fault and merit have been weakened. Thus the Supreme Court soon began to accept voluntarily instituted affirmative action programmes, despite the lack of proven fault on the part of the employer. Instead, the focus is again on the social context in which the equality concept operates: in upholding voluntary affirmative action programmes, the Court has only required sufficient evidence of imbalances and segregation for which the employer appears responsible,[67] not proof of fault against the defendant.

This approach is exemplified in *Johnson v. Santa Clara*[68] which, like *Kalanke* and *Marschall*, concerned a voluntarily instituted affirmative action plan for hiring and promoting women and minorities in a context of severe under-representation of both groups in the workforce. The aim was expressly result oriented, the target being ultimately to achieve a workforce of which about a third of jobs were held by women. The *Johnson* plan was more flexible than that of *Kalanke*, in that the sex of a qualified applicant was only a factor among several to be considered. It was also more controversial in that, as in *Abrahamsson*, a woman could be promoted even if she was marginally less well qualified than a male applicant. The plan was challenged when a qualified woman was promoted ahead of a man to the position of road dispatcher, a grade in which to date none of the 238 positions had been held by a woman. The male employee, who in fact had a marginally better test score, complained of sex discrimination contrary to Title VII. The *Johnson* policy received warm judicial endorsement. Brennan J, giving judgment for the court, declared that it was no violation of Title VII to take sex into account in promoting a woman over a male employee where this was in pursuance of an affirmative action plan to remedy the under-representation of women and minorities in traditionally segregated job classifications.

Similarly, the US Supreme Court has rejected the neutral view of the State, instead upholding both the right and the responsibility of the State to use its public and market powers in remedying discrimination. Thus in

---

[66] *United States v. Paradise* (1988) 480 US 149, 107 S Ct 1053.
[67] *United Steelworkers v. Weber*, above n. 14.      [68] (1987) 480 US 616, 107 S Ct 1442.

*Fullilove v. Klutznick*[69] the Court upheld a policy setting aside 10 per cent of federal funds granted for the provision of public works to procure services from minority owned businesses, even if the latter were not the lowest bidder. Chief Justice Burger stated specifically that in a remedial context, it was not necessary for Congress to act in a wholly colour-blind way. Indeed, substantive reverse discrimination of this sort was viewed as a necessary means to achieve equal economic opportunities.

However, recent cases in the US have been marked by the ascendancy of a far more symmetrical approach. This is reflected in the controversies within the case-law on two main issues: the 'innocent' third party who is discriminated against on grounds of race or sex in the process of preferring minorities or women; and the standard of scrutiny. So far as the 'innocent third party' is concerned, the Court has attempted to reach a balance (not dissimilar to that hinted at by the Advocate General in *Badeck*) whereby individuals who are not members of the target group are not expected to bear too great a burden in redressing the disadvantage of the preferred group. Since no one has an absolute right to a job, promotion or training place, the person refused a position on grounds of sex or race is not unduly burdened. However, loss of an existing job (for example in a redundancy situation) has been held to be too serious a prospect to permit individual interests to be subordinated. The result has been that, except in the case of identified victims of discrimination, the vested interests of 'dispreferred' workers to retain seniority rights and therefore remain in work have generally trumped the goals of achieving and maintaining a balanced workforce. The effects of this compromise are evident in *Wygant v. Jackson Board of Education*,[70] in which a collective agreement was struck down as contrary to the 14th Amendment because it gave preferential protection against layoffs to minority employees. The result was, however, largely to undermine the effects of positive action programmes incorporating under-represented workers: such workers were the 'last in' and therefore inevitably the 'first out'.

The second controversial issue in US case-law concerns the standard of scrutiny which should be applied in affirmative action cases. The Supreme Court has a well developed jurisprudence requiring 'strict scrutiny' of any classifications which burden blacks: such a classification must serve a compelling governmental interest and be narrowly tailored to achieve that aim.[71] In practice, the insistence on strict scrutiny has

---

[69] (1980) 448 US 448, 100 S Ct 2758.    [70] (1986) 476 US 267, 106 S Ct 1842.
[71] *Korematsu v. United States* (1994) 323 US 214, 65 S Ct 193.

outlawed most racist policies or practices discriminating against blacks. This raises the question: does an equally strict standard of review apply to racial classifications which benefit blacks at the expense of whites? US case-law is criss-crossed with deeply conflicting judicial statements on this point. In *Bakke* Powell J, consistent with his symmetrical stance, was unequivocal in his rejection of the argument that strict scrutiny applies only to classifications that disadvantage discrete and insular minorities. Instead, he argued, all kinds of race-conscious criteria should be subject to the 'most exacting of judicial examination'.[72] By contrast four judges (Brennan, White, Marshall, and Blackmunn JJ), taking a substantive asymmetric view, held that a less stringent standard of review should apply to racial classifications designed to further remedial purposes than to pernicious classifications. On this view, it was sufficient for the policy to be 'substantially related' to the achievement of an important government objective, a standard known as intermediate review.[73] The issue remained unresolved until, in two crucial cases in the last decades of the twentieth century, *City of Richmond v. J A Croson*[74] and *Adarand v. Pena*,[75] the exacting standard of strict scrutiny won the day.

However, a closer examination of the judgments in *Adarand* reveals that the dispute between the asymmetric and the symmetric approaches continues despite the triumph of strict scrutiny. While O'Connor J agreed with Thomas J and Scalia J on the standard of strict scrutiny, in fact their interpretation of that standard differed markedly. Thomas and Scalia JJ upheld the strict standard from a strongly symmetrical and individualistic camp. However, O'Connor J, giving judgment for the court, articulated a sensitive synthesis of the difficult opposing views. She was at pains to dispute the notion that strict scrutiny is strict in theory but fatal in fact.[76] Indeed, she held, the federal government might well have a compelling interest to act on the basis of race to overcome the 'persistence of both the practice and lingering effects of racial discrimination against minority groups'.[77] In this respect, her approach incorporates important elements of the clearly substantive view expressed in dissent by Stevens J,[78] who rejected the strict scrutiny standard by reasserting the fundamental difference between a policy designed to perpetuate a caste system and one seeking to eliminate racial discrimination.

---

[72] *Bakke*, above n. 1.                    [73] *Fullilove v Klutznick*, above n. 72 (*per* Marshall J).
[74] (1989) 488 US 469, 109 S Ct 706.
[75] *Adarand*, above n. 2.                 [76] *ibid.*, at 2117.
[77] Rehnquist, Kennedy, and Thomas JJ all agreed.
[78] Joined by Souter, Ginsburg, and Breyer JJ.

In most post-*Adarand* cases, the controversy has primarily occurred in respect of voting rights. The clear discrimination against blacks in the US, effectively depriving them of their votes, led to a systematic positive action programme. This included as a central strategy, the redrawing of electoral districts to give black voters a better opportunity to influence the outcome of elections.[79] The deliberate creation of districts with black majorities has caused deep controversy within the US, particularly in recent years.[80] Not surprisingly, it has led to a spate of litigation,[81] in which the Supreme Court has been required to decide whether such gerrymandering is necessary to ensure that blacks have equal opportunity to elect representatives of their choice; or, whether it reinforces harmful racial stereotypes and impedes progress towards a multi-racial society. The divergence between those members of the Supreme Court who take a substantive approach and those who take a symmetrical approach emerges more clearly than ever. Thus in the 1996 case of *Shaw v. Hunt*,[82] the majority struck down a congressionally mandated redistricting plan on the ground that it was not narrowly tailored to serve a compelling State interest. Rehnquist J for the Court declared emphatically that all laws classifying on racial grounds are constitutionally suspect. This is true even if the reason is benign or the purpose remedial. This fiercely symmetrical approach was countered for the minority by Stevens J, who declared that the sorry state of race relations in North Carolina was sufficient reason to attempt to facilitate greater participation of blacks in the electoral process. The crucial casting vote remained that of O'Connor J, who attempted, as she did in *Adarand*, to use the strict scrutiny test in a way which was sensitive to the range of conflicting interests. Most importantly she has reaffirmed her position that strict scrutiny should not be equated with total prohibition of affirmative action. Thus she declared in *Bush v. Vera* that the State could indeed have a compelling interest in pursuing equality of opportunity of voters to elect representatives of their choice; and that it was possible to find means which were 'narrowly tailored to those ends' by producing electoral districts which aim to produce black majorities, but which do not deviate too much from

[79] Voting Rights Act 1965, amended in 1982 to include a 'results-based' test to ascertain whether the right had been violated.

[80] See, e.g. A. Thernstrom, 'Voting Rights: Another Affirmative Action Mess' (1996) 43 *UCLA Law Review* 2031.

[81] *Shaw v. Reno* (1993) 509 US 630, 113 S Ct 2816; *Miller v. Johnson* (1995) 515 US 900, 115 S Ct 2475; *United States v. Hays* (1995) 5 US 737, 115 S Ct 2431; *Bush v. Vera* (1996) 517 US 952, 116 S Ct 1941.

[82] *Shaw v. Hunt* (1996) 517 US 899, 116 S Ct 1894.

established districting principles.[83] By contrast, the strictly symmetrical
judges (although concurring with O'Connor J) make it extremely difficult
if not impossible to justify deliberate use of race in drawing districts.[84] At
the same time, a vocal minority[85] continues to advocate a more substantive
approach.

## III  AIMS AND EFFECTIVENESS

The discussion above has demonstrated that the principled objections to
affirmative action can be plausibly repudiated. The ferocity of the controversy over its legitimacy has, however, deflected attention away from
an equally problematic issue: what are its aims, and is affirmative action
effective in achieving those aims? The ECJ has made little progress in
explicating means and ends. The *Kalanke* case simply outlaws affirmative
action.[86] *Marschall* although reaching the opposite results, avoids any
sustained discussion either of which aims are legitimate and the extent to
which the means must fit the ends. Although the Advocate General in
*Badeck* explicitly introduces a proportionality test, and the Court in
*Abrahamsson* holds that Article 141(4) must be interpreted as a proportionality measure, neither suggests legitimate ends or the standard of
scrutiny of the means. By contrast, the 'strict scrutiny' test used by the
US courts, requires a demonstration of legitimate State aims, and of
means that are narrowly tailored to achieve those ends. This has forced
the US Supreme Court to grapple with these questions. In the course of
discussion, several aims of affirmative action have been articulated. These
can be grouped under three main headings, namely: (i) the removal of
discriminatory barriers or redressing past disadvantage; (ii) the representation of the interests of the previously excluded group; and (iii) the
fostering of diversity and the creation of role models.

### (I)  REMOVAL OF BARRIERS AND REDRESSING
### PAST DISADVANTAGE

The use of reverse discrimination as a remedy for past discrimination is,
as has been seen, well known in the US. A closer look at the cases of both
*Kalanke* and *Marschall* reveal a similar strategic impulse to remove
discriminatory barriers within the German public services. Despite

---

[83] *Bush v. Vera*, above n. 84, at 1969–70.
[84] *ibid.*, at 1971 (*per* Kennedy J), at 1972–3 (*per* Thomas and Scalia JJ).
[85] Stevens, Ginsburg, and Breyer JJ.
[86] See A-G Jacobs' opinion in *Marschall*, above n. 43.

apparently objective eligibility standards, there are many hidden obstacles to women's advancement.[87] This is because the assessment process in the German public services normally gravitates towards uniform results. Faced with numerous equally qualified candidates, the selectors have created auxiliary selection criteria, the most prominent ones being duration of service, age, and number of dependants. It is well established that all these criteria, despite being equally applicable to both men and women, in practice exclude substantially more women than men. Against this background, the tie-break provisions introduced by the City of Bremen can be seen to be part of a strategic attempt to overcome hidden barriers to women's advancement. Indeed, the ECJ is aware of this process, acknowledging in *Marschall* that the 'mere fact that a male candidate and a female candidate are equally qualified does not mean that they have the same chances' and upholding in *Badeck* the use of criteria which although apparently neutral in practice assist women in countering existing disadvantage.

Redressing past discrimination and removing present barriers are clearly legitimate State interests. More difficult, however, is the question whether the use of gender or race preferences is a means which is 'narrowly tailored' to achieve those ends. On the assumption that, in the absence of barriers, there would be a random spread of men and women, and members of different ethnic groups across the labour force and government, the very fact that a group is seriously under-represented in a sphere or activity is evidence of the subtle operation of often invisible barriers. Yet could this not be dealt with by the familiar principle of indirect discrimination? Indirect discrimination expressly aims to remove apparently neutral barriers which in fact function to exclude more women than men unless they can be justified.[88] However, it has proved to be too clumsy a tool to achieve its aims. As we saw in Chapter Four, the apparently clear legislative definition of indirect discrimination in British law leaves a host of questions unanswered. Must the 'requirement or condition' be an absolute bar? And what is the 'proportion' a proportion of? The whole population or just a part of it, such as the working population, the establishment, or other individuals with the same qualifications? Applicants seeking to prove indirect discrimination have found that the courts give varying and often unpredictable answers to these

---

[87] D. Schiek, 'More Positive Action in Community Law' [1998] ILJ 155; D. Schiek, 'Positive Action in Community Law' [1996] ILJ 239.
[88] Sex Discrimination Act 1975, s. 1(1)(b)(i).

questions.[89] Equally problematic, it is left to an individual victim to initiate court proceedings and argue each of these issues. Finally, even if she
can surmount all these barriers, she may find that an employer successfully shows that the criteria, despite being exclusionary, are justifiable by
reference to the needs of the business.

Affirmative action resolves all of these difficulties. Instead of relying on
litigation by individual victims, the employer takes the initiative. Nor is it
necessary to prove that an exclusionary rule has had a disproportionate
impact. Instead, it is sufficient to demonstrate a clear pattern of under-
representation of women in particular grades or occupations. The complex questions above are unnecessary. Moreover, discriminatory selection
criteria are unequivocally removed: by creating a presumption in favour
of women in conditions of equal merit, it makes it impossible for
such criteria to be reintroduced surreptitiously through subjective
decision-making.

Phrased in this way, affirmative action can be legitimated as an effective
means of overcoming hidden barriers. At the same time, this formulation
reveals its very limited impact. Most importantly, while preference policies may change the gender or racial composition of some higher paid
occupations, they do not challenge the underlying structural and institutional forces leading to the discrimination. As Young argues,[90] because
affirmative action diagnoses the problem as one of maldistribution of
privileged positions, its objective is limited to the redistribution of such
positions among under-represented groups. However, this narrow distributive definition of racial and gender justice leaves out the equally
important issues of institutional organization and decision-making
power. The under-representation of women in higher positions in the
employment ladder, both public and private, is only partially solved by
inserting some women into those positions. While some women 'make it
to the top', the vast majority will remain in poorly paid, low status jobs. It
is not surprising that, in practice, reverse discrimination is often found to
do no more than favour middle class women or blacks who are already
relatively privileged in society. This outcome is particularly striking in
India, where it has been found that the main beneficiaries of affirmative
action programmes reserving benefits for members of scheduled castes
and tribes (SC/ST categories) were those who were already upwardly

---

[89] For a recent example see Case 167/97 *Seymour Smith* [1999] ECR I-623. For further
discussion see S. Fredman, *Women and the Law* (Clarendon Press, 1997), pp. 287–300.
[90] I. Young, *Justice and the Politics of Difference* (Princeton University Press, 1990), p. 193.

mobile and already had some resources. Indeed, Menski points out: 'The benefits of the SC/ST category are now snatched away and appropriated by a thin elite layer of SC/ST members and their offspring, while the vast majority remain as backward and disadvantaged as ever'.[91] For fundamental change to occur, the structural and institutional causes of exclusion need to be changed, including the division of labour in the home, the interaction between work in the family and work in the paid labour force, education and others. Indeed, this insight was recognized and articulated by Attorney General Tesauro in *Kalanke* when he said: 'Formal numerical equality is an objective which may salve some consciences, but it will remain illusory . . . unless it goes together with measures which are genuinely destined to achieve equality . . . In the final analysis, that which is necessary above all is a substantial change in the economic, social and cultural model which is at the root of the inequalities'.[92]

## (II) REPRESENTATION AND PERSPECTIVE

A more dynamic way of justifying the use of affirmative action policies is to argue that the very presence of women or minorities in higher status positions will lead to structural changes. On this argument, women or minorities in such positions will be able to represent the needs and interests of their groups in decision-making, changing both the agenda of decision-making and their outcomes. Women will, for example, be in a position to argue for maternity leave, child-care, and family friendly policies, thus paving the way for more women to enter these positions. This representative function is important, on this view, for both formal decision-making institutions such as legislatures or trade union executive bodies, and for informal decision-making. Managers, civil servants, judges, professionals and chief administrators make a host of decisions, all of which require that the interests of women or minorities be properly represented.

This has indeed been the rationale driving recent moves at EU level to achieve balanced participation of men and women in decision-making. At a conference in April 1999, Padraig Flynn, who was then the responsible Commissioner, emphasized that increasing the numbers of women in decision-making was crucial not only to achieve the 'quantitative objective of a numerical balance of women and men' but also the 'qualitative

---

[91] W. F. Menski, 'The Indian Experience and its Lessons for Britain' in B. Hepple and E. Szyszcak (eds.), *Discrimination and the Limits of the Law* (Mansell, 1992), p. 300 at p. 330.
[92] *Kalanke*, above n. 38, [1995] IRLR 660 at 665.

objective of improving decision-making'. Citing studies which revealed that a critical mass of about 30 per cent of women was needed to 'create the necessary dynamic' to allow women's concerns, needs, and interests to be taken into account, he went on to declare that 'the different but complementary and mutually enriching views of men and women should be reflected in all policies shaping the citizen's life'.[93]

However, more support is needed to underpin the assumption that the mere presence of women will guarantee that women's interests will be articulated. As Phillips puts it, we generally reject a politics of presence in favour of a politics of ideas. 'The shift from direct to representative democracy has shifted the emphasis from *who* the politicians are to *what* (policies, preferences, ideas), they represent, and in doing so has made accountability to the electorate the pre-eminent radical concern'.[94] Two possible arguments could be mounted to justify the renewed emphasis on presence, but both turn out to be problematic. The first is to argue that any woman or minority will inevitably articulate the needs, interests, and concerns of other women or minorities. Her presence is therefore all that is needed. This appears to be the basis of Commissioner Flynn's unhesitating assertion that women and men have different views. However, although there is some evidence that women may have a different moral sense to men,[95] modern feminists are acutely aware of the range of differing interests among women, and indeed of the potential for conflict. Attempts to construct an 'essential woman' merely land up replicating the dominant ideology about women, obscuring crucial differences in class, race, sexual orientation, etc. This is equally true of minority groups: the assumption that black groups share common interests merely veils deep differences based on religion, country of origin, or language.

A second way of justifying the representative function of affirmative action is to accept that the mere presence of women is not sufficient, but to argue instead that women beneficiaries of affirmative action are there as genuine representatives of other women. But this in turn requires some mechanism of accountability. Our experience of the Thatcher years demonstrated clearly that a woman in power is not necessarily a representative of women's interests. Indeed, she may have achieved power partly because she was able to conform to a male ethic and thereby suppress any belief in the importance of articulating women's concerns. There are no

---

[93] See http://europa.eu.int/comm/employment_social/equ_opp/index_en.htm.

[94] A. Phillips, *The Politics of Presence* (Clarendon Press, 1995), p. 4.

[95] See C. Gilligan, *In a Different Voice: Psychological Theory and Women's Development* (Harvard University Press, 1982), especially ch. 5.

mechanisms for accountability in affirmative action plans in public or private employment, and even on decision-making bodies, including the legislature, women decision-makers are not cast as accountable to women constituents. Even if there was such a link, it is not clear that representation of a minority interest could make an impact on decisions. Indeed, minority representation could well consign a group to perpetual defeat.

There is, however, a third and more promising way to justify the use of affirmative action policies to improve the extent to which women's concerns are addressed. This is to argue, as Young does, that decision-making is wrongly conceived of as a process of bargaining between interest groups, each of which represents a fixed set of interests, and whose representatives are mandated to further those interests and to compromise only as a quid pro quo.[96] Instead, it is argued, decision-making is a result of communication and discussion based on more than egotistical impulses, but on a desire to reach a fair and reasoned result.[97] Participants are prepared to recognize others' concerns and beliefs in their own right, not just in order to wrest return favours catering for their constituents' interests. In addition, this approach does not take an abstract, impartial view of rationality, but recognizes that the particular life experience of the decision-maker is reflected in his or her view. Since gender and race remain such strong determinants of a person's life experience, the overwhelming predominance of one gender or race in decision-making fora make it unlikely that the experience and perspectives of the excluded group will be articulated.[98] Indeed, a recent study in Britain demonstrated that the biggest barrier to advancement for ethnic minorities, women and disabled people within the senior Civil Service is believed to be a deeply embedded culture which acts to exclude those who are different from traditional Civil Service employees, who are generally middle class, middle-aged white men.[99] On this view, it is possible to characterize women's presence as functioning to open up new perspectives on decision-making, to cast light on assumptions that the dominant group perceives as universal, and to enhance the store of 'social knowledge'.

Corresponding to the rejection of interest group politics is a rejection of the notion of fixed interest groups. It is worth reiterating Young's argument, seen first in Chapter One, that groups are better understood, not as fixed categories with impermeable boundaries, but as a set of relationships between different people. Such a relational understanding

---

[96] Young, above n. 93, pp. 118–19.  
[97] *ibid.*, pp. 92–4.  
[98] Phillips, above n. 97, p. 52.  
[99] (1999) 87 EOR 4.

moves beyond the notion that a group consists of members who all share the same fixed attributes and have nothing in common with members of other groups. Instead, a group is characterized as a social process of interaction in which some people have an affinity with each other. Assertion of affinity with a group may change with social context and with life changes; and members may have interests which differ from other members of the group but are similar to members of other groups.[100] This approach makes sense of the notion that women or minorities may have distinct perspectives, which the very process of exclusion negates, and therefore which need to be guaranteed a place in deliberative decision-making. But it also makes it unnecessary to conceive of women or minorities as groups with a fixed essence, or indeed to require women to perform a specific representative function. In addition, it demonstrates the necessity for a critical mass both to reflect a diversity within the social group in question and to make the common interests more audible.

### (III) ROLE MODELS AND DIVERSITY

The pursuit of diversity and the provision of role models are related goals which draw on the insights discussed above in relation to the importance of minority perspectives in influencing decisions. A third and related justification for reverse discrimination is that it provides diversity in an educational institution or workplace; and that it facilitates the provision of role models. The justification for diversity as an aim is in fact remarkably similar to that elaborated by Young above. In *Bakke*,[101] Powell J justified affirmative action in university admissions thus: 'An otherwise qualified medical student with a particular background—whether it be ethnic, geographic, culturally advantaged or disadvantaged—may bring to a professional school of medicine, experiences, outlook, and ideas that enrich the training of its student body and better equip its graduates to render with understanding their vital service to humanity'.[102] In other words, where a group has been excluded from a particular setting, be it a workforce or an educational institution, the likelihood is that the perspectives and experiences of members of the excluded group, particularly those relating to its exclusion, will be undervalued, misunderstood, or ignored by the dominant group, making it impossible for the excluded group to change its disadvantaged position. While diversity operates to change the perspectives of the dominant group, the provision of role models operates on the self-perception of excluded groups, piercing

---

[100] Young, above n. 93, pp. 171–2.     [101] Above n. 1.     [102] *ibid.*, at 314, 2760.

stereotypes and giving them the self confidence to move into non-traditional positions.

Both these aims have been highly controversial in US case-law. In *Bakke*, Powell J considered that diversity could be a factor which might tip the balance in favour of a minority student in competition with another similar applicant. However, this did not receive explicit support from the other judgments in the case. More recently, the US Court of Appeals emphatically rejected the argument, put forward by University of Texas law school, that its policy of giving substantial preference in its admissions programme to blacks and Mexican Americans was justifiable on the grounds of the educational benefits that flow from a racially and ethnically diverse student body.[103] Taking a narrowly individualist view of affirmative action, the Court held that diversity contradicts rather than furthers the aims of equal protection. By treating minorities as a group, rather than as individuals, the judge argued, such a policy uses racial criteria unlawfully, undercutting the goal of the Fourteenth Amendment, namely, the end of racially motivated state action. A similar trend is visible in relation to the provision of role models. Thus Powell J in *Bakke* accepted as permissible the goals of supplying more professional people for under-served communities although he did not see this (or educational diversity) as necessitating a quota system. However, in *Wygant*,[104] the defendant Board of Education argued, *inter alia*, that its policy of protecting newly hired minority teachers against lay-offs was justified by the State's duty to reduce racial discrimination by providing minority role models for minority students. This Powell J roundly rejected on the grounds that it would permit affirmative action long past the point of its remedial purpose.

The arguments in both these cases can, however, be countered. The view that using race to promote educational diversity is impermissible is based on an explicit rejection of the ways in which race (or gender) affect a person's life experience, opportunities, and perspectives. According to Circuit Judge Smith: 'To believe that a person's race controls his point of view is to stereotype him'. Yet the same judge was prepared to accept that a university may properly favour one applicant over another because of issues such as an applicant's relationship to school alumni, whether an applicant's parents attended college, or the applicant's economic and social background. As argued above, there is no need to assume that a

---

[103] *Hopwood v. Texas* (1996) 78 F 3d 932 (US Ct of Apps (5th Cir)).
[104] Wygant, above n. 3.

person's race 'controls' her point of view; indeed that would be wrongly to essentialize her. But this is not to say that her particular cultural, social, and personal perspectives have not been influenced by her gender or her race; nor that the perspectives of the dominant group have not been similarly influenced in a way that excludes others. The rejection of the need for role models rests on a similarly tenuous base.

An immensely valuable counter is provided by the Supreme Court of Canada. As Chief Justice Dickson put it in a recent case,[105] the aim of an employment equity programme (in this case setting a quota of one woman in four new hirings until a goal of 13 per cent women in certain blue collar occupations was reached) is not to compensate past victims; but 'an attempt to ensure that future applicants and workers from the affected group will not face the same insidious barriers that blocked their forebears'.[106] He identified at least two ways in which such a programme is likely to be more effective than one which simply relies on equal opportunities or the proscription of intentional prejudice. First, the insistence that women be placed in non-traditional jobs allows them to prove that they really can do the job, thereby dispelling stereotypes about women's abilities. This was particularly evident in the case at hand, in which the quotas ordered by the tribunal concerned traditionally male jobs such as 'brakeman' or signaller at Canadian National Railways. Second, an employment equity programme helps to create a 'critical mass' of women in the work-place. Once a significant number of women are represented in a particular type of work, 'there is a significant chance for the continuing self-correction of the system'.[107] The critical mass overcomes the problem of tokenism, which would leave a few women isolated and vulnerable to sexual harassment or accusations of being imposters. It would also generate further employment of women, partly by means of the informal recruitment network and partly by reducing the stigma and anxiety associated with strange and unconventional work. Finally, a critical mass of women forces management to give women's concerns their due weight and compels personnel offices to take female applications seriously. As the Chief Justice concluded: 'It is readily apparent that, in attempting to combat systemic discrimination, it is essential to look to the past patterns of discrimination and to destroy those patterns in order to prevent the same type of discrimination in the future'.[108]

---

[105] *Action Travail des Femmes v. Canadian National Railway Co* [1987] 1 SCR 1114, 40 DLR (4th) 193.
[106] *ibid.* at 213.        [107] *ibid.* at 214.        [108] *ibid.* at 215.

## (IV) COMPETING CLAIMS: PREFERENCE FOR WHOM?

The above discussion has assumed that it is easy to identify the group which qualifies for preferential treatment. However, in practice this might give rise to some particularly difficult problems. We saw in Chapter Two that groups conveniently classified as 'ethnic minorities' can in fact differ substantially in their social position. Bangladeshis, for example, constitute a group which is significantly more disadvantaged than African Asians. If a Bangladeshi is competing with an African Asian for a position, and if one or both are women, how do we decide which warrants preferential treatment? This problem has led to differing solutions. In India, which has a sophisticated and complex system of preferential treatment a list of groups has been compiled, but this has not been without fierce controversy. It has also been open to manipulation by those who wish to avail themselves of the privileges attached to disadvantaged status. In other countries, it has been left to the courts to resolve difficult questions such as these. A valuable attempt to generate a principled response is found in a recent Canadian case,[109] which concerned a decision to distribute proceeds from a commercial project on reserved lands only to Ontario First Nations communities registered as bands under the Indian Act. The decision was challenged by several First Nation and other groups which were not registered as Indian Act 'bands', and did not have reserve lands. The case was particularly difficult since it was acknowledged that the excluded groups shared the same social and economic disadvantages as the beneficiaries of the schemes. The Canadian Supreme Court, however, held that their equality rights were not breached. The question to be addressed, according to the Court, was whether the measure undermined the aim of the equality guarantee in the Canadian Charter, which is to protect against the violation of essential human dignity. The court steered clear of engaging in a process of comparing disadvantage. Instead it focused on whether exclusion from the programme was likely to stigmatize the excluded group by conveying the message that the group in question was less worthy of recognition and participation in the larger society. In this case, although the project was under-inclusive, it could not be said to undermine the dignity of the excluded groups in this sense. It was tailored to meet a legitimate end, and therefore did not constitute a breach of the applicants' equality rights.

[109] *Ardoch Algonquin First Nation v. Ontario* 2000 SCC 37 (Canadian Supreme Court).

## IV  CONCLUSION

It has been argued above that the objections to affirmative action in principle can be seen to rest on a particular view of equality, namely one that is based on an abstract view of justice, which asserts the primacy of the individual and which assumes a neutral State. By contrast, a substantive conception of equality recognizes that justice must operate within a specific social context, based on the actual patterns of exclusion and disadvantage; that it must take into account the role of groups in influencing individual's life chances, and that it must recognize that the State is necessarily partial. On such a view, a coherent justification for affirmative action can be constructed. However, this is not the end of the matter. The aims of affirmative action need closer scrutiny on the basis of a proportionality principle, which requires an affirmative action policy to be narrowly tailored to meet legitimate ends. The above discussion has shown that there is a set of coherent and mutually reinforcing justifications for affirmative action. This in turn is based on a particular view both of groups and of decision-making: of groups as sets of relationships based on affinity, rather than a self contained and clearly demarcated set of individuals; and of decision-making as a process of communication and deliberation, rather than of interest group bargaining.

At the same time, it is important to stress the limitations of affirmative action as a strategy. The introduction of new perspectives, while an important goal, can only have a limited impact: entrenched structures are often resilient and indeed have powerful conformist pressures. Women or minorities may find themselves forced to hide their views and ignore their own needs and interests in order to ensure that their continued participation is viable. Even if they do articulate their perspectives, the process of recognition and affirmation is halting and erratic. Thus affirmative action needs to be only one part of a broad based and radical strategy, which does more than redistribute privileged positions; but refashions the institutions which continue to perpetuate exclusion.

# 6

# Rights and Remedies: the Limits of the Law

What impact has existing anti-discrimination legislation had on structures of discrimination in Britain? While initial successes fuelled early optimism, deeper structures of discrimination have proved remarkably resilient. Thus the abolition of separate pay scales for men and women led to a dramatic increase in women's pay relative to men in the early years. However, this impact was soon exhausted, and twenty-five years after the equal pay legislation came into force, there remains an unacceptably wide gap between men's pay and that of women. Similarly, although some highly visible women have moved into positions and grades previously monopolized by men, the majority of women remain segregated in low paid, low status jobs. Women are still seriously under-represented in positions of power in society; and women pensioners constitute one of the most disadvantaged groups in the country. Likewise, some ethnic minority groups have significantly improved their social and economic position. However, racial harassment is still widespread: in a recent survey, a third of Black and Asian people reported having encountered race discrimination in the workplace.[1] Particularly disturbing is the institutionalized racism within the police force itself. Authorized discrimination is similarly evident in other bastions of civil society, foremost amongst them the armed forces, which have clung on to openly homophobic and sexist policies. Perhaps the most disturbing is the recent surge of hostility towards asylum seekers, demonstrating that racism lurks very close to the surface of public consciousness. Similarly, religious discrimination remains widespread, with religious minorities reporting that their members experience unfair treatment in education, employment, and the media.[2]

This raises doubts about the role of law in effecting social change. Is law inevitably limited? Or can we refashion legal tools in such a way as to

---

[1] CRE *Race Equality in the North of England*, reported in Equal Opportunities Review No. 97 (May/June 2001) pp.5–6.

[2] *Religious Discrimination in England and Wales*, Home Office Research Study 220, available on www.homeoffice.gov.uk.

play a major part in achieving substantive equality? In order to answer these questions it is necessary to examine not just the conceptual apparatus of equality law, but also the enforcement mechanisms. The primary means of enforcing anti-discrimination laws until very recently has been by means of individual claims to employment tribunals. More recently, however, attempts have been made to fashion a new sort of enforcement mechanism, which goes beyond the individualized and backward looking nature of tribunal claims. These positive duties require more than just a change in enforcement measures. They also require a reformulation of the aim of the law: to move beyond penalizing individual acts of unlawful discrimination and compensating individual victims, towards promoting equality through structural change. This in turn involves striking a delicate balance between individual responsibility, and legal incentives, be they positive or negative. It also involves weighing up different sorts of costs. Discrimination is a cost both to individuals and society. This cost needs to be balanced against the more quantifiable and concrete costs to employers asserting the right to pursue their business needs, and the State asserting the right to make macro-economic policy decisions.

Through all of this, of course, the less visible but equally important educational role of the law should not be ignored. However, it is important that the law conveys the right messages. Anti-discrimination legislation which relies wholly on individual claims to tribunals might well signal to employers, State agents, and other major actors that the function of the law extends no further. As long as they can avoid tribunal claims, and pay out compensation where necessary, the problem of discrimination has been dealt with. Exemptions from the law also give the impression that there is no requirement for such bodies to refrain from discriminating. Thus the finding that the Race Relations Act did not apply to immigration control,[3] nor to police when pursuing and arresting or charging alleged criminals,[4] could well have contributed significantly to the continuation of institutionalized racism in the police and other public services. Similarly, improving maternity rights for mothers without ensuring an equivalent set of rights for fathers could well damage women's employment prospects by reinforcing employers' prejudices against women in the workforce.

This chapter begins by considering existing structures of adjudication

---

[3] *R v. Entry Clearance officer (Bombay), ex p Amin* [1983] 2 AC 818 (HL).
[4] *Farah v. Commissioner for Police for the Metropolis* [1998] QB 65 (CA).

and compensation, and then turns to examine the role and nature of positive duties.

# I ADVERSARIALISM: THE NARROW REACH OF ADJUDICATION

Until very recently, the primary channel for enforcement of anti-discrimination law has been by individual complaint to an employment tribunal. Employment related claims under the equal pay, sex discrimination, race discrimination, and disability discrimination laws lie to employment tribunals. Claims which relate to education or the provision of goods and services lie to the county court, but such cases have been a small minority of the total. There have also been several attempts to harness the judicial review procedure of the High Court, but although some important gains have been made by this route, the courts have been careful to preserve judicial review for genuinely public law cases. Particularly influential has been the reference procedure to the European Court of Justice, according to which tribunals and courts may refer questions of European Union law for a definitive answer. A wider range of judicial options will become available now that the Human Rights Act is in effect, since all courts and tribunals have some jurisdiction under this Act. Below, I consider first the nature of claims to tribunals, and then turn briefly to other types of court.

## (I) TRIBUNALS

The tribunal system was deliberately structured to provide an accessible, cheap, and speedy alternative to the existing court process. Tribunals are also intended to be more sensitive than ordinary courts to employment related concerns. Hence their tripartite structure. Decisions are made by a legal chair and two lay members with industrial experience, one appointed after consultation with trade unions, the other after consultation with employers organizations. The Employment Appeal Tribunal, to which appeals from employment tribunals lie, is similarly tripartite in structure, with a judge in the chair. In race discrimination cases, it is the normal practice to appoint one lay member from a panel designated on appointment as having special knowledge and experience of race relations. A similar practice for disability cases has been urged on the government by the Disability Rights Task force. In sex discrimination cases, it is usual to have one woman on the panel. Tribunals are more informal and accessible than courts: there are no complicated pleadings and tribunals are not bound by strict rules of evidence. Although as we will see there may be in practice an advantage to having legal representation, representatives do not need to be lawyers and applicants can represent themselves. This means that tribunal cases are potentially less expensive than courts. Finally, the large numbers of tribunals throughout the country have made them somewhat quicker than courts.

However, the record of tribunals in discrimination cases has, with some notable exceptions, been disappointing. Compared to the scale of discrimination in society, the number of complaints to tribunals is small, and the number of successes minuscule. During the twelve years from 1976 to 1988, only 12,344 equal pay claims were brought in tribunals; and only 20 per cent of these were won after a tribunal hearing or settled. Of all the sex discrimination cases commenced during the period 1990–99, only 8 per cent were successful at a tribunal hearing. Recent figures show little improvement. In 1998–99, as few as 1,530 equal pay claims were completed in tribunals, and of those which were actually dealt with by a tribunal, only a pitiful 2 per cent were successful.[5] In the same year, only 2,694 race discrimination cases and 4,025 sex discrimination cases were completed.[6] But even these figures vastly overestimate the role of tribunals. About 70 per cent of race discrimination cases and 75 per cent of sex discrimination cases did not make it to a tribunal hearing in that year, but were either settled following ACAS conciliation, withdrawn or disposed of otherwise. Of those that reached tribunal hearings, about a third of sex discrimination complaints were successful, compared with less than one in five race discrimination cases. This means that a mere 7 per cent of all sex discrimination complaints and 6 per cent of race discrimination cases were decided in favour of the complainant.[7] Nor was the expectation of speed and low cost in tribunals met. Instead, the length of the process has been described by the EAT as 'scandalous' and 'a denial of justice to women through the judicial process'.[8] The average time for

---

[5] (1999) 88 EOR 43.

[6] In 1993–4, 1,969 sex discrimination cases were completed, rising to 4,052 in 1994–5. 780 equal pay cases were completed in 1993–4, but only 418 in 1994–5.

[7] In 1994–5, over 80 per cent of sex discrimination cases were conciliated, withdrawn or disposed of otherwise without the need for a tribunal hearing. In the same year, 70 per cent of equal pay cases were withdrawn and a further 23 per cent conciliated. For the handful, success rates are poor. About a third of the Sex Discrimination Act cases which reached a tribunal in 1993–4, and a half in 1994–5, were successful, with compensation being awarded in only fifty-eight and 134 cases respectively. The success rate is even more discouraging. In 1994–5, applicants under the Equal Pay Act were successful in a mere one third of the twenty-five cases heard by tribunals: (1996) 69 EOR 26.

[8] *Aldridge v. British Telecommunications plc* [1990] IRLR 10 (EAT) at 14.

an equal value case is at least eighteen months, and some cases, such as that of 1,280 women against British Coal, have been running for the extraordinary period of fifteen years. The speech therapists' claim was finally concluded after fourteen years.[9]

Several factors have contributed to the discouraging performance of tribunals in the discrimination arena. First, like the ordinary courts, the tribunals depend wholly on the individual claimant to initiate the case, bring the evidence and make the legal arguments. Not only is such a procedure premised on the assumption that discrimination complaints are purely individual. It also places an excessive burden on an individual victim of discrimination, who must muster the courage to face an employer or ex-employer with a discrimination claim, as well as finding the personal and financial resources to pursue it. Moreover, each party bears his or her own expenses[10] and compensation levels are low, so that even a successful applicant could well be out of pocket. This creates a powerful disincentive on individuals to enforce the law through tribunals.

The second and related difficulty concerns the obstacles to obtaining evidence. Direct discrimination is particularly difficult to prove, since, although the motivation of the alleged discriminator need not be proved, most relevant evidence is in the hands of the respondent. Indirect discrimination and equal pay claims have their own difficulties, requiring complex compilation of statistics. Some attempts have been made to mitigate this difficulty, but with only marginal impact. Particularly ineffective is the statutory questionnaire which may be served on the respondent prior to institution of proceedings requesting information about the latter's reasons for his or her actions.[11] Although the answers are admissible in evidence, the employer is under little pressure to respond. At most, if a respondent 'deliberately and without reasonable excuse omits to reply in a reasonable period, or his reply is evasive or equivocal', the court or tribunal may draw any inference it considers just or equitable to draw.[12] A more helpful approach is to shift the burden of proof to the respondent once the applicant has made out a prima facie

---

[9] Figures in this section are taken from B. Hepple, M. Coussey, and T. Choudhury, *Equality: A New Framework* Report of the Independent Review of the Enforcement of UK Anti-Discrimination Legislation (Hart, 2000), paras 4.28 and 4.29.

[10] Unless one party acts unreasonably: Employment Tribunals Rules of Procedure 1993 SI 1993/2687, r.12.

[11] Sex Discrimination Act 1975, s.74; Race Relations Act 1976, s.65; Disability Discrimination Act 1995, s.56 and see also Fair Employment and Treatment (Northern Ireland) Order (FETO) 1998, art. 44.

[12] Sex Discrimination Act 1975, s.74(2)(b); Race Relations Act 1976, s.65(2)(b).

case of discrimination. Most important in this respect has been the development by the ECJ of a set of robust principles which were given statutory endorsement by the 1997 Burden of Proof Directive.[13] This provides that once an applicant has established facts from which it may be presumed that there has been direct or indirect sex discrimination, the burden of proof must shift to the respondent to prove that there has been no breach of the principle of equal treatment. The Burden of Proof Directive, however, applies only in the field of sex discrimination. There has been a parallel but weaker development by the domestic courts to shift the burden of proof in race discrimination cases.[14] This will now need to be strengthened in the light of the new EU directive on equal treatment between persons of different racial or ethnic origin, which contains an identical provision to that of the 1997 directive.[15]

Far more significant would be a reform which took the burden of litigation off the individual claimant altogether. This would involve a recognition that discrimination is not just a question of individual justice. Social discrimination necessarily affects a group of individuals, and there should be legal mechanisms to permit remedial action to be taken on the part of the whole group. In practice, many of the most important claims have been litigated by means of a series of representative actions, co-ordinated by trade unions, pressure groups, law centres, and others. It may also be important to challenge a discriminatory rule when it is not possible to find a worker who has been affected. Women and ethnic minorities may be deterred from applying for certain kinds of jobs because of indirect discrimination; yet such practices should still be open to challenge.[16] The body in the best position to bring such challenges is the relevant equality commission. Hence the Independent Review of the Enforcement of UK Anti-Discrimination legislation has recommended that the relevant Commission should have power to institute proceedings in its own name or jointly with individuals in respect of unlawful discrimination where there is a common question of fact or law affecting a number of persons, whether identified or not.[17]

---

[13] Directive 97/80 [1997] OJ L14/6, extended to the UK by Directive 98/52 [1998] OJ L205/66.

[14] *King v. the Great Britain China Centre* [1991] IRLR 513 (CA); *Zafar v. Glasgow City Council* [1997] 1 WLR 1659 (HL). Instead of placing a duty on tribunals to shift the burden to the employer once a prima facie case has been made out, these cases leave it to the discretion of the tribunal.

[15] Directive 2000/43 [2000] OJ L180/22, Art. 8.

[16] See Hepple, Coussey, and Choudhury, above n.9, para. 4.24.

[17] *ibid.*, para. 4.26, recommendation 44.

The third reason why tribunals have had a limited impact results from the uneasy combination of a procedure which aims to be informal, simple and accessible, with a set of legal provisions which are extremely complex, not least because of the interaction of anti-discrimination statutes with EU law and that of the Human Rights Act. This has prompted any party who can afford it to resort to legal representation. Research has repeatedly shown that a legally represented applicant in a discrimination case is more likely to be successful at a hearing than one who appears in person (although an applicant in person is more likely to be successful than if he or she were represented by a non-legal person such as a trade union). Respondents are also more likely to be successful if they are legally represented.[18] Yet, legal aid has until very recently only been available for advice and assistance and not for legal representation before tribunals.[19] Although the tribunal is meant to assist an unrepresented party, this role creates an awkward tension with its adjudicative function. This problem has been somewhat mitigated by the powers of the Equal Opportunities Commission, Commission for Racial Equality, and Disability Rights Commission to give assistance to complainants, including the funding of legal representation.[20] Assistance is available in cases which raise a question of principle, or where it is unreasonable to expect the applicant to deal with it unaided, having regard, *inter alia*, to the complexity of the case. The budgetary constraints on the Commissions, however, make it inevitable that only a small number of complainants receive financial assistance. In 1998, for example, the CRE gave full legal representation in 163 cases and limited representation in a further 101 cases.

The legal aid framework has now been radically reformed, a development which could provide the opportunity to obtain subsidized legal assistance in discrimination cases. In England and Wales, from April 2000, legal aid is to be substituted by the Community Legal Service, which brings together a range of organizations offering legal and advice services, including solicitors, law centres, citizens' advice bureaux, local authority services, and trade unions. People who meet the eligibility rules and who cannot afford to pay for legal services may receive assistance from these networks. The Lord Chancellor has directed that, the Community Legal Services Fund, which subsidizes these services,

---

[18] *ibid.*, para. 4.34.

[19] Legal Aid Act 1988, ss. 8–9. The amount was generally less than £100. Legal aid was available for representation before the Employment Appeal Tribunal.

[20] Sex Discrimination Act 1975, s.75(1); Race Relations Act 1976, s.66; Disability Rights Commission Act 1999, s.12.

should give priority to certain cases, which include breaches of human rights by public bodies, and employment rights cases, including employment related discrimination cases. With the addition of priority status for non-employment discrimination cases, this could provide significant amelioration of the inequality of arms between parties in tribunals. However, by increasing the role of lawyers in tribunal hearings, the reforms inevitably sacrifice some of the speed, informality, and inexpensiveness of the tribunal system. It could be argued that this does no more than reflect the internal contradiction of the tribunal system. A more radical response to these conflicting tensions would be to enhance the inquisitorial role of the tribunal rather than entrenching its adversarialism.

The fourth factor contributing to the limited impact of the tribunal system is that, again like the courts, the procedure is essentially adversarial, processing the case as a bipolar dispute between two individuals, diametrically opposed, to be resolved on a winner-take-all basis.[21] This all-or-nothing response leaves no room for compromise or synthesis. It is only outside of the court process, in settlements, that compromise may be reached; indeed parties are encouraged to do so by the statutory provision for conciliation on request or on the initiative of an ACAS conciliation officer.[22] However, while the process of settlement may be more flexible than the court, settlement is if anything more intensely individualist than the formal hearing. Its outcome is a private matter between the parties, creating no precedents or guiding principles for society as a whole. The tension between private compromise and public adversarialism is particularly problematic in test cases, when the Commissions or ACAS might be eager to establish a point of principle, while the complainant wishes merely to reach an outcome.

### (II) COUNTY COURTS, THE HIGH COURT AND THE ECJ

Despite their limitations, tribunals still retain an advantage in terms of informality, cost, and speed over the county and sheriff courts, which have jurisdiction over discrimination cases involving education, and the provision of goods, services, and facilities to the public. Of all the procedures, this one has been the object of most widespread dissatisfaction.[23] Only a handful of cases come before the county courts each year, a reflection, according to the EOC, of the formality, cost, and protracted nature of the

---

[21] A. Chayes, 'The Role of the Judge in Public Law Litigation' (1976) 89 *Harvard Law Review* 1281.

[22] Sex Discrimination Act 1975, s.64.

[23] Hepple, Coussey, and Choudhury, above n.9, para. 4.13.

county court process. Similarly, the disability rights group RADAR has argued that the problems associated with county courts are the biggest barrier facing individuals wishing to take up cases under Part III of the Disability Discrimination Act 1995. Indeed, in the first nineteen months of its operation, only nine DDA cases came before the county courts. The greater expense of this avenue of adjudication is in part accounted for by the fact that applicants have to pay court fees and may face an order for costs or expenses if unsuccessful. In addition, county court judges have little knowledge or experience of discrimination claims. It has therefore been suggested that all discrimination claims whether or not they involve employment should be commenced in employment tribunals, with the possibility of transfer to a county court if appropriate or if the parties so request.[24]

More effective is the application for judicial review to the High Court. This procedure departs in significant ways from the traditional adversarial mould. Most importantly, public law remedies have effects well beyond the individual litigant. By striking down the discriminatory decision rather than focusing on the effect on an individual, judicial review can potentially change a discriminatory practice to the benefit of a whole class of present and future victims. The case of *R v. Secretary of State, ex p EOC*[25] is the most dramatic example of the potential of this procedure. In that case, it will be recalled, the requirement that part-time workers work continuously for five years in order to qualify for employment protection rights was struck down under the Equal Treatment Directive. In one fell swoop, all part-time workers were able to benefit. Also of great significance was the decision of the House of Lords that the EOC had standing to initiate judicial review proceedings. This opens up an important arena for public interest litigation spearheaded by the Commissions.

Forays of this sort into the public law arena are, however, unlikely to become commonplace. The courts are fiercely protective of the judicial review procedure, making it unlikely that cases will succeed unless they are based on a claim that the courts characterize as 'public'.[26] Nevertheless, the coming into force of the HRA is likely to open up a new avenue for judicial review. Under the HRA, all courts and tribunals have the duty to subject any executive decision, common law principle, or primary legislation to human rights scrutiny. Although only the High Court,

---

[24] *ibid.*, paras 4.13 and 4.14.      [25] [1995] 1 AC 1 (HL).
[26] *R v. East Berkshire Health Authority, ex p Walsh* [1985] QB 152 (CA).

Court of Appeal, and House of Lords have jurisdiction to declare primary legislation incompatible with Convention rights, all courts must attempt to interpret legislation as compatible with Convention rights, ensure the common law develops consistently with human rights, and subject executive decision-making to human rights scrutiny. To the extent that Article 14 bites, there will therefore be a more extensive judicial role in discrimination law.

More influential has been the ECJ. Under the special reference procedure, any tribunal or court may refer a question of EU law to the Court of Justice for definitive resolution. A number of seminal test cases have been litigated along this route with some important results. There are several difficulties with this route, however. The first is that, until the new Article 13 directives on race, disability, and other grounds come into effect, only sex discrimination cases can be litigated along this route. Second, unless a case is supported by the EOC, it is a daunting project for an individual litigant to persist with litigation which could take years to complete. Third, the procedure before the ECJ itself is very different from that of the domestic courts. The emphasis is on written rather than oral presentations, and a central role is played by the Advocate General, who gives an influential opinion on each case. Finally, no dissenting judgments are given. The pretence at unanimity, or the even more basic notion that the law must be seen to produce only one answer, means that in practice judgments are often a series of compromises, rather than a principled opinion.

## (III) REMEDIES

Probably the most serious failing of the adjudication process has been in the nature of its remedies. Like the adversarial system as a whole, remedies are limited by their focus on the individual. Instead of engaging actively in forward-looking reform of the kind essential to achieve comprehensive restructuring, the primary remedy available to tribunals is in the form of monetary compensation. When employment tribunals (then known as industrial tribunals) were created, it was not thought appropriate to entrust them with an injunctive remedy. Nor do they have the power of ordering reinstatement or re-engagement in discrimination cases, despite having such power in unfair dismissal cases. Instead, tribunals are armed with the timid weapon of a recommendation. Even the recommendation is individualized: rather than reaching into structural causes of discrimination, the tribunal is merely empowered to recommend action to obviate or reduce the adverse effect on the complainant and then only if it appears to the tribunal to be practicable.[27] There is therefore no power to make a recommendation that discriminatory practices be changed where the applicant has left the employment. Thus in *Noone*,[28] the Court of Appeal held that a tribunal did not have the power to order that a victim of race discrimination in the selection process be offered the next available post.[29] Moreover, an employer who fails to comply with the recommendation is treated gently in comparison with the vehemence of the sanction for contempt of an injunction. Failure to comply is only penalized if the employer cannot offer reasonable justification[30] and the standard of such justification is deliberately low.[31] If no reasonable justification is established, the sanction is mild: instead of a hefty fine or even imprisonment, which is the consequence of failure to comply with an injunction, discrimination is penalized merely by an increase in compensation.

This may be contrasted with the mandatory injunction, used in the US in many of the important equal treatment cases. Unlike compensation, which is retrospective, individualized and all-or-nothing, the mandatory injunction operates as a continuing constraint on future action. This challenges the adversarial system in several fundamental ways. First, the court is actively involved in balancing the interests not only of the parties before it but those of others who are inevitably affected. Second, because the focus shifts away from past conduct such as fault and intention, onto future consequences, the nature of the relevant evidence changes. Evidence on social facts is required, and wider interest representation necessitated. Third, the prospective nature of the remedy creates the incentive for parties to reach a compromise. Finally, the judge is no longer a passive arbiter, but an active participant in the process.[32] Most importantly, the judge maintains a continuing role in mediating, supervising, and even managing the operation of the decree. The result is radical. Instead of litigation functioning as a private dispute settlement, it operates as a manner of carrying out a policy.[33] The change has been far from

---

[27] Sex Discrimination Act 1975, s.65(1)(c); Race Relations Act 1976 s.56(1)(c); Disability Discrimination Act 1995, s.8(1)(c).

[28] *Noone v. North West Thames Regional Health Authority (No 2)* [1988] IRLR 530 (CA).

[29] See also *British Gas v. Sharma* [1999] IRLR 101 (EAT).

[30] Sex Discrimination Act 1975, s.65(3); Race Relations Act s.56(4); Disability Discrimination Act 1995, s.8(5).

[31] *Nelson v. Tyne and Wear Passenger Transport Executive* [1978] ICR 183 (EAT).

[32] O. M. Fiss, 'The Forms of Justice' (1979) 93 Harvard Law Review 1, at 16–28.

[33] Chayes, above n.21, at 1288–96.

uncontroversial, raising questions both about the suitability of judges in making policy decisions of this sort, and the legitimacy and accuracy of social science information.[34] Nevertheless, it forms an important attempt to surmount the restrictions of the adversarial approach.

The substitute for dynamic and interactive remedies has been the almost exclusive reliance on compensation, which satisfies the law's neutrality and individualism by granting a one-off remedy to the individual alone. At the same time, there remains an intense ambivalence to the function of compensation. Is it deterrent, or compensatory, or both? The legislation itself has always been partly based on an assumption that only if the party is at fault, can it be right to expect him or her to pay compensation. This is most floridly manifested in the Race Relations Act 1976, which does not permit compensation to be awarded for unintentional indirect discrimination.[35] A corresponding restriction in the Sex Discrimination Act 1975 was finally removed in 1996, after a number of employment tribunals had held that it contravened the Equal Treatment Directive.[36] At the same time, courts and tribunals have been unwilling to use damages in a punitive form, stressing in this context the compensatory nature of damages. Although the Court of Appeal has upheld the award of exemplary damages against a local authority for discriminating on grounds of race and sex against a black woman, this was only because the act fell within the recognized exception for oppressive acts by public authorities.[37] More recently, the EAT[38] has emphatically ruled out the award of exemplary damages in race discrimination cases, while in another case, it refused to countenance the possibility of exemplary damages against the Ministry of Defence for the dismissal of a servicewoman on grounds of her pregnancy, on the grounds that exemplary damages could not possibly apply to a breach of the Equal Treatment Directive.[39] This was despite the fact that the ECJ has stressed that the award of damages should have a deterrent effect. The Law Commission has in fact recommended that punitive damages (the preferred term for exemplary damages) should be awarded in any case, including a discrimination claim, where in committing a wrong or in conduct subsequent to the wrong, the

---

[34] See the discussion in Chayes, above n.21, and Fiss, above n.32.

[35] Race Relations Act 1976 s.57(3): (http://www.hmso.gov.uk/acts/acts1995/Ukpga_19950050_en_3.htm#mdiv8).

[36] The Sex Discrimination and Equal Pay (Miscellaneous Amendments) Regulations 1996 SI 1996/438, r.2(4), repealing Sex Discrimination Act 1975, s.66(3).

[37] *City of Bradford v. Arora* [1991] 2 QB 507 (CA).

[38] *Deane v. London Borough of Ealing* [1993] IRLR 209 (EAT).

[39] *Ministry of Defence v. Meredith* [1995] IRLR 539 (EAT).

defendant deliberately and outrageously disregarded the claimant's rights. Certainly, there are clear fact situations in which the tribunal or court should be able set damages at a level which would both deter the discriminator, and express the strong disapproval of the court.[40]

The primary aim of damages for unlawful discrimination therefore remains compensatory. The measure of damage is similar to that in tort claims, namely, aiming to put the victim into the position he or she would have been in had the wrong not occurred. Until November 1993,[41] compensation was subject to an upper limit, which frequently kept awards far below their real level. The statutory maximum, paralleling that for unfair dismissal cases, was low: it stood at a mere £11,000 in 1994; and tribunals generally kept awards well below the limit.[42] Some progress has been made since the path-breaking case of *Marshall (No. 2)*,[43] which forced a repeal of the statutory limit on the grounds that it infringed the Equal Treatment Directive.[44] Most important was the Court's emphatic restatement of the principle that Member States must guarantee real and effective judicial protection of the right to equality of opportunity in a way that has a real deterrent effect on the employer. The removal of the statutory limit has had an important impact, with compensation levels immediately moving steeply upwards.[45] Most importantly, the removal of the upper limit has permitted some particularly large awards, with the highest awards in 1999 being over £180,000 in a sex discrimination case.[46] Possibly the most notable progress has been made in levels of compensation awarded for injury to feelings.[47] Nevertheless, the median award remains low. In 1999, the median award for race discrimination cases was £6,000, and for disability £5,500. Sex discrimination lagged behind, with a median award of £3,713. It is clear therefore that the levels of compensation awarded are far from adequate to discharge the State's remedial duty. Certainly compensation plays an important role, but only if the levels are satisfactory and they are combined with other sorts of intervention, such as the positive duties described below.

[40] See Hepple, Coussey, and Choudhury, above n.9, recommendation 50.

[41] Sex Discrimination and Equal Pay (Remedies) Regulations 1993 SI 1993/2798.

[42] *Employment Gazette* May 1991 pp.305–6.

[43] Case C-271/91 *Marshall v. Southampton and South West Hampshire Area Health Authority (No 2)* [1993] ECR I-4367.

[44] Directive 76/207 [1976] OJ L39/40, Art. 6.

[45] (1994) 57 EOR 11–21.

[46] (2000) 93 EOR 11–22.

[47] Sex Discrimination Act 1975, s.66; Race Relations Act 1976, s.57(4); Disability Discrimination Act 1995, s.8(4).

## (IV) A CRITIQUE OF THE ADVERSARIAL STRUCTURE

It is arguable that discrimination law, by its nature, requires a departure from the traditional adversarial structure, even in the more informal setting of a tribunal. As Chayes demonstrates, legislation which explicitly modifies and regulates basic social and economic realities challenges the traditional adversarial model.[48] The bipolar structure is particularly inappropriate for public and private interactions which are not bilateral transactions between individuals, but have wide social implications. This in turn requires a transformation of the adjudicative structure from what Fiss calls a 'dispute resolution' model to a model of 'structural reform'.[49] In the dispute resolution model, the victim, spokesperson, and beneficiary are automatically combined in one claimant. In the newer model, the victim is not an individual but a group; and the spokesperson is not necessarily one of the group. In addition, because a beneficiary need not prove individual damage, the class of beneficiaries may well be wider than the victims. Thus all members of a particular racial group might benefit from the institution of prohibitions on racial harassment, even though not everyone has individually suffered from racial harassment. A similar analysis applies to the defendant. Whereas in the dispute resolution model, the defendant is both the wrongdoer and the provider of a remedy, in the model of structural reform, the wrongdoer disappears, and instead the focus is on the body able to achieve reform. In the result, the individualism of the adversarial system is supplanted by a group-based model. Thus the individual no longer bears the burden of enforcing his or her own equality rights.

One way of achieving this reformed approach is the introduction of class actions. Class actions aim to assist claimant's in cases in which an injury simultaneously affects many individuals, and involves law so complex that for any one individual to sue entails disproportionate expense.[50] The class suit is a particularly flexible type of joint action because any member of the injured group may sue on behalf of the whole group. There is no need to organize all the victims before the trial or to prove that the spokesperson is representative. Instead, participation of all claimants is deferred until after the trial: all members of the group are entitled to participate in the end result, and by the same token, all share the burden of expenses on a *quantum meruit* basis.

---

[48] Chayes, above n.21, p.1288.     [49] See Fiss, above n.32.

[50] H. Kalven and M. Rosenfield, 'The Contemporary Function of the Class Suit' (1940) 8 *University of Chicago Law Review* 684.

## II AGENCY ENFORCEMENT

Some of the weaknesses of an adjudicative structure have been addressed by the powers given to the EOC, CRE, and the Disability Rights Commission to initiate and conduct a 'formal investigation' into cases of suspected unlawful discrimination.[51] The formal investigation departs from adversarialism in several key respects. As a start, it is an active rather than passive process. The relevant Commission has the power to initiate the investigation, thus inviting a strategic approach instead of an *ad hoc* series of actions. Moreover, it has strong information gathering powers, including the ability to demand written or oral evidence and the production of documents. The formal investigation also deviates significantly from the individualism of the tribunal procedure. The power is specifically directed at a practice of discrimination rather than a particular discriminatory act against an individual. Nor is the situation characterized as an all-or-nothing bipolar dispute. Instead, the investigation is intended to be an interactive process, during which the Commission aims to secure a change in discriminatory practices through discussion, negotiation, and conciliation. Its remedial powers are therefore essentially forward looking: the Commission has the power to issue recommendations and, ultimately, if necessary, a non-discrimination notice.

However, the novelty of the procedure and the challenge it poses to deeply entrenched visions of adversarialism have led to a reaction against it by the courts. In a series of judicial review cases against the Commission for Racial Equality, the formal investigation was trammelled with a chain of restrictive procedural requirements intended to protect the employer against what was considered to be a harsh and inquisitorial procedure.[52] Lord Denning indeed went so far as to characterize the formal investigation as akin to the Spanish inquisition.[53] This combined with an absence of strategic use of the power by the Commissions[54] has meant that the impact of the formal investigation has been disappointing.

---

[51] Sex Discrimination Act 1975, ss.57–61; Race Relations Act 1976, ss.48–62.

[52] *CRE v. Prestige Group plc* [1984] 1 WLR 335 (HL), *London Borough of Hillingdon v. CRE* [1982] AC 779 (HL) and see generally G. Appleby and E. Ellis, 'Formal Investigations' [1984] PL 236.

[53] *Science Research Council v. Nassé* [1979] 1 QB 144 (CA) at 172.

[54] Appleby and Ellis, above n.52, at p.260.

## III 'FOURTH GENERATION' EQUALITY: POSITIVE DUTIES

The most important response to the individualized, retrospective, and passive enforcement and remedial structure has, however, taken the form of positive duties to promote equality. As we have already seen, positive duties are proactive rather than reactive. The aim is to introduce equality measures rather than responding to complaints by individual victims; and to harness the energies of employers and public bodies to do so. At the root of the positive duty is a recognition that societal discrimination extends well beyond individual acts of racist prejudice. Thus equality can only be meaningfully advanced if practices and structures are altered pro-actively by those in a position to bring about real change.

'Fourth generation' equality laws are being actively developed in several jurisdictions. At EU level, a powerful boost was given to the effectiveness of sex equality legislation by the adoption of the policy of 'mainstreaming'. Mainstreaming means that equality is not just an add-on or after-thought to policy, but is one of the factors taken into account in every policy and executive decision.[55] 'The reactive and negative approach of anti-discrimination is replaced by pro-active, anticipatory and integrative methods'.[56] Within the UK, Northern Ireland has been at the forefront of pioneering legislation on positive duties. Legislation introduced in 1989 imposed a positive duty on employers to take measures to achieve fair participation of Protestant and Roman Catholic employees in their workforces.[57] In the equal pay arena, the most advanced schemes have emanated from the Canadian province of Ontario, where employers have a statutory responsibility to identify pay discrimination and where necessary to initiate and implement pay adjustments.[58] More recently, the emphasis has shifted to duties on public bodies. Once again at the forefront of such developments has been

---

[55] *Incorporating Equal Opportunities for Women and Men into all Community Policies and Activities* Commission Communication COM(96) final; see generally T. Rees, *Mainstreaming Equality in the European Union: Education, Training and Labour Market Policies* (Routledge, 1998).

[56] Hepple, Coussey, and Choudhury, above n.9, para. 3.8.

[57] Fair Employment Act 1989, now contained in Fair Employment and Treatment (Northern Ireland) Order (FETO) 1998, Part VII; C. McCrudden, 'Mainstreaming Equality in the Governance of Northern Ireland' (1999) 22:4 *Fordham International Law Journal* 1696.

[58] Ontario Pay Equity Act 1987, as amended.

legislation in Northern Ireland, where public authorities must have 'due regard to the need to promote equality of opportunity' in carrying out all their functions.[59] In the UK as a whole, by far the most important initiative is contained in the Race Relations Amendment Act 2000, which came into force in April 2001. This explicitly aims to mainstream racial equality by making the promotion of equality of opportunity and good race relations an integral part of the way public functions are carried out. The Act places a general statutory duty on a wide range of public authorities not just to eliminate unlawful racial discrimination, but also to 'promote equality of opportunity and good relations between persons of different racial groups'.[60] As well as the general duty, the Home Secretary is given the power to impose specific duties on listed public authorities 'for the purpose of ensuring the better performance of the general duty'.[61] These specific duties can be tailor-made to meet the requirements of the particular public authority.

The imposition of positive duties changes the whole landscape of discrimination law. The focus is no longer on the perpetrator of a discriminatory act. Instead, the spotlight is on the body in the best position to promote equality. Individual fault becomes irrelevant. One consequence of this is that the respondent is not identifiable simply from the definition of discrimination. Legislation must explicitly define and justify the choice of bodies upon whom to place the obligation. Similarly, the nature of the duty changes. Under the traditional model, individuals are required to refrain from discriminating. If they breach this duty, they are required to pay compensation to the victim. By contrast, the trigger for the duty to promote equality is not self-defining. Legislation must specify both when the duty arises, and its content. The following sections attempt to analyse positive duties under these headings. First, to whom does the duty apply? Second, what triggers the duty and what is its content? Thirdly, who is entitled to participate in the decision-making process? Fourth, how are positive duties enforced, and finally, what are the aims?

---

[59] Northern Ireland Act 1998, s.75; and see C. McCrudden, 'The Equal Opportunity Duty in the Northern Ireland Act 1998: An Analysis' in *Equal Rights and Human Rights— Their Role in Peace Building* (Committee on the Administration of Justice (Northern Ireland), 1999), pp.11–23.

[60] Race Relations Act 1976, s.71(1) (as amended).

[61] Race Relations Amendment Act 2000, s.71(2)–(3).

## (I) TO WHOM DOES THE DUTY APPLY?

The key to the advances represented by positive duties is that they fall, not upon the perpetrator of a discriminatory act, but upon the body in the best position to promote equality. Following this rationale, duties have been imposed primarily on employers and public bodies. Thus the Ontarian equal pay legislation targets employers, while in Northern Ireland, separate statutes place duties on employers and public bodies. Notably, the amended race relations legislation in the UK only applies to public bodies; the unstated assumption being that it would be unfairly onerous to impose positive duties on private employers. This means, in turn, that it is essential to draw a clear dividing line between public and private, a distinction which remains contested in many areas of the law. How should the definition be drawn? Should it be left to the courts, with the attendant uncertainty? Or should the legislation provide a list of bodies, with the risk of rigidity? The former has been the approach under both the equality guarantee in the Human Rights Act 1998, and the duty to refrain from racial discrimination in the rest of the Race Relations Act. Each of these applies to 'public' bodies; and to private bodies with 'public functions', terms which are left to the courts to apply. After much debate, however, it was the latter solution which was chosen for the positive duty, and a list is provided in a schedule to the Act. At present, the list covers the familiar range of public bodies, including government departments; the Scottish Administration; the National Assembly for Wales; the armed forces; the National Health Service; local government; fire, education and transport authorities; and the police.

Given the specificity of the duty to be imposed, the listing solution is clearly the appropriate one. However, the constant shifting of the boundaries between public and private, both in terms of privatization and contracting out of functions, requires vigilance on the part of the appropriate government minister. This issue is addressed in two ways in the Race Relations Amendment Act. First, the public body remains responsible for complying with the general duty even if it has contracted out some of its functions to private or voluntary organizations. Second, the Home Secretary has the power to add further bodies to the list provided they exercise 'functions of a public nature'. As many as 302 new entries have been proposed, most of which are regulatory bodies and non-departmental public bodies set up by statute with advisory or executive functions. In addition, several public corporations are included and, significantly, the public functions of nationalized industries such as the

Radio Authority and the Post Office. Thus, if the list is accepted, the British Medical Association, the Royal College of Nursing, ACAS (the Advisory, Conciliation and Arbitration Service), and the funding research councils, will all be subject to the general duty. However, notably, judicial and quasi-judicial bodies are excluded on the grounds that such a duty would have interfered with the concept of judicial independence.

### (II) THE DUTY: TRIGGERS AND CONTENT

Traditional anti-discrimination legislation requires the victim to identify an act of discrimination, in order to attract a compensatory remedy. Positive duties, by contrast, place the onus of identifying patterns of inequality on the body on whom the duty to promote equality lies. Both the Northern Ireland and the Ontario legislation in this respect provide a neat contrast to earlier generations of anti-discrimination law. Instead of imposing a duty only in response to individual claims of discrimination, employers must take responsibility for discovering discrimination as well as remedying it. The content of the duty is then a direct response to the problem identified. Thus the Northern Ireland legislation requires the employer to monitor the number of existing employees who belong to each community; and to undertake periodic reviews of employment practices. Where fair participation is not evident, the employer must engage in affirmative action (short of reverse discrimination) to improve the representation of the under-represented group. Under the Ontarian Act, employers with more than ten employees are required to examine the pay structures within their establishments for evidence of pay disparities between female dominated groups and male dominated groups doing work of equal value.[62] If a discrepancy is found, the employer must draw up an equity plan or make appropriate adjustments.[63]

Duties placed on public bodies are even more proactive, generally requiring the authority to screen all of its policies and practices for their impact on equality. Thus the guidance provided to public bodies in implementing the positive duties under the new race relations legislation emphasizes that the authority must take the initiative in assessing how its policies and programmes could affect ethnic minorities and identifying any potential for adverse differential impact. Regular monitoring is a

---

[62] If there is no appropriate male comparator class within the establishment, it is possible to claim proportionate pay with groups of men doing work of different value, or to find proxy comparisons with employees of different employers with matching job descriptions.

[63] Depending on the size of the workforce.

crucial component, both to identify disparate impact of policies and practices, and to match such policies to the needs of ethnic minorities. Indeed,
the government is proposing to impose a specific duty on all listed public
employers to ethnically monitor staff in post and applicants for jobs,
promotion, and training. Monitoring the commencement of employment
is, however, not enough. There needs to be ongoing vigilance of the
employment relationship itself, including such issues as discipline and
dismissal, and training. It has therefore also been proposed that public
employers with at least 150 full time employees should have a specific
duty to ethnically monitor grievances, disciplinary action, performance
appraisal which results in benefits or sanctions, training, and dismissals.
Transparency is also considered essential to the process, with a
requirement that the results of ethnic monitoring be published annually.

The trigger for the positive duty is then intimately related to the content of the duty itself. Under the amended Race Relations Act, the traditional negative duty to eliminate racial discrimination is now combined
with the two positive duties, namely, to promote equality of opportunity,
and to promote good relations between persons of different racial groups.
This is essentially a mainstreaming measure. According to guidance provided by the CRE, the aim of the general duty is to make the promotion
of equality of opportunity and good race relations an integral part of the
way public functions are carried out. This is a duty, not a discretion:
public authorities do not have the option to ignore racial equality. At the
same time, the duty is not absolute, but proportionate. Legislation
requires the authority to have 'due regard' to the need to promote equality of opportunity and good race relations. The duty does not necessarily
trump other requirements, but must be given due weight, proportionate
to its relevance.

All of these factors appear explicitly in the specific duties which the
Home Secretary has the power to impose on listed public bodies. According to proposals, public bodies should prepare and publish a Race Equality Scheme setting out how it intends to meet its obligations to promote
race equality. It should assess which of its functions and policies are
relevant to the duty, with regular subsequent reviews; set out its arrangements for assessing and consulting on the impact on the promotion of race
equality of policies it is proposing for adoption; set out its arrangements
for monitoring for any adverse impact on the promotion of race equality
of policies it has adopted; and set out its arrangements for publishing
the results.

## (III)  PROCESS OF DECISION-MAKING:
### PARTICIPATORY DEMOCRACY

The nature of the positive duty in the discrimination field is such that the process of decision-making is as important as the outcome. One approach is to institute a highly centralized scheme, with government or a public agency dictating in detail the steps to be taken and enforcing standards through legal proceedings. However, it has been shown that the effectiveness of equality strategies depends on convincing those who implement the plan of its appropriateness and value; and ultimately changing the culture itself. More can be achieved by enlisting the self-interest of employers and providers than through unilateral control.[64] This has led to the evolution of mechanisms to facilitate a dialogue between the relevant equality commission and those who are being regulated. The powerful US Office of Federal Contract Compliance Programs, for example, always attempts to reach a formal conciliation agreement, or enlist binding undertakings, failing which there is negotiation and conciliation. It is only if all fails that the legal process is enlisted and the ultimate sanction of debarment invoked. It is in a sense a mark of the success of the OFCCP in enlisting the energies of employers that only a handful of contractors have been debarred since the scheme was instituted. A similar pattern can be seen in the formal investigation process under the UK sex and race discrimination legislation. As was seen above, the investigation is intended to be an interactive process, during which the relevant Commission aims to secure a change in discriminatory practices through discussion, negotiation, and conciliation.

But harnessing the energies of the employer or provider is not sufficient. It has been shown that the quality of regulation improves significantly by incorporating those affected both into the decision-making process and its implementation. This would include trade unions, community organizations, and public interest groups. The importance of this dimension is clearly evidenced by the experience of the operation of the Ontario Pay Equity Act. The Ontario scheme required recognized trade unions to be involved in the pay equity process; whereas in workplaces in which female job classes were not organized, employers were entitled to proceed alone. Non-binding advice by the Pay Equity Commission to set up a pay equity committee including workers and management was generally ignored. The results were striking. In workplaces without recognized trade unions, there was substantial employer

---

[64] Hepple, Coussey, and Choudhury, above n.9, para. 3.5.

manipulation in order to minimize the costs and impact of pay equity. This could be done because of the inevitably subjective nature of job evaluation, and the open-textured definitions of key terms such as the establishment within which pay equity was to be achieved, the definition of job classes and the choice of appropriate comparators. McColgan notes that unions were in a position to resist such manipulation, for example by ensuring that the values assigned to job classes reflected a genuine and gender neutral assessment; that the definition of 'establishment' was such as to include comparators for female job classes; and to influence the characterization of job classes as male or female.[65] Unions were even able to negotiate above the minimum required by the Act, using a combination of industrial muscle and threats to invoke the legal process to support their claims. The result was that organized workers benefited far more from the process than their unorganized colleagues. It is similarly arguable that the success of mainstreaming at EU level has been enhanced by the participation of vocal women's groups.

### (IV) ENFORCEABILITY

Although enforceability appears to be an absolute concept, in fact there is a spectrum of different types and degrees of enforceability. At the one end of the spectrum are wholly voluntary codes of conduct, with 'good practice' guidelines produced by a public agency. The incentive to comply is provided simply by persuasion, focusing in particular on the extent to which equality can promote the business needs of employers. At the other end of this spectrum is a tightly regulated system, requiring on-going monitoring by a central agency and carrying judicially enforced sanctions including mandatory injunctions and fines. In between there are a range of different degrees of enforceability, including financial incentives such as the award of or refusal to award government contracts. Moreover, the enforcement could arise at different stages, from the keeping of records to the introduction of new practices.

Enforcement clearly differs as between duties placed on public bodies and duties in the private sector. There is no truly voluntary code for public bodies: they are constitutionally bound to follow directions, even if there is no specific sanction attached. Nevertheless, in the absence of a formal external agency to press for compliance, change is unlikely unless

---

[65] A. McColgan, 'Equal Pay: Lessons from Ontario's Pay Equity Unit' Working Paper No. 5 *Independent Review of the Enforcement of UK Anti-Discrimination Legislation* November 1999, para. 3.31.

there is a commitment by those involved in delivering the policy, reinforced, where possible, by vocal pressure groups representing the under-represented groups. This pattern is evident in the approach to mainstreaming of sex equality issues at EU level. The guiding document issued by the Commission requires commitment and motivation from public actors themselves. It is up to pressure groups and State actors to ensure that equality has been pursued. In practice, at EU level, there has been important evidence that equality concerns have been taken into account in formulating policies, particularly in respect of education and training, and measures to tackle unemployment.

Without a fundamental culture change, purely voluntary requirements may well have little effect. This is illustrated by considering the lack of impact of the targets set for increasing ethnic minority recruitment in the police forces in Britain. In 1999, only 2 per cent of police officers were from ethnic minorities, despite the fact that they comprise 7 per cent of the population. The few who were appointed were twice as likely to resign, three times more likely to be dismissed and had to wait longer to be promoted. This prompted Home Secretary Jack Straw to announce targets for the recruitment and retention of ethnic minorities, the aim being for every force in England and Wales to reflect its local ethnic minority population within ten years. In addition, retention and promotion targets were set.[66] This would entail an average yearly increase of over 800 officers. However, compliance was left entirely in the hands of the superior officers in particular forces. The result was that recruitment fell woefully below the targets. In the first year after the targets were set, the number of ethnic minority police officers in the forty-five forces increased by only 209. While some forces showed significant increases, in some, such as West Yorkshire, the number in fact fell.

At the opposite end of the spectrum is the establishment of an external agency with strong compliance responsibilities. Recognizing the deficiencies of the voluntary approach, the Northern Ireland Act gives extensive powers to the Northern Ireland Equality Commission to function as the engine driving change in public bodies within its purview. Thus the Act does not simply require public authorities to draw up equality schemes; it goes further and requires all such equality schemes to be submitted for approval. If the scheme is not approved, it is referred to the Secretary of State, who may draw up a scheme to be imposed on the public authority, or request the public authority to make a revised scheme.[67] The

---

[66] (1999) 85 EOR 23–24.     [67] Northern Ireland Act 1998, s.75 and sched. 9.

Commission also has powers to investigate the extent of compliance; and, if non-compliance is found, to refer the matter to the Secretary of State who can issue directions to the authority, or to lay a report before Parliament and the Northern Ireland Assembly.

Representing a synthesis of these alternatives is the proposal by the Independent Review of the Enforcement of Anti-Discrimination legislation for the UK. Instead of close scrutiny by a commission, the Review prefers enforcement through building mainstreaming into the government's performance management frameworks. The primary impetus should come from government itself, using regular monitoring and progress reports, with a residual power only in the Commission to enforce compliance, either on receiving a formal complaint or on its own initiative. As a very last resort power, the Commission should be able to issue an enforcement notice, and if necessary apply to a tribunal for an order requiring compliance.[68] It should be stressed that to be effective, these strategies must include proper training and an attempt to imbue the micro culture with a commitment to the value of equal opportunities. Not only can line managers easily subvert policies, but it is difficult to achieve any more than formal compliance unless there is an appropriate ethos.

Compliance mechanisms provided to enforce the new duty on public authorities introduced by the Race Relations (Amendment) Act 2000 reflect this approach to some extent, representing a hybrid of the purely voluntary and the regulatory approaches. No specific compliance mechanism is provided for the general duty. The guidance produced by the CRE makes it clear that an individual cannot institute proceedings, except perhaps by way of judicial review; the only recourse being to draw the default to the attention of the CRE. By contrast, a detailed regulatory enforcement mechanism is provided in respect of specific duties. The CRE is empowered to issue a compliance notice to any public authority that fails to fulfil a specific duty imposed by order to promote race equality. The notice may require the authority to comply with the duty and provide information to the CRE of steps taken to do so. If the Commission considers that a person has not complied with any requirement of the notice within three months it may apply to a designated county court for an order requiring the person to comply with the requirement of the notice. Audit bodies such as the Audit Commission would also be subject to the duty to promote race equality. It is striking that no details appear

[68] Hepple, Coussey, and Choudhury, above n.9, paras 3.21–3.22.

in the Act itself of how the CRE is to monitor compliance and therefore on what basis it can come to its conclusion that a non-compliance notice is required.

Private sector enforcement requires a different technique. It is well established that a system based entirely on self-regulation will have little effect. Employers who consider that equal opportunities advance their business needs will comply in any event. Those who have no such incentive will safely avoid taking responsibility for advancing equality. Moreover, the formal adoption of equal opportunities policy may simply be 'an excuse for complacency. Management . . . seems particularly prone to a conviction that equal opportunity "now exists" '.[69] Nor is it sufficient for government to issue a code of practice without any enforcement mechanisms. This has been clearly evidenced by the experience in the area of age discrimination. The political decision to do no more than introduce a code of practice has yielded few results. A recent survey of 800 companies indicated that only 1 per cent had introduced change as a direct result of the Code of Practice on Age Diversity in Employment, and only 4 per cent thought that future change was likely. The main reason given was the belief that company policy or practice already met government guidelines. By contrast, a study of British residents over 50 found that a large majority believed that employers discriminated against older workers.[70] This contrasts strikingly with research showing that almost nine out of ten firms have developed or revised their employment policies as a direct result of the Disability Discrimination Act 1995.[71] This merely reinforces extensive research demonstrating that, while it is important to harness the positive goodwill and energy of major actors, some enforcement mechanism must be available to keep all actors in line.[72] The Report of the Independent Review of the Enforcement of Anti-Discrimination Legislation therefore recommends an enforcement pyramid, which assumes voluntary compliance and co-operation but establishes progressively more deterrent penalties until there is compliance.[73]

Extensive experience of specific mechanisms has already been gained in the US, Northern Ireland, and Ontario. Possibly the most effective sanction in the private sector is that of contract compliance. Introduced in 1961 by President Kennedy, this approach required contractors of the

---

[69] J. West and K. Lyon, 'The Trouble with Equal Opportunities: The Case of Women Academics' (1995) 7 *Gender and Education* 51 at 60, cited in Rees, above n.55, at p.42.

[70] (2000) 93 EOR 8.     [71] *ibid.*

[72] Hepple, Coussey, and Choudhury, above n.9, para. 3.3; Rees, above n.55, p. 36.

[73] Hepple, Coussey, and Choudhury, above n.9, para. 3.4.

federal government to increase the representation of racial minorities in their workforces as a condition for the award and the continuation of the contract.[74] These requirements have been extended to cover sex and religion,[75] and there are also schemes for persons with disabilities and disabled war veterans. Enforcement in race and gender cases lies with the powerful Office of Federal Contract Compliance Programmes (OFCCP), which has extensive investigatory powers, including routine compliance reviews; pre-award compliance reviews; individual complaint investigations, and class complaint investigations.[76] Most importantly, the threat to the economic well-being of private contractors by the sanction of withdrawal of lucrative federal contractors has been crucial in securing the effectiveness of the positive duties. The OFCCP has a range of measures at its disposal to ensure compliance, culminating in the power to declare contractors ineligible to receive further contracts and to interrupt progress payments on existing contracts. In practice, this power has rarely been used: both the threat of debarment and the risk of bad publicity have functioned as a sufficient deterrent. The importance of this deterrent is acknowledged by affected employers. Indeed, all the US employers interviewed in a recent study said that they would not have been able to sustain the significant increases in the representation of women and minorities which had taken place in their organizations without the compulsory affirmative action requirements.[77] The result is that this strategy, which applies to approximately 300,000 Federal contractors, employing about 40 per cent of the working population, has had a significantly more powerful influence on employers than individual complaint-led investigations.

A more closely controlled and comprehensive strategy has been used more recently in Northern Ireland, involving a combination of criminal, civil, and economic sanctions. As we have seen, legislation introduced in 1989 imposed positive duties on employers to take measures to achieve fair participation in their workforces of Protestant and Roman Catholic employees.[78] The Equality Commission plays a central role in ensuring compliance. Registered employers are required to send a monitoring return each year to the Commission including details of the number of

---

[74] Executive Order 10925.          [75] Executive Order 11246.

[76] The facts in this paragraph are taken from Hepple, Coussey, and Choudhury, above n.9, paras 3.23–3.29.

[77] *ibid.*, paras 3.23–3.24, 3.29.

[78] Fair Employment Act 1989, now contained in Fair Employment and Treatment (Northern Ireland) Order (FETO) 1998, Part VII.

existing employees who belong to each community, the composition of applicants for employment; and in relevant cases, those ceasing to be employed. Notably, criminal sanctions are used to enforce the obligation to serve a return. But the Commission also has a range of other sanctions at its disposal. Although the employer is required to initiate and conduct its own periodic reviews, and draw up its own affirmative action plans in response, the Commission may make recommendations as to the affirmative action to be taken; it can serve directions on an employer who fails to give written undertakings where appropriate, and serve a notice about goals and timetables. Enforcement is also complemented by recourse to the tribunal, for example to enforce a written undertaking. Finally, the Commission also has economic sanctions, which include denial not only of government contracts, but also of financial assistance.[79]

Far more dependent on employers' goodwill has been the otherwise highly innovative pay equity legislation in the Canadian Province of Ontario. It is striking that, despite the complexity of the obligations placed on employers, minimal supervisory and enforcement powers are provided. Unlike the provisions in Northern Ireland, the Ontarian provisions do not place an enforceable obligation on employers to file the results of their monitoring exercises or the resulting pay equity plan. Nor does the Pay Equity Commission have powers to initiate investigations. Instead, intervention by the PEC depends upon an employee complaint. This inevitably suffers from some of the deficiencies of the individual complaints-led process discussed above. The individual employee in an establishment where an employer has chosen not to post a pay equity scheme can only complain if the employer could be shown to have made no adjustments or adjustments which were smaller than required. Yet this requires not only great individual effort, but also access to information more likely to be in the hands of the employers. In practice, this has proved to be a serious deficiency of the Act. Research in Ontario showed that many large employers failed to meet their deadlines—indeed only 30 per cent of employers had posted plans or made equity adjustments within or close to their deadline. Among small private sector employees, there has been substantial non-compliance.[80] It has indeed been stressed that the case for proper enforcement is much stronger for pay equity than employment equity; largely because of the direct costs involved.[81]

---

[79] FETO 1998, arts. 55–68.     [80] McColgan, above n.65.
[81] Hepple, Coussey, and Choudhury, above n.9, para. 3.45.

## (V) AIMS AND OBJECTIVES

The radical nature of positive duties makes it tempting to view their introduction as an end in itself. Yet is it is crucially important to consider what each strategy is aiming to achieve. In particular, which conception of equality is being utilized? Several different notions of equality were discussed in Chapter One and the implications of these differences have been pursued in relation to various aspects of discrimination, such as affirmative action. Clearly, the notion of a positive duty aims to do more than eliminate individual prejudice. This section considers and evaluates several possible objectives: (i) economic efficiency; (ii) fair participation; (iii) substantive equality of opportunity; and (iv) structural change. Most schemes, it will be seen, have elements of distributive equality, but the benefits to be redistributed vary in scale and depth. Some schemes pursue more than one objective, and these may either be mutually exclusive or conflicting. The results are therefore not only complex but often fluid. This section therefore can do no more than begin to sketch the main issues that arise.

### (a) Economic efficiency goals

During the 1980s and early 1990s, equality was set up in conflict with economic efficiency goals. Fuelled in particular by the neo-liberal governments of Thatcher and Major, it was argued that equal opportunity policies imposed by the State were a burden on business and could only lead to greater unemployment. However, in a powerful response to this approach, it began to be argued that in fact equal opportunities, properly focused, would improve efficiency. Cutting pay and equal opportunities would not yield a competitive advantage; instead the future lay in the development of a highly skilled, motivated, and integrated workforce. It was this approach which grounded the policy of the EU during the 1990s.[82] And since it was women who formed the majority of the economically inactive and unskilled potential labour force, the development of women's skills came to be regarded as highly significant in the overall economic policy aimed at creating a skilled workforce.[83] It was this objective which was at the basis of many of the most important positive action programmes at EU level, such as the provision of funding to Member States to promote vocational training and employment for women. It was

---

[82] European Commission, *Growth, Competitiveness, Employment: The Challenges and Ways Forward into the 21st Century* (1994) Bulletin of the European Communities, Supplement 6/93.

[83] Rees, above n.55, p.63.

a major contributing factor to the commitment to mainstreaming at EU level.

This approach has some important strengths. Indeed, as will be seen below, this imperative has had the effect of creating some important substantive gains towards equal opportunities for women. However, the fact that equality is ultimately subservient to the market imperative means that it is inevitably limited. As soon as equality is considered to be too costly, it gives way to other priorities. For example, training programmes are resourced only to the extent that this is judged to produce efficiency gains. Many of the Community initiatives such as NOW (or New Opportunities for Women) were given only limited funding, and the proportion of the total budget of the EU which is spent on equality issues is tiny. The subservience of equality to economic objectives is also starkly illustrated by the fact that the positive action programmes have been focused on women, excluding equality on grounds of race, ethnic minority, religion, sexual orientation, and disability. The integration of these groups into the labour market has, until very recently, simply not been considered to be necessary to serve the predetermined economic aims. It was only when such aims could be seen to be served by equality for these groups that legislative moves in that direction were possible. It is particularly striking that the most recent directive on equality for racial and ethnic minorities states in its preamble that discrimination based on racial or ethnic origin may undermine the achievement of the objectives of the EC Treaty, stressing, *inter alia*, the attainment of a high level of employment and of social protection.[84] Moreover, the 'economic prism' could well make it appear that there is a competitive conflict between different disadvantaged groups. Policies to absorb women may well entail fewer opportunities for migrant work, and a corresponding strengthening of immigration control.

The subservience to the market perspective also means that structural change need not be contemplated. As Rees puts it, there is a crucial difference between mainstreaming equality and transforming the mainstream.[85] Although mainstreaming requires that equality objectives be integrated into all policies, it does not require restructuring. Thus the model of full time working, mobility, and job continuity continues to dominate policy formation; and ingrained assumptions about women's work and their marginal role in the workforce are deeply influential in shaping education and training. Even gestures towards restructuring,

---

[84] Directive 2000/43, preamble para. 9.    [85] Rees, above n.55, p.69.

such as the acknowledgement of fathers' parental responsibilities through the provision of parental leave, are undermined by the refusal to accept the added cost of an entitlement to pay during leave.

## (b) Fair participation

The second and often most readily identifiable aim, is to increase the participation of under-represented groups in employment or public office. Thus the explicit aim of the Northern Ireland provisions is to achieve proportionate participation of Roman Catholics and Protestants in all types of employment, levels of employment, and extent of employment. Employment equity schemes with similar aims have been introduced in several other countries, such as Canada, Australia, and South Africa. In addition, it was with the express aim of increasing the participation of women in the public sector that the reverse discrimination schemes described in the previous chapter in Germany and Sweden were introduced.[86] Within Great Britain, there are several public sector initiatives to achieve better representation of ethnic minorities in the public services. Nor has the aim of achieving fair participation been confined to employment. It extends too to representation in public office, including the judiciary, Parliament, and the other decision-making bodies. The most important such initiative is at EU level, where a commitment has been made to achieve balanced participation for men and women in public life and in particular in all levels of decision-making.

This aim is attractive in that it is easily quantifiable. Targets can be set and achievement measured by properly structured monitoring. However, closer consideration shows that more is needed before this aim can be coherent. Most importantly, fair participation can conceal differing conceptions of the equality to which these measures are being directed, which in turn affect the definition of legitimate means and the appraisal of success. A substantive view of equality of results, for example, would value the redistribution of jobs to a disadvantaged group more highly than individual merit or fault. This would permit the institution of reverse discrimination or preference policies in order to achieve fair participation, as has been done in the US, Germany, Sweden and, most radically, in India.[87] By contrast, a conception of equality based on an individualized view of equality of opportunity would continue to stress individual merit, and instead focus on the removal of barriers to recruitment. Improving the level of representation is not seen as an end in itself,

---

[86] See Chapter Five.    [87] *ibid.*

but a reflection of the degree of success in achieving true equality of opportunity. This is clearly seen in the Northern Ireland provisions, which forbid reverse discrimination. As the Fair Employment Commission stressed, any measure taken must be consistent with the principle of appointing the best person for the job.[88] The measures to be taken therefore focus on encouraging more applicants from the under-represented group, and improving selection practices so that the proportion of appointees reflects the composition of applicants.[89] However, these provisions do not include substantive measures to improve the ability of members of the group to attain the goal; the procedural measures established in Northern Ireland stop short of substantive intervention of this sort.

The goal of increasing participation has many strengths. But its limitations should not be overlooked. In particular, merely changing the colour, gender, or religious composition of a workforce may not achieve structural changes. Those who succeed in attaining positions may have done so at the cost of conforming to existing structures, be they long working hours, a Christian calendar, dress requirements, etc. Cultural change, crucial to a conducive working environment may not be achieved. The result is either that targets remain stubbornly unattainable or that participation rates give an illusion of change. Alternatively, the change in gender or colour composition may mask a diminution in status or pay of the jobs in question. Feminization of jobs has often accompanied such a diminution. This is clearly demonstrated in the advance of women into managerial positions, particularly in catering and other services. The pay of women in such positions has been shown to be below the national average.

Both the strengths and weaknesses of fair participation can be demonstrated by considering the Northern Ireland schemes respectively. In Northern Ireland, significant progress has in fact been made in improving the representation of the Catholic community in previously under-represented areas. Indeed, the total Catholic participation in the workforce increased by 4.2 per cent between 1990 and 1998, standing at 39.1 per cent in that year.[90] Although there is still some way to go before it reflects the availability figure of 42 per cent, it is clearly a significant achievement. Particularly notable is the increase in the appointment of

---

[88] Fair Employment Commission Annual Report 1998, para. 1.4.                    [89] *ibid.*
[90] Figures in this section are taken from the Fair Employment Commission Monitoring Report No. 9 (1998).

Catholic women to professional positions in both the public and private sectors. However, a closer look at the figures shows that this improvement has been more marked in some sectors than others. There is still a substantial under-representation of Catholics in security related occupations, which increased by only 1 per cent to 8.4 per cent between 1990 and 1998. In addition, progress has been closely related to the degree of growth in the economy. Thus the most marked rises in Catholic participation have been in expanding sectors such as managers, administrators, and professional occupations in the private sector. Conversely, the decline in manufacturing has meant that the change in Catholic employment in these occupations has been more static. Equally important, the fair employment provisions have had little impact on unemployment, where the Catholic figures are still substantially higher than those of Protestants.

### (c) Substantive equality of opportunity

The limitations of the focus on fair participation suggest that there is a role for more substantive measures. Instead of simply opening the door to greater opportunity, it is necessary to improve the ability of members of the under-represented group to go through the door, for example, by enhancing their qualifications or providing child-care. Indeed, a recent survey in Northern Ireland highlighted the substantive obstacles to employment rather than the procedural issues on which the Fair Employment legislation has focused. Respondents to the survey, which aimed at elucidating perceived obstacles to finding employment, stressed the depressed nature of the economy, lack of educational qualifications, and lack of training. More Catholics than Protestants mentioned lack of qualifications, training, and work experience as the main obstacles to finding employment. Notably few mentioned obstacles rooted in the religious tensions of Northern Ireland, such as religion, prejudice based on living in a predominantly Catholic or Protestant area, and the fact that jobs were only available in dangerous areas.[91]

Thus an important aim of positive action programmes could be seen to be the provision of substantive equal opportunities. This is particularly important in that it not only removes barriers to participation, but equips the under-represented to make use of the newly expanded opportunities. Central among such strategies would be the provision of education and

---

[91] A. M. Gallagher and P. Daly, 'Fair Employment in Northern Ireland: Attitudinal Evidence' (Northern Ireland Equality Commission, 1999).

training, child-care facilities, and family leave. It is notable that the EU provisions, while on one level serving the aims of economic efficiency, have simultaneously assisted to some extent in the provision of substantive equal opportunities. In Britain, the child-care strategy instituted by the Labour government after 1997 would constitute substantive positive action of this sort. The same is true for the provision of subsidized maternity pay (called statutory maternity pay) and the institution of tax incentives for employers to establish workplace nurseries.

Properly conceived, the provision of substantive equality of opportunity could have important and long-term effects. At the same time, such achievements will be limited unless accompanied by structural change. Subsidized maternity pay without the provision of equal subsidies for paternity and parental leave reinforces the status quo which gives primary responsibility for child-care to mothers rather than fathers. Training schemes which do not themselves adapt to women's needs for flexible hours and child-care will have little impact. Research has shown that in practice many training schemes are residential or do not provide for child-care. Similarly, substantive equality of opportunity, while making an important contribution on the supply side, will only succeed if accompanied by corresponding changes on the demand side. The definition of skill, for example, would need to be adapted on the demand side before training programmes can be adopted to achieve structural change.

## (d) Structural change

The above discussion has pointed to the urgent need for positive duties to include an element of restructuring rather than being restricted to movements within the existing framework. Instead of attempting to adapt members of other under-represented groups better to fit in with the existing framework, it is crucial to transform the existing framework in order to reflect the norms of the excluded 'other'. Long working hours need to be adapted to achieve a better home–work balance, not just for women, but for men too. The welfare system needs to be restructured to reflect a genuinely egalitarian society. The exclusively white male dominated culture of the police, armed forces, and fire services needs to be transformed before real change will be achieved. The linkage of work-free days with the Christian calendar needs to be severed and dress codes based on a Christian tradition removed; accommodation for disability needs to extend beyond tolerance for longer leave, shown to be the main form of accommodation so far, to adaptation of premises and working places, and beyond that to changes in transport systems, media images, and welfare payments.

At first sight, pay equity schemes based on a comparable worth or equal value approach seem to come closest to structural change. The concept of job evaluation requires a radical re-configuration of accepted wage rates and relativities, particularly where this extends to a proportional readjustment. Women in jobs which were previously of low value and status can be seen to be doing work which is equivalent to that done by men in well organized and high status positions, and to be rewarded accordingly. However, the extent of restructuring which can be achieved through pay equity has been limited, largely because of the dependency on equality itself. That is, women have only been able to compare their jobs with 'male' jobs within the existing framework, leaving women in segregated workplaces without a remedy. In addition, the concept of value itself is infinitely manipulable and easily shaped to reflect no more than the established values. Even radical re-evaluations, such as that instituted within local authorities during the 1980s, have been unable to stand up to powerful social and economic currents. Thus radical restructuring which brought home-helps up to the level of garbage collectors was not enough to maintain equality of pay: differential productivity and overtime bonuses soon re-established the pay gap.[92] Finally, perceived economic constraints have limited the reach of pay equity schemes. Some of these are built into the Ontarian scheme: no more than 1 per cent of pay-roll output needs to be spent on equity adjustments, and small workplaces are not affected. Some operate externally and only semi-visibly. Thus the institution of pay equity in the public sector in Ontario coincided with severe budgetary cut-backs. The cost of pay equity was therefore borne by increased redundancies. A hollow victory indeed.

## IV CONCLUSION

In surveying the limits of law through the prism of enforcement, we have come full circle conceptually. What does equality mean, and what are we hoping to achieve? The questions asked in Chapter One have received a range of different answers. Indeed, it is not just the answers, but also the questions, which have changed. As equality law faces new and increasingly complex challenges, so the conceptual apparatus has been adjusted

---

[92] See further S. Fredman, *Women and the Law* (Clarendon, 1997), p.243.

and its legal manifestations re-examined. But the responses, although innovative, have often represented incomplete solutions; progress has been evident, but uneven. Those dedicated to equality still face an exacting, but ultimately deeply rewarding, task.

# Index